The Complete Guide to
Investing in Real Estate
Tax Liens & Deeds

*How to Earn
High Rates of Return — Safely*

REVISED 2ND EDITION

Alan Northcott

THE COMPLETE GUIDE TO INVESTING IN REAL ESTATE TAX LIENS & DEEDS: HOW TO EARN HIGH RATES OF RETURN - SAFELY REVISED 2ND EDITION

Copyright © 2015 Atlantic Publishing Group, Inc.
1405 SW 6th Avenue • Ocala, Florida 34471 • Phone 800-814-1132 • Fax 352-622-1875
Website: www.atlantic-pub.com • E-mail: sales@atlantic-pub.com
SAN Number: 268-1250

No part of this publication may be reproduced, stored in a retrieval system, or transmitted in any form or by any means, electronic, mechanical, photocopying, recording, scanning, or otherwise, except as permitted under Section 107 or 108 of the 1976 United States Copyright Act, without the prior written permission of the Publisher. Requests to the Publisher for permission should be sent to Atlantic Publishing Group, Inc., 1210 SW 23rd Place, Ocala, Florida 34471

Library of Congress Cataloging-in-Publication Data

Northcott, Alan, 1951-
  The complete guide to investing in real estate tax liens & deeds : how to earn high rates of return--safely / Alan Northcott. -- Rev. 2nd ed.
     p. cm.
  Rev. ed. of: The complete guide to investing in real estate tax liens & deeds : how to earn high rates of return-safely / Jamaine Burrell. c2006.
  Includes bibliographical references and index.
  ISBN 978-1-60138-899-5 (alk. paper) -- ISBN 1-60138-899-3 1. Real estate investment--United States. 2. Real estate investment--Law and legislation--United States. 3. Tax liens--United States. I. Burrell, Jamaine, 1958- Complete guide to investing in real estate tax liens & deeds. II. Title. III. Title: Complete guide to investing in real estate tax liens and deeds.
  HD255.B875 2012
  332.63'24--dc23
                            2012015618

LIMIT OF LIABILITY/DISCLAIMER OF WARRANTY: The publisher and the author make no representations or warranties with respect to the accuracy or completeness of the contents of this work and specifically disclaim all warranties, including without limitation warranties of fitness for a particular purpose. No warranty may be created or extended by sales or promotional materials. The advice and strategies contained herein may not be suitable for every situation. This work is sold with the understanding that the publisher is not engaged in rendering legal, accounting, or other professional services. If professional assistance is required, the services of a competent professional should be sought. Neither the publisher nor the author shall be liable for damages arising herefrom. The fact that an organization or website is referred to in this work as a citation and/or a potential source of further information does not mean that the author or the publisher endorses the information the organization or website may provide or recommendations it may make. Further, readers should be aware that Internet websites listed in this work may have changed or disappeared between when this work was written and when it is read.

TRADEMARK DISCLAIMER: All trademarks, trade names, or logos mentioned or used are the property of their respective owners and are used only to directly describe the products being provided. Every effort has been made to properly capitalize, punctuate, identify, and attribute trademarks and trade names to their respective owners, including the use of ® and ™ wherever possible and practical. Atlantic Publishing Group, Inc. is not a partner, affiliate, or licensee with the holders of said trademarks.

Printed on Recycled Paper

Printed in the United States

Reduce. Reuse.
RECYCLE.

A decade ago, Atlantic Publishing signed the Green Press Initiative. These guidelines promote environmentally friendly practices, such as using recycled stock and vegetable-based inks, avoiding waste, choosing energy-efficient resources, and promoting a no-pulping policy. We now use 100-percent recycled stock on all our books. The results: in one year, switching to post-consumer recycled stock saved 24 mature trees, 5,000 gallons of water, the equivalent of the total energy used for one home in a year, and the equivalent of the greenhouse gases from one car driven for a year.

Over the years, we have adopted a number of dogs from rescues and shelters. First there was Bear and after he passed, Ginger and Scout. Now, we have Kira, another rescue. They have brought immense joy and love not just into our lives, but into the lives of all who met them.

We want you to know a portion of the profits of this book will be donated in Bear, Ginger and Scout's memory to local animal shelters, parks, conservation organizations, and other individuals and nonprofit organizations in need of assistance.

*– **Douglas & Sherri Brown**,*
President & Vice-President of Atlantic Publishing

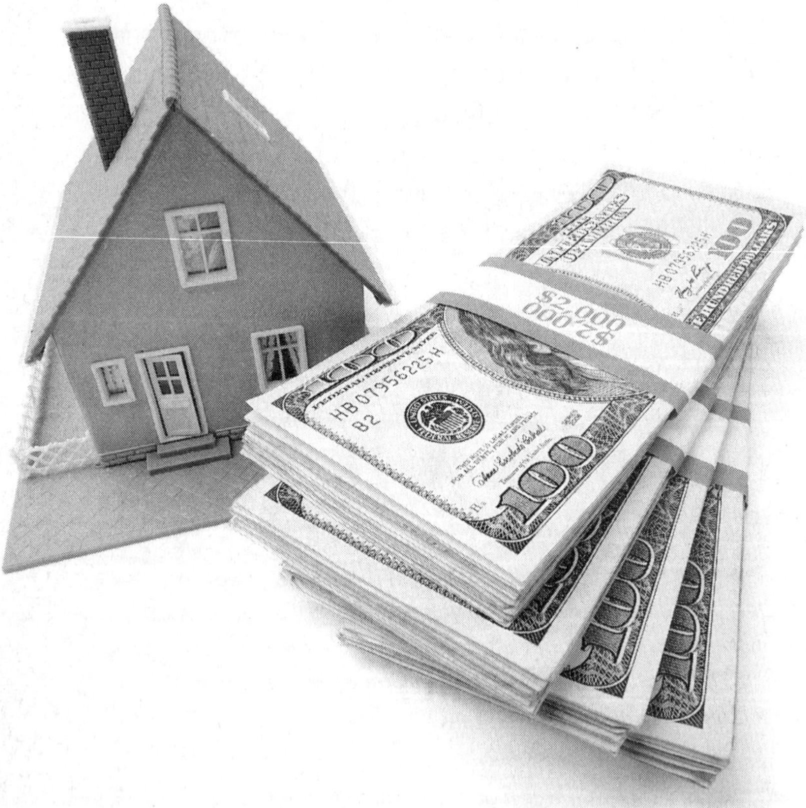
$2,000

Table of Contents

Preface to Revised Second Edition   11

Chapter 1: What Is a Tax Lien Certificate?   15

Tax Deed States...16
Tax Lien States..19
Tax Lien Certificates..20

Chapter 2: Delinquent Properties   27

Single-Family Housing Units...28
Multiple-Family Housing Units...28
Homestead Properties...29

Mortgaged Properties 29
Worthless Properties 31

Chapter 3: Income and Growth Potential — 35

Risk Factors 36

Chapter 4: The Annual Tax Sale — 43

Tax Sale Listings 43
Registration 44
Meeting the Schedule 47
Keeping Pace 49
Restrictions on Bids 50
Opportunities to Invest 50
Payment 54
Obtaining Deed 56

Chapter 5: Bidding on Tax Lien Certificates — 59

Competitive Bidding 59
Noncompetitive Bidding 65
Over-the-Counter Tax Certificates 69

Chapter 6: Investing in Tax Lien Certificates   71

Ownership as the Objective 71
Return as the Objective 76
Investors 79

Chapter 7: Obtaining Investment Dollars   81

Tax Considerations 81
Retirement Programs 86
Partnerships 88
Partnership Agreements 90

Chapter 8: Return on Investment Dollars   97

Interest Rates 98
Percentage Yield 100
Flipping 106
Assignment 108

Chapter 9: Steps To Purchasing Tax Lien Certificates   109

Step 1: Understand State Laws and Procedures Governing the Taxing Municipality 110

Step 2: Eliminate States That Are Not Likely
to Have Certificates Available for Offer 114

Step 3: Seek Over-the-Counter Lien Certificates
in Order of the Oldest to Newest 121

Step 4: Determine the Bidding Systems Used 123

Step 5: Bid Where the Bidding Process Does
Not Significantly Affect Price 126

Step 6: Acquire the Listing of Delinquent Properties 133

Step 7: Determine Properties Less Likely to Be Redeemed 135

Chapter 10: Making Use of Tax Lien Certificates — 147

Tax Lien Certificate Assignments 147

Collecting Redemption Amounts 148

Chapter 11: Foreclosing Unredeemed Properties — 155

Administrative Filing of Foreclosure 156

Force of Sale Foreclosure 159

Quiet Title 160

Hindrance to Foreclosure 160

After Foreclosure 170

Chapter 12: What Next? — 171

Choose the State...172
Pick Your County...172
Research Properties...173
Inspect the Properties..173
The Auction..174

Conclusion — 175

Appendix 1: State Laws — 177

Bibliography — 281

Author Biography — 283

Index — 285

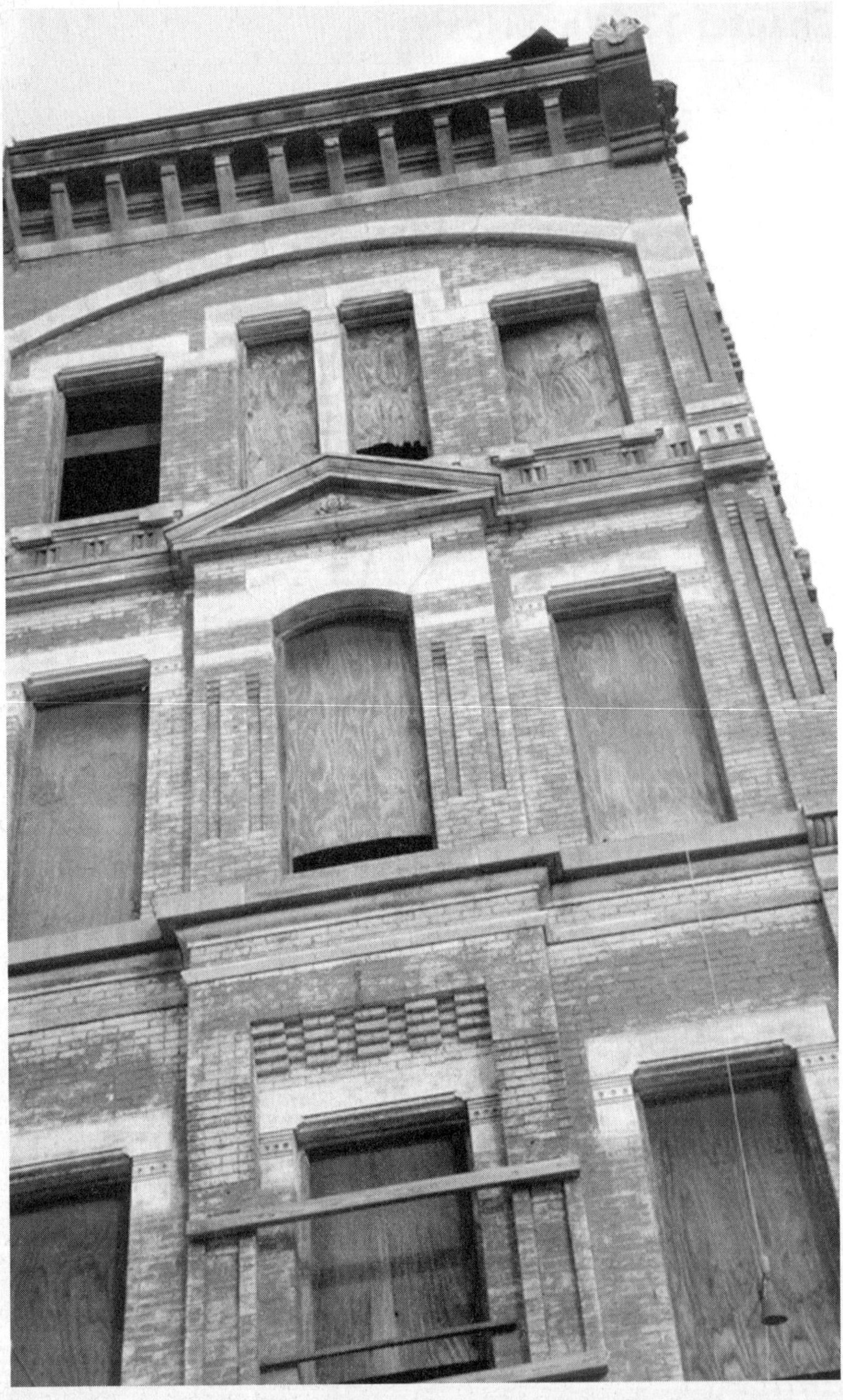

Preface to Revised Second Edition

My initial encounter with the tax lien process was from the other side. I had owned my first house in a small Arizona town for about ten years when I decided that I could pay off the mortgage. Up until that time, as is the practice with residential mortgages, the mortgage company had been taking care of taxes through the escrow account, and I had been duly noting the amount from the annual statements to claim on my tax returns.

We paid off the mortgage in August of one year, and when I came to prepare my tax returns for the following year, fortunately in February long before they were due, I noticed that I had no property taxes on the closing statement from the mortgage company to claim. I checked with the county taxation department, who informed me that my taxes were going to auction on the following week in the tax lien sale.

Needless to say, I was shocked, outraged, confused, and a host of other feelings, particularly as I do not make a practice of not paying my bills. I did not understand how they could be "selling my debt" so quickly and how I had had no idea that a payment was due. I also was concerned what this would do to the credit rating I had nurtured so carefully. I was working away from home at the time, so I had to pay additional costs for overnighting a cashier's check to the collector to prevent the auction taking place.

A multitude of factors figured into causing this distressing situation. I had not realized, having not owned property before, that I should have been receiving a tax statement every year, even though I was not paying it directly. The address on file was incorrect in two respects — it was a physical street address, when our small town had no delivery and only post office boxes, and it even was addressed to the adjacent municipality, not my own. Presumably, each year the tax statement had been returned to the county as "undeliverable," but as they firmly told me, there was no requirement for the county to do other than send the statement, not to track down the owner. The onus is on the owner to pay, whether or not a statement is received. I was in the telephone book and frequently in the local paper from my involvement in town government, but the county made no effort in this regard.

My other question was why a tax lien should be sold so quickly following nonpayment. There is a lesson here in devious interpretation of the rules. The county assured me that I was recorded as delinquent for two years, even though it had only been one annual payment missed for just five months. Under their rules, the taxes that should have been paid in September were those charged for the previous year. That meant that I was recorded as not paying for the previous year, and when January came I also owed for the year just gone, despite the fact that in normal circumstances that would not be due for payment for another six months.

But this experience turned into a positive one. Through it, I became aware of the "profit from tax liens" industry. The fact is that it takes some effort and perhaps many attempts in order to invest successfully in tax liens or tax deeds, and the popular Internet course I purchased glossed over many of the details. Unfortunately, at that time, I had not discovered the book you now hold in your hands, which at a far lower cost goes into considerably more detail. And the other positive outcome was that my positive credit rating remained intact, as Maricopa County in Arizona had a policy of not reporting delinquency to the credit rating agencies. You should note that I am not sure if this applies to any other jurisdiction or if it still applies in Maricopa County.

The first edition of the book was already a thorough reference work, but there were little niggles that needed addressing.

Sometimes, for example in Louisiana, the sheriff's department may be responsible for the sales, and I have attempted to list the most useful sites, although you might need to click through or call to get the information you seek. Even so, it is my hope that the details given will be of value. I have personally viewed each of the sites listed for current relevance. And yes, there are 3,143 counties or equivalents (such as Louisiana's parishes) in the United States. The most common county name is Washington, which is in more than 30 of the states.

In addition, the final chapter, which runs through the basic process of taking part in tax lien and tax deed auctions, has been added. Although every municipality has its own process, a general framework is given that can be followed easily and adapted to local regulations. This outline details the necessary dealings that make up this method of investment.

— Alan Northcott

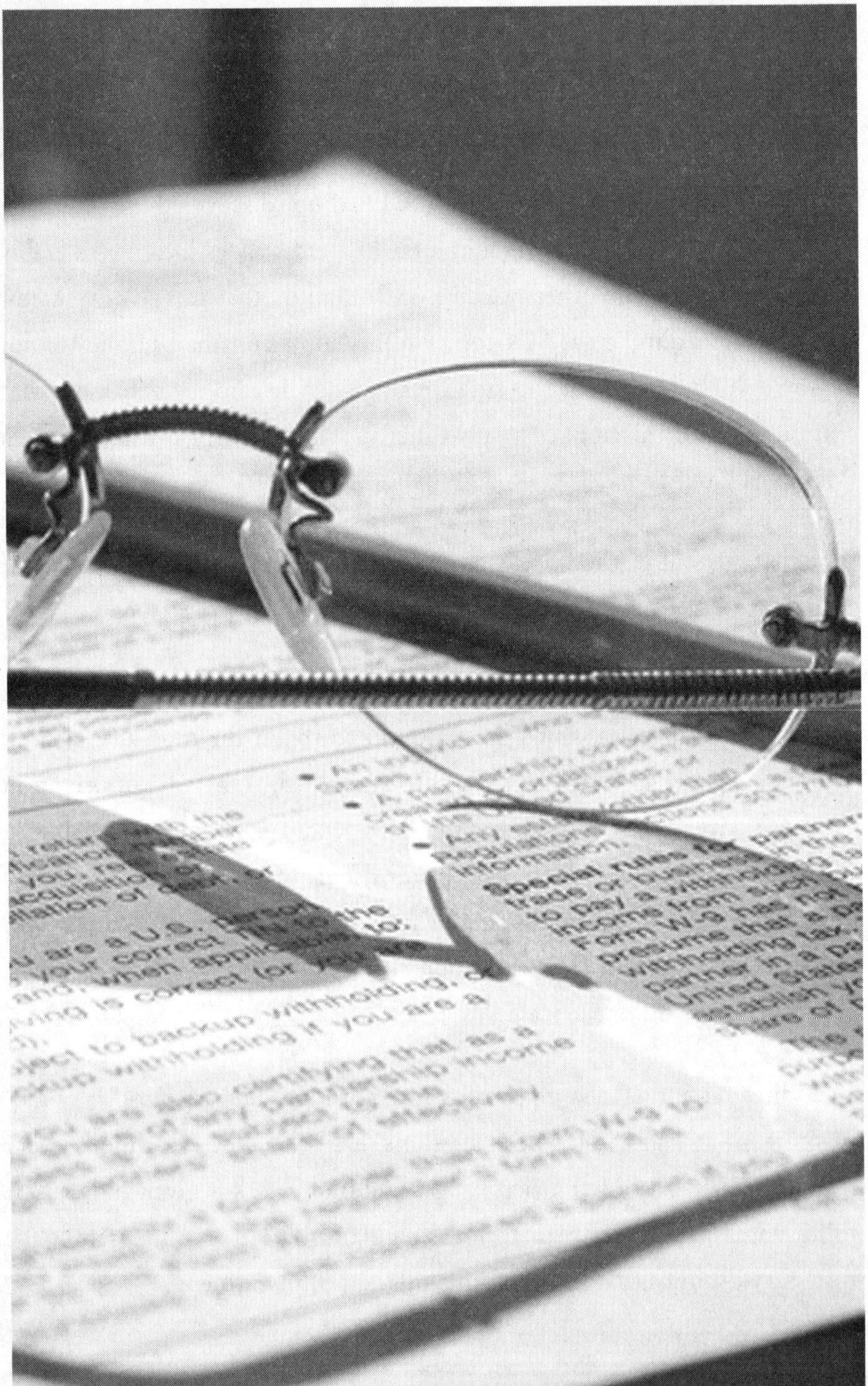

Chapter 1

What Is a Tax Lien Certificate?

In general, when property owners fail to pay the required property tax assessed on real property, the property may be auctioned and sold at a real property tax sale, though real property is not always sold at tax sales. Some states engage in the sale of deeds to real property to recoup losses from delinquent property taxes. Other states engage in the sale of liens against real property to recoup the losses. A lien is simply a security interest in real property. That means the debt is secured by the property, which may, as the ultimate recourse, be seized in payment of that debt.

The purchase of a tax deed is significantly different from the purchase of a tax lien. States that engage in the sale of tax deeds are considered tax deed states. The bidder bids for immediate possession of deed and title to a property. A tax deed is issued or assigned in return for the payment of unpaid real property taxes as well as associated penalties, interest, and costs of the tax sale. States that engage in the sale of tax liens are considered tax lien states. The tax sale initiates a process or system by which an investor pays the delinquent tax on behalf of the property owner. The property owner is then given an opportunity to repay the investor or be forced to relinquish title and deed to the property in the future. A certificate that indicates payment of the tax lien is issued or assigned in return for the payment of unpaid real property taxes as well as associated penalties, interest, and costs of the tax sale.

Tax Deed States

In tax deed states, the winning bidder at a tax sale purchases ownership to a property, as specified by a tax deed. The bidder becomes the property owner upon payment of the delinquent tax amount and any other costs and fees assessed against the property. In some tax deed states, the sale is not immediately final, as the previous property owner is given an opportunity to redeem the property from the newly established owner. The redemption period varies among the states, but generally ranges from six months to two years. These states are considered hybrid tax deed states. Hybrid tax deed states include ten states and the territory of Guam, as follows:

- Connecticut
- Delaware
- Georgia
- Guam
- Hawaii
- Louisiana
- Massachusetts
- Pennsylvania*
- Rhode Island
- Tennessee
- Texas

*Pennsylvania engages in a hybrid tax sale system for improved properties that are legally occupied at least 90 days before the tax sale. Otherwise,

Pennsylvania does not provide an opportunity for the previous property owner to redeem the property from the new owner. In hybrid tax deed states, even though the sale of a tax deed transfers ownership to the tax deed purchaser, the purchaser has no right of possession to the property. Hybrid tax deed states allow property owners to retain all rights of possession.

Other tax deed states do not provide the previous property owner with an opportunity to redeem a property and regain ownership. Because property owners are not allowed an opportunity to redeem their properties, there is no redemption period or interest rates and penalties applied to redemption amounts. These states are considered "pure" tax deed states and are listed below.

- Alaska[2]
- Arkansas
- California[1]
- Idaho
- Kansas
- Maine
- Michigan[2]
- Minnesota
- Nevada[2]
- New Hampshire[1]
- New Mexico
- New York[1]
- North Carolina
- Ohio[1]
- Oregon
- Utah
- Virginia
- Washington
- Wisconsin[2]

[1] Some tax deed states have statutes that allow for the sale of tax certificates rather than or in addition to tax deeds. These states are considered tax deed states because they are inconsistent in engaging in the sale of tax lien certificates across the entire state.

California is relatively new to tax sales and never has sold a tax lien certificate, even though state legislation includes statutes authorizing each of its 58 counties to do so.

Massachusetts statutes have been exercised only in certain towns.

New Hampshire statutes are rarely exercised.

New York statutes have been exercised only in certain cities and counties.

Ohio statutes allow for the sale of tax liens in municipalities with populations greater than 200,000.

[2] Some tax deed states engage in peculiarities that should be noted.

Alaska offers tax deeds for sale only to the municipality in which the property is located. If the property owner fails to redeem the property from the municipality within one year, the municipality offers the property for sale, usually at the fair market value.

Arkansas allows property owners to redeem their properties within 30 days of the tax sale.

Michigan and **Wisconsin** offer properties for sale after they have been foreclosed by judgment.

Nevada uses tax lien certificates to foreclose special assessments or improvements, such as repairs to sidewalks, curbs, gutters, and the like.

Tax Lien States

In tax lien states, no deed or title transfers are executed as a direct result of a tax sale. The winning bidder purchases a tax lien certificate, and a parcel of property is used to secure the lien. The delinquent property owner retains ownership of the property and is allowed an opportunity to redeem the tax lien held against the property. Some states consistently rely upon the sale of tax lien certificates to recoup losses due to delinquent property taxes. These states are considered "pure" tax lien states. Twenty-two states as well as the District of Columbia (D.C.) and the commonwealth of Puerto Rico are pure tax lien states, as follows:

- Alabama
- Arizona
- Colorado
- D.C.
- Florida
- Illinois
- Indiana
- Iowa
- Kentucky
- Maryland
- Michigan
- Mississippi
- Missouri
- Montana
- Nebraska
- New Jersey
- North Dakota
- Oklahoma
- Puerto Rico
- South Carolina
- South Dakota
- Vermont

- West Virginia
- Wyoming

Different tax lien states have differing systems for recouping delinquent real estate tax. Florida is a tax lien state, but the established tax sale system does not allow a tax lien holder to foreclose the property owner's right of redemption. The sale of tax lien certificates is strictly an offer to investors to collect interest on the cost of a tax lien certificate in return for paying the delinquent property tax. If the property owner fails to redeem a tax lien certificate during the redemption period, the deed to the property is offered for sale at a second auction. During this phase of the Florida tax sale system, Florida converts to a tax deed state.

Tax Lien Certificates

A tax lien certificate is a real estate document that serves as evidence of indebtedness against a parcel of real estate. When tax lien certificates are sold, the parcel of real estate serves as collateral to secure the purchase of the tax lien certificate. Tax lien certificates are sold by tax lien states and in specific jurisdictions of some tax deed states. Different states refer to the document by various names that include the following:

- Tax lien certificate
- Tax sale certificate
- Tax sale receipt
- Tax lien
- Tax claim
- Tax certificate
- Lien certificate
- Certificate of purchase
- Certificate of sale
- Certificate of delinquency
- Receipt showing the amount paid
- Receipt for the purchase money

Form 1 (see page 22) shows a sample of a tax lien certificate purchased in Iowa during a 2001 tax sale. In Iowa, a tax lien certificate is issued as a certificate of purchase.

When an individual purchases a tax lien certificate, that individual is, in effect, making a loan to the property owner for the payment of delinquent property taxes. The tax lien certificate indicates the particular individual making the loan and assigns the specified property as security against the loan. The particular parcel of property may serve as collateral in part or as a whole. The property owner must repay the loan in an amount equal to the delinquent tax and associated penalties, interest, and costs of the sale to maintain ownership of the property. As long as a tax lien is outstanding, the property owner may not borrow against the property; nor may the property owner trade, sell, or otherwise dispose of the property. If the property owner fails to repay the loan within a predetermined period of time, the tax lien certificate holder is entitled to foreclose the property owner's right to redeem the property or the property owner's right to redeem the portion of the property held and assigned as collateral. Foreclosure permits the transfer of title to the deed from the property owner to either the tax lien certificate holder or both the lien holder and property owner. When a tax lien certificate is secured by less than 100 percent of the real property, foreclosure transfers the title of the property to both the lien certificate holder and property owner as tenants in common.

The sale of tax lien certificates benefits the taxing municipality, the property owner, and the purchaser. The taxing municipality benefits from the sale process by collecting the delinquent tax amount needed to fund government services. The timeliness of payments from investors not only allows the government to fund services, but also allows the government to provide uninterrupted services to the taxpaying community. The property owner who is delinquent in paying taxes benefits from the tax sale process because he or she is given an extended opportunity to pay delinquent property taxes. However, the inclusion of penalties, interest, and costs increases the amount that must be repaid to the lien certificate holder. The investor benefits by receiving, in most cases, either a high return on investment dollars used to acquire the tax lien certificate or ownership of the property if the loan is not repaid. The return on investment dollars is realized from the interest, penalty, or both that is required for redemption of the tax lien certificate. Ownership is realized once the investor engages in specific procedures to foreclose the right of redemption and obtain the deed and right of possession to the property.

```
               CERTIFICATE OF PURCHASE AT TAX SALE NUMBER 01-1772
                  TREASURER'S OFFICE, SHELBY COUNTY, STATE OF IOWA

I,                       , TREASURER, DO HEREBY CERTIFY THAT ON THE 18 DAY
OF JUNE,     2001, AT THE REGULAR       TAX SALE PUBLICLY HELD ON THAT DATE,
THE FOLLOWING PROPERTY SITUATED IN SHELBY COUNTY WAS SOLD TO:

FOR THE AMOUNT OF TAXES, INTEREST AND COSTS DUE AND REMAINING UNPAID.

DIST SH-CP                      TAXED TO:
ASSHC   PARCEL 832916000003

LEGAL DESCRIPTION:     33-78-40                   PT NW SW

YEAR TYPE  RECEIPT    AMOUNT      INTEREST      COSTS        TOTAL
1999 RE   90998.0     838.00       76.00         4.00        918.00
                                  SUBTOTAL                   918.00
                                  CERTIFICATE FEE             10.00
                                  GRAND TOTAL                 928.00

***********************************************************************
THIS BID WAS FOR A 100% INTEREST IN THE PROPERTY.
***********************************************************************

WITNESS MY HAND:
DATE JUNE 18, 2001     _____
                       TREASURER OF SHELBY COUNTY,

***********************************************************************
ASSIGNMENT: FOR THE PAYMENT OF $_____, AS PER AGREEMENT, I HEREBY
ASSIGN ALL RIGHTS, TITLE, AND INTEREST IN THIS CERTIFICATE TO:
                                                     SS_____

DATE    _____    _____
01-1772                           ASSIGNOR
```

Form 1: Sample Tax Lien Certificate

Different states have different methods of enforcing the laws pertaining to delinquent real estate taxes and tax lien certificates. State laws dictate the particular processes for conducting the annual tax sale. State laws, for example, may allow the tax sale to take place at any given time, on a specific date, or within some specified period. The particular city or county treasurer is responsible for determining where and when the tax sale is held, though the treasurer may allow an outside entity to actually host the sale on his or her behalf.

Tax lien certificate costs

Statutes that dictate the process for delinquent property tax sales, the assignment of tax lien certificates, the redemption of tax lien certificates, and the foreclosure process govern most states. In states that do not have statutes governing the annual tax sale, a reputable governing body is responsible for defining the process and entities responsible for the sale. The treasurer of each state municipality usually makes a determination of the cost to be applied to tax lien certificates. The cost may include any of the following:

- Delinquent property tax amount
- Other delinquent fees assessed against the securing real property
- Penalties
- Interest
- Administrative fees
- Cost of the tax sale
- Cost of issuing the tax certificate

The delinquent property tax amount always is included in the cost of a tax lien certificate. Other delinquent fees may include unpaid costs assessed for water and services provided by the governing body. Either state statute or a governing body of the particular jurisdiction establishes penalties, interest, administrative fees, and the cost of auctioning tax lien certificates at the tax sale. Each municipality's determination of the combination of costs is the advertised opening bid amount offered when tax lien certificates are auctioned at the delinquent property tax sale. The opening bid amount usually represents the minimum amount that must be bid.

Right of redemption

The sale of a tax lien certificate does not indicate a transfer of ownership to the tax lien certificate holder; nor does it allow the certificate holder any right of possession to the property that secures the tax lien certificate. States allow property owners to hold title to their property during the redemption period. This is inclusive of the property owner, mortgage lenders, and other lenders that may hold a deed of trust against the property. The delinquent property owner owns the property and has all rights of possession to the property until the lien certificate holder is able to foreclose the property owner's right of redemption. Even then, the owner still may hold partial ownership if the tax lien certificate was purchased by competitively bidding down ownership in the property.

Anyone can pay the redemption amount on behalf of the property owner, but only the bidder at the tax sale or the over-the-counter purchaser is able to purchase a tax lien certificate. The tax lien certificate holder, however, may assign his or her interest in the tax lien certificate to another party by entering into a contractual agreement with the other party or assignee. Contractual assignments are common among institutional investors that send hired representatives to tax sales. A representative bids on behalf of the company, using his or her own identity and transfers interest in any lien certificates acquired to his or her employer. The assignment is recorded with the taxing authority, and upon redemption, the last recorded assignee is paid the redemption amount.

The treasurer or tax collector is responsible for handling the redemption of tax lien certificates. He or she collects the redemption amounts and notifies the last assigned and recorded certificate holder of the redemption. Upon receipt of such notice, the tax lien certificate holder is required to return the tax lien certificate to the treasurer or tax collector. The treasurer or tax collector is then responsible for paying the redemption proceeds to the party to which the certificate is assigned.

Redemption period

The delinquent property owner has a responsibility to redeem the tax lien certificate from the tax lien certificate holder by paying the delinquent tax assessed against the property plus interest, penalties, fees, and costs of the sale within a specified time. This period is known as the redemption period, and it may range from 60 days to four years depending upon the particular state's statutes. The start of the redemption period usually is established as the day of the tax sale and may be applicable to tax lien certificates sold over the counter or auctioned later.

Interest and penalties may be applied to the redemption amount. Annual interest rates generally range between 6 and 24 percent of the tax lien plus associated costs, as established by state statute or a governing body. Penalty amounts also are established by state statute or a governing body and usually are set at a fixed percentage of the tax lien amount. Estimates indicate that property owners will redeem between 95 and 98 percent of all tax lien certificates offered for sale during the redemption period.

No right of redemption

In all states except Florida and Kentucky, if no one redeems a tax certificate within the specified redemption period, the certificate holder may follow prescribed procedures to foreclose the right of redemption and obtain title to the deed and right of possession to the property. Both Florida and Kentucky have processes in place to prevent a transfer of deed due solely to delinquent property taxes.

Florida state laws prohibit individuals from taking deed to property because of delinquent property taxes by including an additional step in the tax sale process. When a tax certificate is not redeemed during the redemption period, the property is auctioned again at a public oral bid foreclosure auction. The sale of tax lien certificates is really an offer to investors to profit from the redemption amount in return for paying delinquent taxes that are needed to fund government services. With this particular type of auction, the actual real estate is sold to the highest bidder, which may or may not be the tax lien certificate holder who has no additional rights to the property because of his certificate.

In Kentucky, if a tax lien certificate is not redeemed within one year of the tax sale, the tax lien holder is required to take legal action against the property owner for the amount paid to secure the tax lien certificate, the right to foreclose the right of redemption, or both. If the tax lien holder seeks to foreclose the right of redemption, the property must first be appraised and offered for sale at a public oral bid foreclosure auction. If there is no purchaser at the auction, the state commissioner may make deed to the tax certificate holder. If the tax lien certificate specifies a percentage of ownership, the winning bidder is deeded the applicable percentage of the tenancy-in-common. Kentucky laws further stipulate the following:

- If the foreclosure auction does not result in proceeds equal to two-thirds of the appraised value of the property, the property owner is given an additional year to redeem the property at the original purchase price of the tax lien certificate plus 10 percent of that purchase price.

- During the new redemption period, the property owner receives a writ of possession and a deed with a lien in favor of the owner.

- Upon paying the newly established redemption amount to the court that ordered the judgment, the state commissioner may make deed to the property owner.

Chapter 2

Delinquent Properties

With the exception of Indian reservations, real property taxes are assessed for all real property in the United States. Each state requires real property owners to pay real property taxes for each parcel of improved or unimproved property owned. Property taxes are ad valorem taxes, which means that the tax is based on the value of the property. Each state and each municipality within the state has its own method of calculating the value of property and the associated tax amount required from its taxpayers. Real property taxes are assessed against residential homes, rental homes, vacant lots, commercial properties, and industrial properties. The state and taxing municipalities that provide services and functionality to the various jurisdictions use these taxes to maintain and provide services to the community. Real property taxes are assessed by the governing municipality and billed to the property owner for payment. Payment is required within a specified period each year. When real property taxes are not paid within the specified time frame, the tax on the property becomes delinquent. Delinquent property taxes create a shortfall for the governing municipality, interrupting its ability to provide needed and vital services. To encourage property owners to pay the necessary property taxes, municipalities assess penalties, interest, and costs against the delinquent property when the tax is not paid on time. Furthermore, governing bodies may offer the property or a lien against the property for sale at the particular municipality's real property tax sale.

Single-Family Housing Units

Single-family units continue to make up the largest percentage of properties with tax lien certificates offered for sale. Single-family housing units provide living space for a single-family unit. These properties offer profit potential when the assessed property taxes become delinquent because individuals are likely to redeem the tax lien held against a property they own. Single-family homes that are also owner-occupied offer the greatest chance of being redeemed by the owner-occupants. Homeowners are not likely to allow the loss of their investment and living space for the relatively small cost of property taxes. When a single-family unit is also a rental unit, the property is used to generate income for the property owner. To continue receiving income from the property, the property owner is likely to redeem the tax lien certificate. Because the delinquent tax amount represents the tax for a single property, the property tax lien is often more affordable than tax liens for multiple family units. Property owners are not only likely to redeem such small debts against the property, but they are also more likely to redeem the tax lien quickly.

Multiple-Family Housing Units

Companies, as opposed to individuals, usually own multiple-family housing units, such as duplexes and apartment buildings. This type of property usually is held as an income-producing investment, and any tax lien held against the property is likely to be redeemed to maintain the investment.

Multiple-family housing units composed of one to four family units offer the most profit potential, as the tax liens held against properties of this magnitude are far more affordable than those of larger housing units that provide living space for many more family units.

Homestead Properties

A homestead property is an occupied property for which the occupants have filed an exemption to paying property taxes. If the occupants qualify for the exemption, the municipality deducts a fixed amount from the appraised value of the property and uses the newly established value in determining the real property tax to be paid on the property. A homestead property indicates that a property serves as a principal residence. Homestead properties offer profit potential, as the property is likely to be the only residence of the property owner, and he or she is not interested in losing such accommodations, particularly at the reduced property tax amount. Homestead property owners are likely to redeem any tax liens held against the property as quickly as possible and offer a high rate of return on investment dollars.

Mortgaged Properties

The mortgage lender is almost guaranteed to redeem mortgaged properties. These properties provide security for the mortgage loan held by the property owner. When the property owner fails to pay required property taxes and allows the property to go to tax sale, the mortgage company risks having the mortgage wiped out should the tax lien certificate holder foreclose the property owner's right to redeem the tax lien certificate. Because tax liens are senior to mortgage and other lender liens held against a parcel of property, a foreclosure by the tax lien certificate holder wipes out any lender liens. Mortgage companies have a vested interest in redeeming tax lien certificates so they, not the tax lien certificate holder, are in the position of being able to foreclose the property owner's right to the property. A mortgage company is not going to have its loan erased for the relatively small cost associated with delinquent taxes unless it is upside down in the property, which implies that the loan amount exceeds the property value by a significant amount. Otherwise, the mortgage company will redeem the tax lien certificate and exercise its right to foreclose the property owner's right to the mortgage loan due to failure to pay property taxes. The property owner then would be put in the position of having to pay the delinquent property taxes and any arrearages to reinstate the mortgage loan. If the property owner is not capable of paying, the mortgage company will foreclose the property and resell it. To prevent property owners from defaulting on property tax payments, mortgage lenders generally require that property owners pay into a tax and insurance escrow account as part of their monthly mortgage payments. The mortgage company, not the individual, is then responsible for withdrawing funds from the escrow account to pay any real property taxes when they become due. Many states allow property taxes to be paid semiannually. In such instances, the mortgage company will disburse funds from the escrow account on a semiannual basis in line with the state's payment schedule.

Trust deed

Rather than a traditional mortgage, some states allow lenders to engage property owners with a trust deed against the property. A trust deed is a contract used as security for a loan. The property owner, by engaging in a trust deed, transfers legal title to his or her property to a trustee for the duration of the loan. The trust deed gives the trustee the power to sell the property if the property owner does not live up to the terms of the trust deed agreement. Even though the property owner transfers legal title to the property, he or she retains possession of it for the duration of the loan.

Worthless Properties

Without making a visual inspection of properties offered for sale at the annual tax sale, the investor has no way of knowing whether a lien certificate is secured by a valuable piece of property, a vacant lot, or an abandoned and dilapidated property. The objective of investing in tax lien certificates is to profit from high redemption amounts or to gain property ownership. When a worthless parcel of property secures a tax lien certificate, the certificate is also worthless. That is why investors are encouraged to research properties to determine the suitability of a property for investment purposes. A given in investing in tax lien certificates is that raw land or vacant lots require more research and investigation than improved properties. In most instances, it is safe to assume that an improved property provides some use even if its current use is not the best use of the property. A vacant lot, on the other hand, may not prove to be of much use.

The Internet can be useful in performing an initial sieve of likely properties. A program such as Google Earth™ is a free way to see street views of many roads, so you can see the area and the particular address. Although properties can change and the pictures might be from a year or two ago, this can save a lot of needless travel. A personal visit and inspection always will be advisable for properties of interest.

Vacant lots

Vacant lots may be valuable to investors seeking to develop land, but they must be suitable for a development effort and must not be landlocked, which means that a parcel of property has no method of entry or departure, except through someone else's property. Landlocked and vacant lots also may be positioned so they are not served by utilities and are far out of the path of any utility-servicing entities, such as those that provide gas and electricity. For the investor seeking to profit from redemption amounts or the investor seeking to gain ownership of a useful or valuable property, a vacant lot may prove to be a worthless investment. A truly worthless property that serves no use or no longer supports its intended use is not likely to be redeemed by the property owner. Such a property will be just as worthless to the investor who forecloses and obtains ownership. This is common with properties that are situated in the desert, on mountainous terrain, or in flood plains. Vacant lots usually are sold at the low end of bid prices. Some tax collectors attempt to prevent the sale of worthless properties by not selling liens on properties with delinquent tax amounts under a certain threshold, say $100. Most tax collectors, on the other hand, put the responsibility for researching properties on the investor and sell tax lien certificates on worthless and landlocked properties.

A vacant lot may not be developable if the development effort violates the zoning regulations of the local government. The responsibility for researching the zoning regulations that apply to a particular parcel of land falls on the investor. The investor also should research any proposed or contingent plans of the municipality to determine what will be done with the land in the near future. If the municipality is in the process of zoning a potential parcel of land for industrial use or it is planning to zone the areas surrounding the parcel for industrial use, the investor needs to know that before acquiring the land for the development of residential homes.

An investor must determine whether the land has any access to water or a sewage disposal system. In many urban areas, a developer simply hooks into the existing systems. However, some areas are not near such systems. The owner may need to provide water for the land if the land has no usable ground water or install a leach field for the property when access to a public sewage disposal system is not attainable. These could be expensive and time-consuming processes if the local municipality does not service the land. Trying to make use of a watershed that is owned by someone or installing a leach field on land that cannot accommodate the system could complicate the investment strategy by creating additional legal and environmental issues.

An investor also must determine if the property lies in a flood plain or is in the path of any historical mudslides. Properties affected by these and other types of natural occurrences may not show any visible signs of damage. Events such as flooding may occur only during specific times of the year. If flooding is excessive during summer, it may not be obvious to the investor during the winter months. A check of the records held by the local planning department may indicate any special designations, such as flood plains, that are recorded. Also, the library or other sources of reference materials may indicate any historical events that may have affected the area.

Abandoned properties

Tax lien certificates may be sold when they are secured by worthless properties with vacant and dilapidated structures. Some of these properties may be identified by the small amount of delinquent taxes assessed against them, which assumes that advertised properties are in their first year of delinquency. That is not always the case. Some states allow property taxes to accrue on abandoned properties for years, even if the property has been partially or completely destroyed. The delinquent tax amount advertised for tax sale purposes may have accrued over years and can be misleading to the investor who is not familiar with the community. Proper research of advertised properties will indicate whether the delinquent tax amount represents a fair amount or an amount in excess of the property's worth. Assessments may not be accurate, as assessors are not immune from making mistakes or recording the wrong information for their valuations. Proper assessments also are not made as frequently as jurisdictions claim they are. It is not uncommon for properties to have undergone major renovations, restructuring, or damage that is not considered in valuation assessments.

Commercial properties

Commercial properties also can be worthless for the investor who is not skilled in commercial real estate. These properties may include structures that indicate a useful business purpose. However, the structures and property may prove to be inadequate for establishing a business operation. The property may be in violation of zoning and other regulations and environmental, health, and building codes. It may have served its previous owners well until new laws and regulations were enacted, but it may be too expensive to bring it into compliance with new codes and standards. Institutional investors usually invest in these types of properties because they have the capital to maintain the properties or revitalize those that have deteriorated.

Chapter 3

Income and Growth Potential

An investment in tax lien certificates is considered a safe investment because the investment is secured by real estate. Tax lien certificates offer income and growth potential that is more consistent than that of other investment opportunities, such as real estate, stocks, bonds, certificates of deposit, and money market funds. The risks are also relatively small compared to other investments. When investors invest in residential real estate by purchasing the property on the real estate market, for example, the property has no income potential unless it is used as a rental property. That parcel of residential real estate, on the other hand, offers profit potential as either a personal residence or rental property. The growth in profit, however, depends upon an expected increase in the property's value over the years of ownership. Overall, residential property values had a history of steady increases, which fuelled the interest in investment at least until the "housing bubble" of recent years, and there is no guarantee that increases will take place for a particular parcel of property securing a tax lien certificate. It is hoped and expected that foreclosing a property owner's right to redeem a tax lien certificate will leave the investor with a residential property that increases in value during ownership. The investor then would be capable of selling the property at a profit over the amount invested. When investors invest in tax lien certificates secured by residential properties, the tax lien certificates guarantee both income potential and growth potential. Income potential is realized when a property owner redeems a tax lien certificate. The property owner has to pay, at a minimum, the delinquent tax amount plus any assessed interest and penalties. The tax lien certificate purchaser is guaranteed to collect the investment amount with interest at the established rate. The interest continues to accrue throughout the redemption period and offers growth potential throughout this period. Even if the property owner should fail to redeem the tax lien certificate, the investor may foreclose the right of redemption and gain ownership of the property at a fraction of the property's value. The newly owned property offers the investor both income and growth potential, as the property either may be sold at market value for an amount in excess of the amount spent to acquire the property, or it may be rented to produce income over time.

Risk Factors

In all investments, including investments in tax lien certificates, there are risks. Since there is no way to avoid all investment risk, the smart investor must develop strategies to manage and minimize risk. Following good investment practices by consulting with or hiring an experienced accountant and attorney is the first step in eliminating and minimizing investment risk. Another successful method of minimizing risk is to engage in practices of risk management. At first thought, it would seem that the only way to truly avoid investment risk is to avoid making investments. After all, accumulated monies that are left "under the mattress" are safe from loss and taxation. The money incurs no tax obligations because there is no income from the money, no gain for the owner, and no amount to tax. However, taxes are just one aspect of an investment. The money never will be lost unless, of course, someone steals it from under the mattress. Notwithstanding any type of theft, the same amount of money put under the mattress will be available when the money is taken from under the mattress. However, the value of money kept under the mattress will decrease over time due to inflation. So, rather than avoiding risk, money left under the mattress really generates a loss. Even if such funds were deposited into a bank savings account, the low interest rates applied to savings also would create a loss over time. The interest rate paid by banks is usually not sufficient to keep up with inflation, and it certainly does not compare to the high interest rates applied to the redemption of tax lien certificates.

An investor must weigh all options responsible for creating the various types of risk and determine the level of risk appropriate for the particular type of investment opportunity. An investor also must consider the effect that investing will have on employment, assets, and other life factors. A young investor, for example, may want to commit huge sums of money in investment opportunities with the expectation of huge returns in the future. The theory behind this type of investment strategy is that the young investor will be vested for many years and, thus, is guaranteed to profit on those investments in later years. There is one problem with this type of strategy. Longevity is not guaranteed. The young investor, by engaging in this type of strategy, may incur other losses during his or her young life and not benefit from the profits promised for the future. The young investor, for example, may accumulate huge lines of credit during the investment years that will consume the profits made from investing in later years. Even worse, the investor may not live long enough to collect on the profit. The smart investor must use techniques of risk management

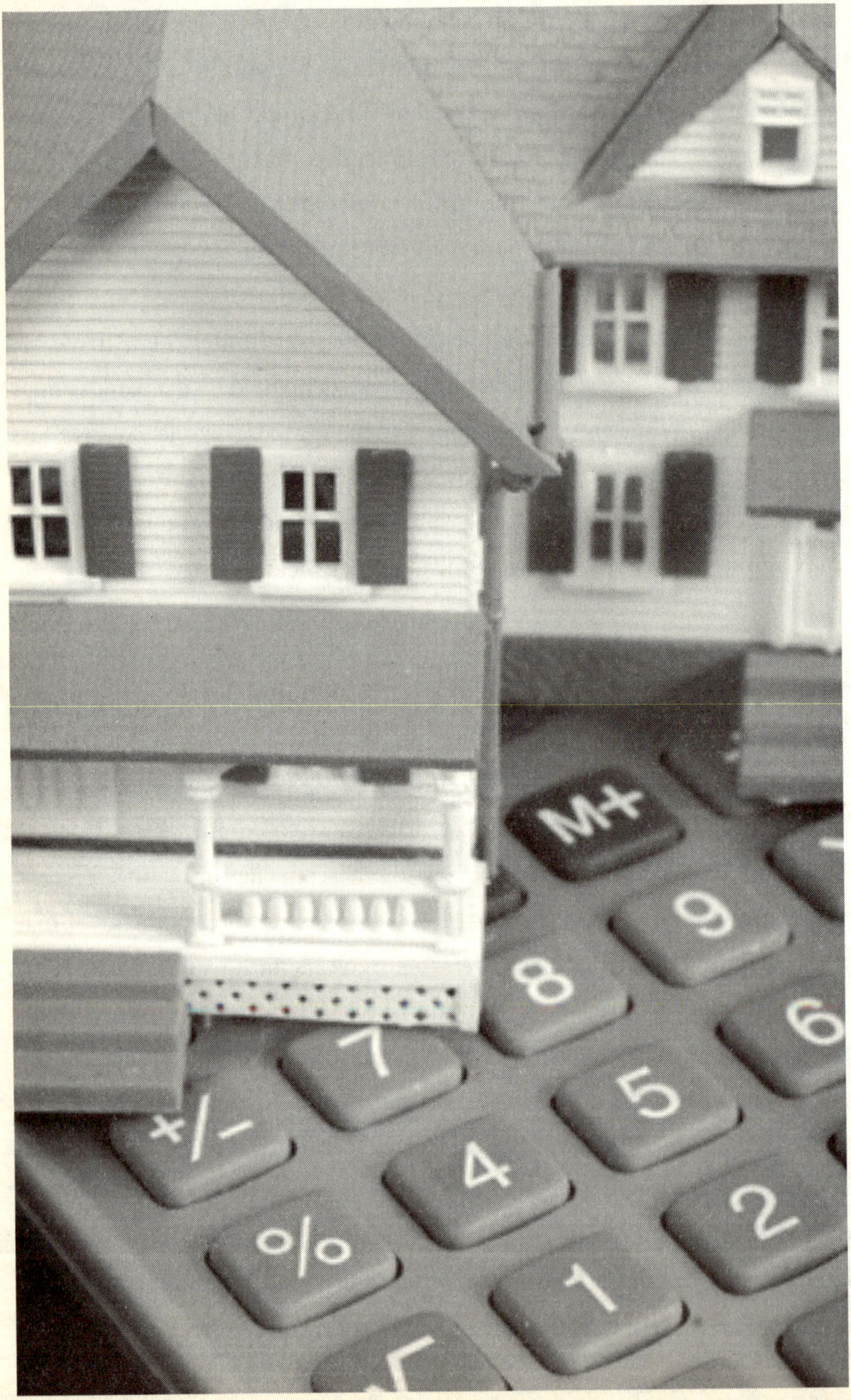

that will reduce the likelihood of all losses. These techniques must include methods of diversification and dollar cost averaging, but one of the most important techniques involves choosing quality markets to invest in. Some markets are more capable of protecting investors against loss than others. The investor should dedicate time and resources to finding the appropriate, quality markets and understand when he or she is allowed to enter them and when he or she should or is able to get rid of them. Investments in tax lien certificates are protected against loss, because the investment dollars are secured by real estate, which if properly chosen, provides more worth than the dollars invested.

Market risk

Market risk means that an investment may sell in the marketplace for less than the amount that was invested to acquire it. Using the stock market as example, an investor may purchase stock in a company that offers unlimited growth potential. The investor makes the purchase when the stock is at its high point and later discovers that the value of the stock is on a constant decline. The investor then sells the stock at a much lower amount than its purchase price and accepts the resulting loss. Market risks may be caused by a number of factors that are internal and external to a business entity. The decline in the value of stocks is such a risk. Tax lien certificates, on the other hand, offer negligible market risk because established laws require the property owner to pay the interest and other costs required for redemption or risk losing their property, which is usually worth far more than the debt. The tax lien certificate holder is guaranteed to receive a return on the investment through either the interest-bearing redemption amount paid by the property owner or the right to foreclose and take ownership of the property itself.

Safety risk

Safety risk is the risk of investing in an investment that is not secured. Certificates of deposit, for example, may be backed by a federal insurance agency, which seems to indicate a safe and secure investment opportunity. However, such agencies have been known to have internal issues that deplete the agency of its funds. If the federal government chooses not to replenish the fund, the security of the investment is lost. Tax lien certificates, on the other hand, are secured by real estate. In particular, the parcel of real estate for which a tax lien certificate is assigned acts as the security for the tax lien certificate. In addition, the cost of a tax lien certificate is rarely in excess of the value of the property. With the inclusion of penalties, interest, fees, and other costs that are added to the cost of a lien certificate, the certificate usually represents only a fraction of the property's market value. As such, the amount invested in tax lien certificates is safe whether the tax lien certificate is redeemed or the right of redemption is foreclosed. In the case of foreclosure, the investor may incur additional expenses to complete the foreclosure process, but the total costs are usually much less than the fair market value of the property that would be received if the property were sold. Many investors are likely to sell the property to recover the costs and to make a profit. Properties often are sold at less than fair market value, and the investor still is able to recover, as a minimum, the total investment amount. Other investors may rent the property to recover the cost and profit from the investment.

Liquidity risk

Liquidity risk is the risk that the investment is not capable of being quickly converted to cash. Some markets are structured so it is not easy to convert the investment to cash when needed. Certificates of deposit, for example, must be held until maturity or the investor is required to pay penalties for early withdrawals. The penalty amount along with the tax consequences may wipe out any profit from the investment, and in the worst case, an early withdrawal could create an investment loss. As another example, the income generated from investments such as money market accounts is dependent upon interest rates. When interest rates fall, investment dollars may be transferable to other types of investments, but the investment dollars may not be liquidated without paying a penalty for the withdrawal of funds. If the money is withdrawn rather than transferred, not only is a penalty applied, but the investor also is obligated to pay taxes on the amount withdrawn. Tax lien certificates, on the other hand, offer limited liquidity, as the return on investment dollars cannot be realized until the property owner redeems the tax lien certificate, a foreclosure takes place and the foreclosed property is sold, or the tax lien certificate holder assigns the certificate to another party for a fee. No matter how long the investor waits for redemption, the established interest rate remains constant and will not fluctuate as stock prices do. The return is guaranteed to exceed the cost of acquiring the tax lien certificate. When certificates are assigned to another party, the assignee pays an amount in excess of the amount spent to acquire the tax lien certificate. The proceeds from both redemption and assignment of a tax lien certificate are liquid. Likewise, when a foreclosure takes place, the property may be sold or rented for amounts that exceed the amount spent to acquire the certificate and to foreclose. The proceeds from a foreclosure sale or from renting a foreclosed property are liquid.

Overhead risk

Overhead risk is the risk of taking a loss in the operation of a business entity. In some business ventures, the amount of overhead expenses consumes any profits that are made, and the cost never is recovered. Labor, travel, research, and investigation are necessary overhead expenses that accrue regardless of the outcome of the investment opportunity. In most businesses, these types of overhead expenses are a deductible expense. The laws pertaining to tax lien investment opportunities are not so clearly defined. The consensus is that the expenses associated with traveling to various tax sales in search of tax lien certificates and the cost of researching and investigating properties that secure tax lien certificates are not considered overhead expense but part of the cost of investing. Only after a tax lien certificate is purchased and assigned are such expenses considered deductible overhead expenses. The investor should consult with his or her accountant or lawyer for the specifics of the tax law.

Tax lien certificates offer minimal risks compared to other investment opportunities. Table 3 below outlines a comparison of tax lien certificates versus other forms of investment.

Table 3
COMPARISON OF INVESTMENT OPPORTUNITIES

Investment	Income Potential	Growth Potential	Market Risk	Safety	Liquidity	Overhead
Tax lien certificates	Yes	Yes	Minimal	Yes	[1]No	High
Residential real estate	No	Inconsistent	High	Yes	[2]No	High
Rental real estate	Inconsistent	Inconsistent	High	Yes	[2]No	High
Stocks	Inconsistent	Inconsistent	High	Inconsistent	Yes	Minimal
Bonds	Yes	Inconsistent	High	Yes	Yes	Minimal
Certificates of deposit	Yes	No	Minimal	Yes	[1]No	Minimal
Money market funds	Yes	No	High	Yes	Yes	Minimal

[1]Liquidity requires redemption.
[2]Liquidity requires the sale of the investment.

Chapter 4

The Annual Tax Sale

Most tax deed states hold periodic delinquent property tax sales. Depending on the taxing jurisdiction of the state, sales may be held as often as weekly, or the range of sales may extend to monthly, quarterly, or biannually. Most tax lien states, on the other hand, hold annual property tax sales. The annual sale is a process of auctioning available tax lien certificates to the public. In order to participate and bid on properties offered for auction, individuals must register and obtain a bidder number and bidder card. Auctions are held throughout a period predetermined and set aside by the taxing authority to complete the offering of tax lien certificates. Some smaller jurisdictions are capable of completing the tax sale in a single day. Larger jurisdictions usually set aside a period of days for the annual tax sale.

Tax Sale Listings

A listing of properties with delinquent property taxes precedes the annual tax sale. Most municipalities publish the listing in a local newspaper weeks before the tax sale takes place. Municipalities that do not have a local newspaper may publish the listing in some other form of print media, or they may be required to post it at some public location. In recent years, some municipalities have published tax sale listings on the Internet. The city or county treasurer is usually responsible for the tax sale and serves as the primary point of contact for information regarding the publication of a municipality's tax sale listing. Newspaper listings are most likely to be published in the legal section of the newspaper, along with other public and legal notices. Most listings include a parcel number, a legal description, and the amount of delinquent taxes. The listing also contains the name and address of the property owner. Some advertised properties also might have designations that indicate specific characteristics of the property. Some tax assessors have websites that may provide the investor with general characteristics of a property, such as zoning information, square footage, the year in which structures were built, and the property's appraised value. Investors should understand that an assessor's appraised valuation is not necessarily the same as the property's market value.

Registration

Bidders are required to register before participating in an annual tax sale auction. Registration involves requiring participants to provide their Social Security or tax identification number (TIN), together with other identifying information, to the taxing municipality. Different municipalities have differing rules and procedures with respect to registration, but most require a Social Security number or TIN. States may require bidders to complete Internal Revenue Service (IRS) Form W-9, "Request for Taxpayer Identification Number and Certification." The identifying Social Security number or TIN is necessary so the municipality can meet its legal obligation to report interest received from redemptions to the IRS. Interest received from the redemption of a tax lien certificate is income to a certificate holder. Registrants also may be required to pay a registration fee before bidding, or they may be required to make a minimum deposit.

When a deposit is required, it is applied to the total dollar amount of lien certificates purchased by a particular bidder. If a bidder does not purchase any tax lien certificates, the deposit is refunded. Some taxing authorities require participants to register for the tax sale as much as a month in advance of the auction. Others allow participants to register in advance of the sale or on the day of auction. Although a tax sale may be held at a town hall or convention center, it usually is situated so that the auction is held in a different area than the registration. Registered bidders are assigned a bidder number and given a bidder card to be used at the auction, usually an oral bid type auction in which bidders must convey their bid amounts orally to the auctioneer.

Some municipalities allow bidders to acquire multiple bidder numbers and bid for multiple tax lien certificates. In Los Angeles, for example, an individual may register on behalf of another person as long as a notarized copy of the power of attorney, as granted to the bidder, is provided along with a valid photo ID. A sample of the bidder registration form used in Los Angeles is shown in Form 2 (see page 46). Los Angeles also allows individuals to register on behalf of a company, corporation, public agency, or partnership as long as notarized copies of the documents granting the bidder authority to register and bid on behalf of the particular entity are provided along with a valid photo ID. Such documentation may include a power of attorney, a resolution showing the corporate seal, a partnership agreement, or corporate minutes showing the corporate seal. The form of a document used to authorize an individual to act on behalf of another entity is shown in Form 3 (see page 47). Bidders must be clear in indicating the manner in which they are bidding on behalf of another entity. Should a property owner fail to redeem a tax lien certificate, the deed conveying title to the property will be vested in the same manner as the registration was vested to purchase the certificate.

Los Angeles County
TREASURER AND TAX COLLECTOR

BIDDER REGISTRATION FORM

Attention Bidders: Persons wishing to bid at the tax sale must pre-register **in-person**. A deposit of $1,000 in the form of a Cashier's Check or bank issued Money Order payable to the Los Angeles County Tax Collector is required at the time of registration. A Bidder Registration Form must be completed and submitted in-person with your deposit. Valid picture identification (driver's license, military identification or state identification card) is required for all registering parties. If you register or request vesting for someone else, you must provide a notarized copy of the power of attorney for each person you represent, along with your valid picture identification. If you register or request vesting for a public agency, company, corporation, or partnership, you will need to provide **notarized copies** of the document that gives you the authority to register and bid on their behalf, along with your valid picture identification.

BIDDER'S NAME: _____
signature(s) required below   REQUIRED FIELD (PLEASE PRINT CLEARLY)

8:00 AM TO 5:00 PM PHONE NUMBER (___)_____
                                    REQUIRED FIELD

VESTING NAME: _____
signature(s) required below

ADDRESS: _____

_____
CITY   STATE   ZIP

PLEASE SHOW HOW TITLE IS TO BE VESTED

_____ HUSBAND AND WIFE AS JOINT TENANTS   _____ A SINGLE MAN
      (REQUIRES BOTH SIGNATURES)

_____ AS TENANTS IN COMMON   _____ A SINGLE WOMAN
      (REQUIRES SIGNATURES OF ALL PARTIES)

_____ A MARRIED MAN AS HIS SOLE & SEPARATE PROPERTY   _____ AN UNMARRIED MAN

_____ A MARRIED WOMAN AS HER SOLE & SEPARATE PROPERTY _____ AN UNMARRIED WOMAN

_____ A MARRIED MAN   _____ A CORPORATION
                                                        (REQUIRES ARTICLES OF INCORPORATION
_____ A MARRIED WOMAN   AND ORDER BY AUTHORIZED MEMBER OF THE
                                                        BOARD OF DIRECTORS GIVING YOU AUTHORITY
                                                        TO BID & VEST PROPERTY.)

_____ A WIDOWER (MAN)   _____ A PUBLIC AGENCY
                                                        (REQUIRES CERTIFIED ORDER FROM THE
_____ A WIDOW (WOMAN)   GOVERNING BOARD GIVING YOU
                                                        AUTHORITY TO BID & VEST PROPERTY)

_____ OTHER

BIDDER'S SIGNATURE _____

OTHER SIGNATURES _____

DATE _____

PLEASE NOTE THAT THE PURCHASE OF TAX-DEFAULTED PROPERTY MADE IS AT YOUR OWN RISK. VESTING INFORMATION CANNOT BE CHANGED AFTER THE REGISTRATION PERIOD HAS CLOSED.

Form 2: Bidder Registration Form

> To: Treasurer Name
> Jurisdiction County Treasurer
> 123 Municipal Avenue
> Anytown, USA 12345
>
> **AUTHORIZATION TO REPRESENT BIDDER**
>
> I / we, (please print)
>
> _____
> (Bidder's name, as it appears on the registration form)
>
> authorize (please print)
>
> _____
>
> to act as my / our personal representative at the Harrison County Tax Sale held on June 18, 2006.
>
>
> _____
> (Signature)
>
> _____
> (Address)
>
> _____
> (City, State, Zip Code) Date:

Form 3: Authorization to Represent Bidder

Meeting the Schedule

Municipalities have established times and schedules for completing the tax sale process and either are mandated or courteous in publishing the schedule to be followed for the tax sale as well as the listing of properties with delinquent taxes. However, tax sale auctioneers and officials have a tendency to fall behind schedule, particularly in those municipalities that engage in competitive bidding and those that are mandated to sell their tax lien certificates during the tax sale. When the auctioning gets behind schedule, modifications to the schedule either are announced during the tax sale or distributed to the participants, but not formally published in the newspaper. Likewise, new listings may be generated but not formally published and distributed to the public. The published tax sale schedule usually allows breaks to enable bidders and officials ample time to handle administrative and other issues during the tax sale process. However, tax sale officials often rotate auctioneers to keep the process flowing during breaks or extend the tax sale day beyond the published and advertised hours to meet their schedule. Thus, tax sales may continue throughout the day with no breaks, or the sales may extend until 7 or 8 p.m. — well beyond the published and documented end of the tax sale day.

The sale also may continue until all available and scheduled certificates are offered for sale. In many instances, tax sale officials may switch the bidding system being used in an attempt to meet their schedules. The state of Florida, for example, allows competitive bidding on the percentage of interest to be paid upon redemption. When auctions are behind schedule, however, officials have been known to resort to random methods of choosing winning bidders. This switch in bidding systems usually occurs at or near the end of the tax sale day and on the final day of the tax sale. When this happens, the auctioneers and tax sale officials have some indication as to whether they will be capable of meeting the goal of offering a certain number of tax liens for sale. If they perceive that the day's "quota" cannot be met using established procedures, they may, without notice, switch to a quicker method of bidding.

Keeping Pace

Auctioneers, like bidders, are human and must deal with the fast, repetitive process inherent in oral bid auctions. Most auctions follow some sort of tempo, but, generally, auctions move at a fast pace, particularly when the auctioneers have several hundred or several thousand tax lien certificates to sell within a matter of days. As with most auctions, once a property is introduced and an opening bid is announced, bidders must be prepared to offer their bids because, in most instances, a pause in the bidding ends the bidding for a particular tax lien certificate. Once a winner has been announced, the auctioneer will not go back.

Bidders must be both patient and alert to avoid becoming distracted. A distracted bidder may not realize that the bidding for a particular property has ended. He or she then jumps back into the process, but ends up bidding on the wrong property. In some states, if a bidder realizes his or her mistake and makes the auctioneer or official aware of it before the bidding ends for the day, he or she may be relieved of the obligation to pay for the tax lien certificate. In most instances, however, bids are final. They may not be exchanged or refunded. In some states, failure to pay the bid amount and associated fees can lead to a penalty, imprisonment, or both. The county of Marion, Indiana, for example, stipulates that bidders who fail to pay the bid price in acceptable funds will be charged a penalty equal to 25 percent of the bid amount and may be subject to prosecution. The city of Los Angeles stipulates that all sales are final and that payment must be made immediately upon winning the bid. Bidders and any co-registered bidders who fail to pay the bid amount on bids less than $5,000 have their bidder cards confiscated and voided and forfeit their right to participate further in the sale. Bids over $5,000 require a minimum deposit equal to the greater of $5,000 or 10 percent of the bid amount. The balance must be paid within 30 days of tax sale day. If the balance of the bid is not paid within the 30-day period, the bidder forfeits his or her total deposit.

Restrictions on Bids

States may impose restrictions on the number of bids that a bidder can make at auction by requiring one or more of the following:

1. A deposit for each bid opportunity
2. A different Social Security number or tax identification number for each bidder number
3. One bid per bidder number

The most restrictive auctions implement all three. Only investors who are capable of bringing associates to the auction may overcome such restrictions, and even then, he or she would need to have an associate for each bid to acquire multiple tax lien certificates. As an alternative, the investor and his or her associates may register and bid at auction, leave the auction area, and reregister to bid with a different bidder number. This process would continue until all lien certificates of interest had been bid. This is particularly useful for investors who are restricted by a municipality that insists on one bid per bidder number. Even when a municipality requires a different Social Security or tax identification number for each bidder number, an investor can use his or her own Social Security number to represent himself or herself, a tax identification number to represent a corporate interest, and the Social Security numbers of children, relatives, or associates to overcome such restrictions. The acquired tax lien certificates then may be assigned to the investor for a nominal charge.

Opportunities to Invest

One of the disadvantages of tax sales for investors is that most are held annually. In addition, in many states, the counties hold their annual tax sales on the same day, which makes it impossible for investors to be present at multiple auctions. This limits the number of opportunities investors have to invest in tax lien certificates. Investors are able to maximize their investment dollars if they can reinvest funds received from redemption amounts in new tax liens. But, again, because most tax sales only are offered annually, the opportunity to reinvest in a particular municipality's lien certificates is lost unless that municipality offers over-the-counter sales of unsold lien certificates. In municipalities that offer attractive interest rates, it is highly unlikely that any such tax lien certificates will be available for offer after the tax sale has ended.

Public oral bid

Most states still engage in the traditional method of offering tax lien certificates at auction using a public oral bid system. This type of system requires bidders or their authorized representatives be present at the sale during the time that properties of interest are offered. Some states such as Missouri have residential requirements, too. Tax lien certificates usually are offered in the order in which they are publicized in the tax sale listing. Listings may be ordered by block and lot number, street address, or some other classification established by the treasurer of the municipality. If an investor is interested in multiple properties located in different areas of the municipality, the properties of interest are likely to be distributed throughout the tax sale listing. In larger municipalities, the investor may have to attend the tax sale for multiple days in order to bid personally on properties of interest. Larger municipalities may have so many tax lien certificates for sale that their auctions may take days to complete. In smaller municipalities, the tax sale may be completed within hours or within a day. Adequate research will uncover the smaller municipalities with fewer lien certificates for sale. The very organized and mobile investor may be capable of attending multiple auctions in a single state during the state's auctioning period. In all public oral bid auctions, the investor is limited to the choice of lien certificates available during his or her attendance.

Over-the-counter sales

In most states, when tax lien certificates are not sold at the annual tax sale, those certificates are offered afterward over the counter. When tax lien certificates are offered over the counter, there are no competitive bidders to bid against one another. Tax lien certificates are purchased for the minimum amount, which includes the delinquent tax amount and incurred penalties, interest, and costs. There is no premium amount added to the cost of tax lien certificates. The interest and penalty rates applied to redemption amounts are usually the same as those applied to tax lien certificates sold at the annual tax sale for all states, except those states that engage in the competitive bidding down of interest rates. Because there is no competitive bidding, the interest and penalty rates applied to redemption amounts are set at the maximum rates established by state statute or the maximum rate established by the governing body of the municipality. Some municipalities even allow investors to purchase over-the-counter lien certificates through the mail, which eliminates the need for investors to be physically present for the sale. This creates additional opportunities for an individual to invest in tax lien certificates and reduces an investor's traveling expenses.

In some municipalities, the demand for over-the-counter certificates is more intense than the demand for lien certificates offered for sale at the annual tax sale. In the tax deed state of Michigan, for example, a tax lien certificate is assigned to the winning bidder at auction. The property owner is given one year to redeem the tax lien certificate, or the lien certificate holder may surrender the certificate for a tax deed. The interest rate for tax lien certificates is 15 percent annually and increases to 50 percent annually in the second year of delinquency. The bidding system used at tax sales provides for bidders to bid down the percentage of ownership in a property. The investor becomes a tenant-in-common with the property owner if no redemption takes place. If, however, lien certificates are offered over the counter after the tax sale, the investor is entitled to purchase the certificates without bidding down ownership. Should the property owner fail to redeem the certificate, the investor may foreclose the right of redemption and follow procedures to gain 100 percent ownership of the property. Even more attractive to investors are over-the-counter certificates secured by properties in the second year of delinquency when the interest rate applied to redemption amounts is maximized to 50 percent.

Online auctions

As an alternative to traditional oral bid auctions that require bidders to be present physically, some municipalities are engaging in online Internet auctions. Companies have been set up that specialize in this process, and in some states, many counties use the same online provider. This type of auction is relatively new, and the investor must rely upon his or her ability to research the systems used in municipalities of interest to understand the system. The state of Florida, for example, has implemented online auctioning for many of its larger jurisdictions.

Using the traditional oral bid auction system, the state of Florida used to hold its 67 annual tax sales during the months of May and June. A deposit of $1,000 was required to obtain a bidder number and the right to bid for tax lien certificates. In larger counties, tax sale officials allowed bidders to be invoiced for the amounts bid at auction. Invoices were mailed to bidders within two weeks of the tax sale. Some municipalities allowed bidders an additional two weeks to pay the remaining bid amount in certified funds. Other municipalities allowed bidders an additional one to two days to make a certified payment.

Orange County, Orlando, is one of the larger municipalities in Florida where the traditional oral bid auction has been replaced by an online system. The online system now is used to handle the bid-down auctioning system used by Orange County. The process is as follows:

1. Bidders register online at the specified website.

2. Advance payment of $1,000 per bidder number is paid to Orange County.
3. Registrants search tax liens published with the particular lien amount and parcel identification number.
4. Bidders enter a bid percentage for a desired property.
5. At the specified time during the auction, a computer algorithm chooses the winning bid and bidder.
6. In a tie, the computer algorithm makes a random pick of the winner.

Online auctions promise to increase the efficiency of auctioning systems. Investors accustomed to the interaction of traditional oral bid auctions will have to adjust to the convenience of bidding online rather than traveling to various locations to participate in the auction process. The Internet also promises to provide more efficiency and accuracy in listing properties for sale and eliminating properties from the listing when redemption occurs soon before the tax sale.

Payment

Each taxing municipality establishes and publishes rules and guidelines to be followed during the auction process. When tax lien certificates are purchased, payment is made to the taxing jurisdiction responsible for the tax sale. The rules and guidelines dictate how payments for the certificates are to be made to the particular taxing municipality.

Most tax collectors request that payments be made with certified funds during the tax sale auction. Some municipalities require that deposits be made with certified funds before the tax sale auction. All municipalities require either full or partial payment for tax lien certificate amounts on the day they are auctioned. Some municipalities may accept personal checks, and most will accept cash payments. However, investors, particularly those who bid on multiple properties, are not always capable of determining the amount needed to secure the tax lien certificates purchased at a particular tax sale. Investors may attend the tax sale with a select list of potential lien certificates to purchase, but during the bidding process, the desired certificates may be awarded to someone else. Investors also may invest in more or fewer lien certificates than anticipated, depending upon the bidding competition. Under such circumstances, the amount that the investor had anticipated spending changes. Municipalities often provide investors with some period for obtaining the necessary funds to cover the cost of purchases required at the tax sale. This may range from a couple of hours to one day or some other period established by the taxing authority.

The state of Indiana, for example, does not require investors to make a deposit to register for the tax sale. The jurisdictions of Indianapolis require that the full amount of a tax lien certificate be paid upon winning the bid. Investors have been known to make a large deposit to a municipality to cover the anticipated costs of bidding during the auction. Form 4 (see page 56) shows a receipt provided to a bidder in return for the deposit of funds to be used during the bidding process. Any unused balance is refunded to the bidder once an accounting of all bids is made. Likewise, the state of Iowa does not require bidders to make a deposit for registration. However, some jurisdictions are allowed to charge a fee in the range of $75 to $100 for bidder cards. Payment for tax lien certificate purchases then is required in certified funds by the end of the day of auction.

In the district of Washington, D.C., bidders must make a minimum deposit of 10 percent of the tax lien certificates purchased. If an investor attempts to purchase tax lien certificates that total more than his or her deposit of 10 percent of the estimated purchase amount, he or she is required to make an additional deposit before continuing with the purchase of lien certificates. The full amount for all bids is required by the end of the tax sale day.

Some large jurisdictions in Florida require a $1,000 deposit. Others invoice the bidder for the balance of lien certificates purchased and provide the bidder with a two-week period to make payment in full. Still other jurisdictions require full payment for all lien certificates purchased within one to two days. Some jurisdictions, particularly the smaller jurisdictions, may allow the bidder to pay using a personal check.

Form 4: Receipt for Bidding Deposit

Obtaining Deed

When a property owner fails to redeem a tax lien certificate, an investor may foreclose the property owner's right of redemption. However, the investor must follow specific procedures to obtain the deed before engaging in the process of foreclosure on the property. Some states issue the investor what is termed a grant deed. Other states issue a warranty deed, and some states issue both. A grant deed uses the term grant in the language of the deed. A grant deed transfers the title from the property owner to the investor with two implied warranties. The first warranty implies that property owner has not previously transferred title to another party. The second warranty implies that the title is free from encumbrances. A grant deed also transfers any title acquired by the property owner subsequent to delivery of the grant deed. A warranty deed transfers title from the property owner to the investor. A warranty deed differs from a grant in that warranty deed guarantees the title to be in the condition specified and documented in the warranty deed. The property owner agrees to protect the investor from all claims to the property. All tax lien states and tax deed states, with the exception of the commonwealth of Puerto Rico and the territory of Guam, issue a grant deed, a warranty deed, or both. Puerto Rico and Guam issue special deeds peculiar to their tax sale system. The language of the deed used in Puerto Rico is likely to be written in Spanish. Table 1 shows the types of deeds that are used in each state.

Table 1
TYPES OF TAX DEEDS LISTED BY STATE

STATE	CLASSIFICATION	TYPE OF DEED
Alabama	Tax lien	Warranty deed
Alaska	Tax deed	Warranty deed
Arizona	Tax lien	Grant deed
California	Tax deed	Grant deed
Colorado	Tax lien	Warranty deed
Connecticut	Hybrid tax deed	Warranty deed
D.C.	Tax lien	Grant deed
Delaware	Hybrid tax deed	Grant deed
Florida	Tax lien	Warranty deed
Georgia	Hybrid tax deed	Warranty deed
Guam	Hybrid Tax Deed	Special Deed
Hawaii	Hybrid tax deed	Warranty deed
Idaho	Tax deed	Warranty deed
Illinois	Tax lien	Grant deed, warranty deed
Indiana	Tax lien	Warranty deed
Iowa	Tax lien	Warranty deed

STATE	CLASSIFICATION	TYPE OF DEED
Kansas	Tax deed	Warranty deed
Kentucky	Tax lien	Warranty deed
Louisiana	Hybrid tax deed	Warranty deed
Maine	Tax deed	Warranty deed
Maryland	Tax lien	Warranty deed
Massachusetts	Hybrid tax deed	Warranty deed
Michigan	Tax deed	Warranty deed
Minnesota	Tax deed	Warranty deed
Mississippi	Tax lien	Warranty deed
Missouri	Tax lien	Warranty deed
Montana	Tax lien	Grant deed
Nebraska	Tax lien	Warranty deed
Nevada	Tax deed	Grant deed
New Hampshire	Tax deed	Warranty deed
New Jersey	Tax lien	Grant deed, warranty deed
New Mexico	Tax Deed	Warranty deed
New York	Tax deed	Grant deed
North Carolina	Tax deed	Warranty deed
North Dakota	Tax lien	Grant deed, warranty Deed
Ohio	Tax deed	Warranty deed
Oklahoma	Tax lien	Grant deed
Oregon	Tax deed	Warranty deed
Pennsylvania	Hybrid tax deed	Grant deed
Puerto Rico	Tax lien	Special
Rhode Island	Hybrid tax deed	Warranty deed
South Carolina	Tax lien	Grant deed, warranty deed
South Dakota	Tax lien	Warranty deed
Tennessee	Hybrid Tax deed	Warranty deed
Texas	Hybrid tax deed	Grant deed
Utah	Tax deed	Warranty deed
Vermont	Tax lien	Warranty deed
Washington	Tax deed	Warranty deed
West Virginia	Tax lien	Grant deed
Wisconsin	Tax deed	Warranty deed
Wyoming	Tax lien	Warranty deed

Chapter 5

Bidding on Tax Lien Certificates

Generally, the public is allowed to participate in auctions and bid on all properties in a jurisdiction that have been identified as having delinquent property taxes. The minimum bid for a tax lien certificate offered for sale is termed the opening bid. In general, the opening bid is an amount equal to the delinquent back taxes, penalties, and interest on the delinquent tax amount and fees and costs associated with offering and issuing the tax lien certificate. However, some states, such as Wisconsin, set a minimum bid of the appraised value, or some percentage of it, which means that there are no obvious rock-bottom "bargains," although good buys still can be found. The bidding process is different in every jurisdiction but generally involves some form of competitive or noncompetitive bidding.

Competitive Bidding

In states such as Wyoming, tax liens may be assigned based on a competitive bidding process. In competitive bidding, the bidder may engage in either a process of bidding up the cost or bidding down the return of a tax lien certificate. Bidding up the cost is also known as premium bidding. It is a simple process of auctioning a tax lien certificate and assigning it to the bidder who is willing to pay the highest amount above the opening bid amount. A process known as late-entry bidding, explained later, also is used to bid up the cost of tax lien certificates by taking advantage of the bidding process. Bidding down the return on tax lien certificates is a bidding process that allows bidders to bid down the percentage of ownership in the property held as security for the tax lien certificate or to bid down the percentage of interest to be paid upon redemption.

Bidding up the premium

Bidding up the premium is a process that involves bidding up the cost of the tax certificate. The cost of acquiring a tax lien certificate is a bid beyond the minimum cost necessary to satisfy the tax lien amount or opening bid amount. The amount of the bid in excess of the opening bid amount is considered the premium bid amount. The bidder willing to pay the highest premium amount is the winning bidder. States that allow bidding up of the premium amount on tax lien certificates may use the following methods of applying interest to the redemption amount to be paid to the investor:

- Applying the same rate to both the opening bid amount and the premium bid amount
- Applying different rates to the different amounts
- Applying interest to the opening bid amount, but not the premium amount
- Applying interest to the premium bid amount, but not the opening bid amount
- Not refunding the premium amount as part of the redemption amount

Chapter 5: Bidding on Tax Lien Certificates

The premium amount is held by some states to help defray the cost of providing government services to the taxpaying community. Other states provide for the premium amount to be refunded to the tax lien certificate holder upon redemption or to the property owner upon foreclosure.

The state of Indiana engages in premium bidding. Redemption of a tax lien certificate does not require the property owner to pay interest as a part of the redemption amount. Instead, a penalty is assessed against the opening bid amount; no penalty is assessed against the premium amount. The penalty varies depending upon when the tax lien certificate is redeemed. If it is redeemed within the first six months following the tax sale, the penalty is 10 percent of the opening bid amount. If it is redeemed after six months but before one year has elapsed, the penalty is 15 percent of the opening bid amount. If it is redeemed after one year, the penalty is 25 percent of the opening bid amount. The premium amount is refunded to the tax lien certificate holder upon redemption. Subsequent taxes and assessments that may accrue during the redemption period have interest applied upon redemption at 12 percent annually. If the property owner fails to redeem the certificate, the certificate holder may file a claim for the premium amount that was paid to acquire the certificate. If the premium amount is not claimed within five years of the foreclosure, it is forfeited to the municipality's general fund.

The state of Mississippi also engages in premium bidding of tax lien certificates. Redemption requires an 18 percent annual interest rate (1.5 percent per month) to be applied to the opening bid amount. A one-time penalty of 5 percent of the opening bid amount also is required for redemption. No interest is applied to the premium amount, and the taxing municipality retains it. It is not refunded to the tax lien certificate holder or the property owner.

Bidding down ownership

In the process of bidding down ownership, tax lien certificates are sold and assigned to the bidder wishing to pay the lesser percentage of interest in the property. The bidder who bids to purchase a 95 percent interest in a property used to secure a tax lien certificate is chosen over the bidder who bids to purchase 100 percent interest in the property. Bidders compete until one bidder reaches a minimum percentage that no other bidder will drop beneath.

If a property owner fails to redeem a tax lien certificate during the predetermined redemption period, the bidder may foreclose the property with a transfer of title to a treasurer's deed. A treasurer's deed allows both the bidder and original owner to hold tenancy-in-common interest in the property. The bidder holds interest at the percentage that he or she bid at auction. The original owner holds the remaining percentage of interest in the property. For example, a winning bidder purchases a tax lien certificate for 85 percent interest in the securing property. Upon foreclosure, the tax lien certificate holder owns 85 percent of the property, and the original property owner owns 15 percent. The two parties become tenants-in-common. Competitive bidding down for tenancy-in-common ownership provides an opportunity for the original property owner to retain partial ownership in the property and to control the disposition of the property. The original property owner's percentage of the tenancy-in-common, however small, restricts the new partial owner from selling or financing the property. For either party of the tenancy-in-common to sell or secure financing against the property, both parties must agree to the action or initiate a partition action, which is a request to the courts to sell the property and split the proceeds from the sale in proportion to each party's percentage of interest. For example, a bidder acquires a property tax lien certificate for 97 percent interest in the property value. The property owner retains the remaining 3 percent interest. A completed partition action allows the bidder to secure

97 percent of the net proceeds from the sale of the property and the owner to secure 3 percent of the net proceeds.

The state of Missouri provides for bidders to competitively bid down ownership in a property. Missouri's tax sale is limited to residents of the particular municipality. In order for persons residing outside the municipality to participate in the bidding, the outsider must designate a resident agent to act on his or her behalf. The resident agent, like all other bidders, must be a resident of the taxing municipality.

The state of New Hampshire also engages in a tax sale system that allows bidders to competitively bid down ownership in a property. The winning bidder is required by state law to notify the mortgage lenders of record of the purchase within 30 days of making the purchase. The notification is necessary for the sale of the tax lien certificate to be valid. Part property owners are allowed to redeem their share of the tax lien certificate to retain their share of tenancy-in-common ownership should foreclosure occur. All property owners are allowed to make partial payments of the redemption amount during the two-year redemption period.

Bidding down interest

Some states also allow bidders to competitively bid down the percentage of interest to be paid upon redemption of the tax lien certificate by the property owner. A bidder may purchase a tax lien certificate with the stipulation that the property owner may redeem the tax certificate by paying less than the amount established by state statute for redemption.

Arizona, for example, has state statutes that specify the redemption interest amount to be paid by the property owner as 16 percent annually. In competitive bidding down, the bidder who bids to purchase a tax lien certificate with a 12 percent redemption interest is chosen over the bidder who bids to purchase it at 14 percent redemption interest. For a particularly desirable property, it is not unknown for the interest rate to be bid down to zero, that is, no interest will be paid, in the hopes that the owners will not redeem and the property can be foreclosed. In Arizona, property owners are allowed to redeem tax lien certificates after the established redemption period has ended and foreclosure has been initiated. The property owner's right to avoid foreclosure does not end until a foreclosure judgment has been made and recorded by the courts. When the property owner redeems after the redemption period has ended, but before a foreclosure judgment is made, the property owner is required to pay additional costs. Property owners also are required to pay reasonable attorney's fees, in addition to the 16 percent interest applied to the cost of the tax lien and subsequent taxes as well as fees and costs associated with the sale of the certificate. Municipalities of Arizona calculate interest such that any fraction of a month is counted as a whole month.

The state of New Jersey also allows bidders to competitively bid down the interest to be paid upon redemption. The statutory redemption interest is 18 percent, but the bidder may bid the percentage down to as low as 1 percent. When the bidding reduces the interest to 1 percent, the state engages in a system of competitively bidding a premium amount. To the benefit of investors, the state also imposes a penalty on the redemption that varies depending on when the redemption takes place. If the redemption occurs within ten days of the tax sale, no penalty is assessed. If the redemption occurs after ten days, the property owner is required to pay the cost of the tax lien, the bid interest, any subsequent taxes, and municipal liens and penalties based on the amount of the redemption amount. If the redemption amount is in excess of $200, the assessed penalty is 2 percent of the redemption amount. If the redemption amount is in excess of $5,000, the assessed penalty is 4 percent of the redemption amount. If the redemption amount is in excess of $10,000, the assessed penalty is 6 percent of the redemption amount.

Late-entry bidding

Late-entry bidding is more of a psychological technique than an established bidding process. A late-entry bidder is usually a seasoned bidder who takes advantage of the bidding frenzy that builds during auctions. He or she allows bidders to compete for bid amounts. When the frenzy has subsided and the final frenzy bidder has made his or her offer, the late-entry bidder makes an offer at a large increase above that of the highest previous bidder. By the time bidders involved in the frenzy are able to readjust their thinking and consider whether they want to top the offer made by the late-entry bidder, the auctioneer recognizes the relatively long pause as the end of bidding. The late-entry bidder takes advantage of the fast pace with which bids are awarded and essentially shocks the last frenzied bidder who was psyched into believing that his or her bid had won. Late-entry bidding is possible in almost every tax sale auctioning system.

Noncompetitive Bidding

In states such as Oklahoma and Wyoming, the bidding is noncompetitive, and the bid amount remains constant. Tax lien certificates are offered on a first-come, first-served basis. When more than one bidder offers to pay for the same tax lien certificate, the treasurer is responsible for implementing his or her own fair and impartial method of choosing a winning bidder. In Wyoming, treasurers have established four noncompetitive methods for selling tax certificates. These methods are not unique to Wyoming and are used in other states that engage in noncompetitive bidding.

First-come, first-served methods

A first-come, first-served method means that bidders form a line outside the location where the tax sale is held and wait their turn to make bids. Individuals are allowed to purchase all available tax lien certificates that have not been sold until all are sold. Alternatively, bidders register for the tax sale, are assigned bidder numbers, and indicate the properties for which they wish to purchase tax lien certificates. If more than one bidder wishes to purchase a tax lien certificate secured by the same property, the earliest registered bidder wins the bid.

Another first-come, first-served method is unique to the county of Johnson, Wyoming. Each bidder is assigned a bidder number upon registration for the tax sale. The auctioneer assigns tax lien certificates according to the sequential order of the bidder number. Bidder number one gets first pick of a single tax lien certificate of his or her choice. Bidder number two gets to choose one of the remaining tax lien certificates and so on until either all bidders' numbers have been exhausted or all tax lien certificates have been sold. If the number of available tax lien certificates exceeds the number of bidders, the assignment of tax lien certificates begins again, starting with bidder number one. If there is a second round, bidders get an opportunity to purchase a second tax lien certificate, and this process continues until all possible tax lien certificates have been sold.

Lottery-type methods

A lottery-type or random method provides for each bidder to be assigned a bidder number. A bingo machine, hat, or other container is used to randomly select a bidder number for each available tax lien certificate. The selected bidder may accept or refuse the draw of his or her bidder number for a particular tax lien certificate. If the bidder accepts the draw, he or she wins the bid. If he or she rejects the draw, additional bidder numbers are drawn randomly until a bidder number is drawn that corresponds to a bidder who wishes to purchase the certificate. After a certificate is sold, all bidder numbers are put back into the "pot" to be drawn randomly for the next available tax lien certificate.

Another lottery-type method used when more than one bidder wishes to purchase an available tax lien certificate is to collect bidder numbers for all parties interested in a particular certificate. A winning bidder then is selected randomly from the pool of bidders interested in the certificate.

Chapter 5: Bidding on Tax Lien Certificates   67

The complications associated with bidding down percentages of ownership in a property make investors reluctant to participate in the process. Most taxing authorities also are biased against the complicated bid-down scheme. To avoid this competition in selling tax lien certificates, city and county treasurers have resorted to various first-come, first-served, and lottery-type methods of selecting bidders. State statutes regarding tax lien certificates in Wyoming provide for competitive bidding for a percentage of ownership in a property. However, the effect of implementing one of the above methods is the same as if the state did not engage in competitive bidding or the selling of percentages of ownership in property. It should be noted that this type of bidding is not applicable to the sale of irrigation assessments. State statutes allow for the noncompetitive bidding of 100 percent interest in the sale of irrigation assessments in Wyoming. The bid is awarded to the first bidder offering an amount sufficient to cover the assessment as well as associated penalties, interest, and costs, not to the bidder offering to purchase the lowest percentage of ownership in the property.

The established bidding methods used by tax lien states are shown in Table 2 below. Table 2 also shows the bidding method used by those tax deed states that allow property owners an opportunity to redeem tax deeds held against their property. Interest rates, penalties, and redemption periods also are shown.

Table 2
BIDDING METHODS FOR TAX LIEN STATES AND TAX DEED STATES WITH REDEMPTION PERIODS

	Bid Method	State	Classification	Interest Rate	Penalty	Redemption Period
1	Bid down interest	Arizona	Tax lien	16%		3 years
2	Bid down interest	Florida[1]	Tax lien	18% (tax liens & deeds)		2 years
3	Bid down interest	Illinois	Tax lien	24% scavenger sale	18% per 6 months tax sale	2–3 years

	Bid Method	State	Classification	Interest Rate	Penalty	Redemption Period
4	Bid down interest	Louisiana	Hybrid tax deed	12%	5%	3 years
5	Bid down interest or premium	New Jersey	Tax lien	18%	2%–6%	2 years
6	Bid down interest	North Dakota	Tax lien	9%–12%		3 years
7	Bid down interest or premium	Rhode Island	Hybrid tax deed		10%	1 year
8	Bid down ownership	Massachusetts	Hybrid tax deed	16%		6 months
9	Bid down ownership	Michigan	Tax deed	15% 1st year	50% 2nd year	1 year
10	Bid down ownership	Missouri	Tax lien	10%		2 years
11	Bid down ownership or random	Nebraska	Tax lien	14%		3 years
12	Bid down ownership	New Hampshire	Tax deed	18%		2 years
13	Premium	Alabama	Tax Lien	12%		3 years
14	Premium	California[1]	Tax deed	18% (tax liens)		2 years (tax liens)
15	Premium	Colorado[2]	Tax lien	9% plus FDR		3 years
16	Premium	Connecticut	Hybrid tax deed	18%		1 year
17	Premium	D.C.	Tax lien	18%		6 months
18	Premium	Delaware	Hybrid tax deed		15%	60 days
19	Premium	Georgia	Hybrid tax deed		10%–20%	1 year
20	Premium	Guam	Hybrid tax deed	12%		6 months
21	Premium	Hawaii	Hybrid tax deed	12%		1 year
22	Premium	Indiana	Tax lien		10%–15%	1 year
23	Premium	Kentucky	Tax lien	12%		1 year
24	Premium	Maryland	Tax lien	6%–24%		6 months
25	Premium	Mississippi	Tax lien	18%	5%	2 years
26	Premium	New York	Tax deed	14%		1 year
27	Premium	Ohio[1]	Tax deed	18% (tax liens)		15 days (tax deeds) 1 year (tax liens)
28	Premium	Pennsylvania	Hybrid tax deed	10%		1 year
29	Premium	Puerto Rico	Tax lien		20%	1 year

	Bid Method	State	Classification	Interest Rate	Penalty	Redemption Period
30	Premium	South Carolina	Tax lien	3%–12%		1 3/4 years
31	Premium	South Dakota	Tax lien	12%		3–4 years
32	Premium	Tennessee	Hybrid tax deed	10%		1 year
33	Premium	Texas	Hybrid tax deed		25%	6 months–2 years
34	Premium	Vermont	Tax lien	12%		1 year
35	Premium	West Virginia	Tax lien	12%		18 months
36	Premium	Wisconsin	Tax deed			2 years
37	Random	Iowa	Tax lien	24%		1 3/4 years
38	Random	Montana	Tax lien	10%	2%	3 years
39	Random	Oklahoma	Tax lien	8%		2 years
40	Random or bid down ownership	Wyoming	Tax lien	18%	3%	4 years

[1]States that sell both tax deeds and tax lien certificates regardless of the classification.
[2]Interest rates are based on the Federal Discount Rate (FDR).

The remaining 13 tax deed states include Alaska, Arkansas, Idaho, Kansas, Maine, Minnesota, Nevada, New Mexico, North Carolina, Oregon, Utah, Virginia, and Washington. These states offer no redemption period for property owners to regain ownership of their properties. Tax deeds are offered for sale by bidding up the premium cost of tax deeds.

Over-the-Counter Tax Certificates

Many state municipalities hold tax sales on the same date making it impossible to acquire tax lien certificates for multiple properties, in multiple jurisdictions. In most states, if a tax certificate is not sold at the tax sale, the certificate is bought and held by the city, county, or state responsible for the sale. In some states, tax lien certificates are offered for resale at public auction later. In most other states, the unsold tax lien certificates are made available for resale, over the counter, to the public on a first-come, first-served or other basis. Tax lien certificates sold over the counter are not subject to the bidding process, so they are bid neither up nor down. They are sold for 100 percent interest in the securing real estate. Investors often choose to purchase tax lien certificates over the counter after the tax sale has ended as an alternative to buying them at tax sales. Purchasing tax lien certificates over the counter offers many other advantages, as outlined below:

- Personnel at the treasurer's or tax collector's office have more time to assist with property issues than they do in days preceding and during the annual tax sale.

- There is an extended period for the investor to focus on and research any potential issues with the property.

- In states that engage in competitive bidding down during the tax sale, purchasers only may be capable of securing a percentage of ownership in properties. Likewise, in states that engage in premium bidding during the tax sale, purchasers are likely to purchase tax lien certificates above cost. Certificates sold over the counter after the tax sale, however, are sold at the opening bid amount for 100 percent ownership in the property.

- Certificates not sold at tax sale may be purchased at any time of year. In most states, no matter when the tax lien certificate is purchased, the redemption period begins on the day of the annual tax sale. Thus, when a tax lien certificate is purchased later, the redemption period is shortened. The shortened redemption period offers the benefit of reducing the time before foreclosure can be initiated to obtain the deed to the securing property. If a property owner redeems the certificate, the reduced waiting time reduces the time necessary to receive a return on investment, thereby increasing the investor's rate of return.

Chapter 6

Investing in Tax Lien Certificates

nnual tax sales are open to the public, but the tax sale process is thought to be rather complex and is not thoroughly understood. As such, attendees at tax sales usually are limited to apprehensive citizens and investors. Apprehensive citizens include those individuals with a vested interest in particular properties and those citizens who are curious about the sale process. The majority of attendees, however, are those involved in the investment opportunity presented by tax lien certificates. Investors purchase tax lien certificates for one of two reasons. They either attempt to use tax lien certificates as a method of gaining ownership of valuable property for pennies on the dollar, or they attempt to profit from the high rate of return realized by redemption amounts.

Ownership as the Objective

Tax lien certificates offer investors a relatively safe and reliable investment opportunity. They are administered and controlled by state governments, secured by real estate, and in most instances, offer a fixed rate of interest on the investment amount. One possible investment objective is to take ownership of valuable property for pennies on the dollar. To maximize the return on investment dollars, the investor attempts to invest in lien certificates are secured by valuable property and to purchase certificates that are least likely to be redeemed by the property owner. One of the biggest obstacles in this approach to investing in tax lien certificates is in determining those tax lien certificates least likely to be redeemed. Most cities and counties offer far more tax lien certificates for sale than any one individual or group of individuals possibly could investigate. Because it is impossible for investors to determine with accuracy the probability that the property owner will redeem a tax lien certificate, they are encouraged to rely on the law of averages and invest in certificates that have as little as a 10 percent chance of not being redeemed. The law of averages implies that if an investor invests in ten tax lien certificates with a 10 percent chance of not being redeemed (10 x 10% = 100%), then there is a 100 percent chance that the investor will invest successfully in at least one tax lien certificate that the owner will fail to redeem.

The law of averages, however, is more theoretical than practical. Property owners redeem most tax lien certificates offered for sale during some point of the redemption period. Even when a tax lien certificate is redeemed, the investor's only loss is access to the money used in the investment during the redemption period. In most states, the investor, at a minimum, has his or her investment dollars returned with interest, as determined by the particular state.

Ownership before the tax sale

Though tax lien certificates usually are acquired at tax sales or over the counter after a tax sale, opportunities exist to invest in the sale of certificates before the sale begins. An investor is free to contact the owners of properties listed in the tax sale listing. If the property owner agrees, the investor can offer one of three opportunities for settling the delinquent tax amount, as follows:

Buying equity

The investor may offer to buy the owner's equity in the property and take ownership of the property. In exchange for a mutually agreed upon price, the property owner provides the investor with ownership by issuing the investor a quitclaim deed to the property. This option works best for property owners who are seeking to rid themselves of a property or are seeking a buy out of a property. The investor usually agrees to pay or assume any debt or liens against the property and negotiates with the property owner for a selling price that is less than the property's fair market value. As an example, a property owner may have an $80,000 outstanding mortgage on a property valued at $200,000. The property owner is also delinquent in paying $4,200 in property taxes. In exchange for the owner's equity of $115,800, the investor may offer to pay the delinquent tax amount, the loan balance, and $50,000 cash to the property owner. In return, the property owner provides the investor a quitclaim deed to the property. The investor becomes the new property owner for an amount equal to the following:

Equity offer:	$ 50,000
Loan balance:	80,000
Delinquent property tax:	4,200
TOTAL	$134,200

The investor owns the property and has about one-third equity in the property.

Investor's Equity
$200,000 − $134,200 = $65,800
$65,800 / $200,000 = 32.9%

Sharing equity

Rather than offering a property owner an option that relieves him or her of home ownership, the investor may offer to share equity with the property owner. Using the terms of the previous example, the investor offers to pay the delinquent tax amount for a 50 percent equity position in the property. Because the property owner has $115,800 equity in the property, the investor would pay the $4,200 delinquent property tax, which increases the shared equity to $120,000. The shared equity is 50-50, so both the investor and the property owner would hold $60,000 equity in the property. Both parties of the shared equity would pay an equal share of the $80,000 outstanding loan balance. Though the example presented here represents a 50-50 equity-sharing agreement, it does not have to be equal. Shared equity can be 25-75 or any division agreed upon and specified in the terms of an equity-sharing agreement.

The percentage of sharing and other terms of the equity-sharing plan must be spelled out clearly in a contract agreement. In most instances, property owners are allowed to maintain possession of the property. The most common equity-sharing agreements provide for the property owner to pay fair market rent to the investor in return for having the investor pay the debts held against the property. The investor is, in effect, renting the property to the property owner, but instead of engaging a typical landlord-tenant type of arrangement, the tenant is part owner. An advantage to this type of arrangement is that the tenant-owner is more likely to maintain the property than a tenant in a typical tenant-landlord relationship. The expenses of the property, including the outstanding mortgage, are split according to the equity percentage. In a 50-50 arrangement, the expenses are divided evenly between both parties. If the arrangement were such that the investor held 75 percent equity and the property owner held 25 percent, the expenses would be divided 75-25 accordingly. The owner-occupants usually are able to deduct their share of the interest on any loan amounts as well as the property tax. The investor deducts his or her share of any interest on loan amounts, property taxes, and any other expenses of the property. The investor also depreciates his or her share of ownership in the property and deducts one-half of the rents received.

Reverse lease option

The investor also may offer to purchase the property and lease it back to the property owner with an option allowing the property owner to repurchase the property at a future date. This option is similar to lease options offered for rental properties in which the tenant agrees to pay rent to the landlord with an option to buy the rental unit in the future. A portion of the monthly rents is reserved and applied to the down payment when the purchase takes place. The specifications of a reverse lease option must be clearly defined by contractual agreement. A legal instrument must define the terms of the payment and time frame for purchase of the property.

Ownership after the tax sale

For a tax lien investor to gain ownership of a property that secures a tax lien certificate, the property owner must fail to redeem the tax lien certificate during the redemption period. But even when the property owner fails to redeem, ownership is not automatic. The investor must follow prescribed processes and procedures to foreclose the property owner's right to redemption and acquire deed and title to the property. Various states and the individual municipalities require different processes and procedures. Some municipalities will allow the investor to engage in a rather simplistic administrative filing of foreclosure. Other states require the investor to engage in what is often a lengthy and complicated judicial method of foreclosure. Judicial foreclosures involve the time, use, and expense of legal counsel and the courts. It is important to note that in many jurisdictions the tax lien holder loses all rights and value to the lien if he or she does not take action within a certain period.

Return as the Objective

When tax lien certificates do not lead to ownership, another reward for investing in them is the high rate of return offered by redemption. When property owners redeem tax lien certificates, the property owner must reimburse the certificate holder for paying the delinquent tax amount that created the tax lien. In addition to the delinquent tax amount, the property owner may be required to pay interest, penalties, and fees as well as costs associated with the establishment and offering of the tax lien certificate.

Different states have differing methods of determining the additional penalty, interest, fees, and costs to be added to the delinquent tax amount. In some states, a penalty may be imposed as a flat amount to be applied annually during the redemption period. States also include interest on the delinquent tax amount, the penalty amount, or both. The interest rates may range from 6 to 24 percent, and they usually are applied annually. The redemption period also varies by state, but generally ranges from six months to four years. The combination of penalties and interest that accrue over the redemption period draws investors to invest in tax lien certificates. Other fees and costs that are reimbursed as part of the redemption amount are an added benefit. Some of the costs include legal fees that may be quite costly in some jurisdictions.

Illinois, for example, is a favorable state for tax lien certificate investing. The typical redemption period for tax lien certificates is two years; however, the tax lien certificate holder may file notice with the particular municipality to extend the redemption period to three years. The state requires redeeming property owners to pay interest and penalties in addition to the delinquent tax amount upon redemption. The statutory interest rate is 18 percent for six months, but state statutes provide for bidders to bid down the interest rate to be applied to redemption amounts. Penalties are applied as a percentage of the bid amount and are staggered throughout the redemption period.

- If a tax lien certificate is redeemed within the first two months, the penalty amount is 3 percent of the cost of the certificate.

- If a tax lien certificate is redeemed after the expiration of two months, but before six months, the penalty amount is equal to the percentage of interest that was bid. For example, if a winning bid were bid down to 2 percent interest upon redemption, the penalty also would be 2 percent during this period. If the winning bid were bid down to 10 percent interest, the penalty amount would be 10 percent.

- If a tax lien certificate is redeemed after the expiration of six months but before one year, the penalty amount is double the bid-down interest rate. That is, if the winning bid were bid down to 10 percent interest upon redemption, the penalty would be 20 percent during this period.

- If a tax lien certificate is redeemed after the expiration of one year but before 18 months, the penalty is triple the bid-down interest rate. So, if the winning bid were bid down to 10 percent interest upon redemption, the penalty would be 30 percent during this period.

- If a tax lien certificate is redeemed after the expiration of 18 months but before two years, the penalty is four times the bid-down interest rate. If the winning bid were bid down to 10 percent interest upon redemption, the penalty would be 40 percent during this period.

- If a tax lien certificate is redeemed after the expiration of two years but before the requested and approved three-year redemption period has expired, the penalty increases 6 percent per year. If the winning bid were bid down to 10 percent interest upon redemption, the penalty would be 46 percent during this period.

The preceding rates apply to tax lien certificates purchased at the annual tax sale. When the certificates are not purchased at the tax sale, the unsold certificates are offered for sale at a scavenger sale. The bidding method used at scavenger sales is premium bidding to the highest bidder. The bidder is not reimbursed for the premium amount used to win the bid, and interest is not applied to the premium amount. Nevertheless, the redemption interest rate still offers a favorable return. The interest rate for tax lien certificates purchased at the scavenger sale is 12 percent for six months (24 percent annually) for the first four years. An additional 6 percent per year is added after the expiration of four years.

Investors

There are two primary types of investors: independent investors and institutional investors. Independent investors are small investors with limited funds to invest. Institutional investors are large corporate investors with millions of investment dollars.

Independent investors

Independent investors are individuals or groups of individuals that purchase tax lien certificates as an investment opportunity. They usually do not have millions of dollars to invest but may have hundreds, thousands, or more to invest. They usually invest on behalf of themselves and are selective with the limited funds they have to invest.

Institutional investors

Institutional investors consist of banks, mortgage companies, brokerage houses, and other large institutions with millions of dollars available for investment purposes. Institutional investors usually are composed of several individuals acting on behalf of the institution. Their research usually is replete with detailed notes specifying available properties to bid on and the optimal range of bidding to maximize yield. Institutional investors are skilled in the bidding process and may be identified at tax sales by some or all of the following characteristics:

- Arrive at the tax sale on time

- Sit at the front of the auction room

- Favor tax sales in large municipalities with many thousands of tax lien certificates available for sale

- Bid on tax lien certificates that are secured by more valuable properties. Property taxes usually are assessed between 1 and 2 percent of the fair market value of a property. Institutional investors are more focused on lien certificates above certain thresholds, generally $1,000 to $1,500. These thresholds are used to identify properties that are likely to have market values in excess of $100,000 and $150,000, respectively.

- Bid down the interest on redemption amounts. The goal of institutional investors is to raise the overall yield on investments and continue to invest in more properties, which further increases their yield. Institutional investors are willing to accept the lower interest on redemption in exchange for the higher yield from properties that are likely to redeem quickly and properties that have penalties attached to the redemption amount.

- Seek properties that are homestead properties. Homestead properties are likely to be redeemed, because the designation indicates that (1) the property serves as a personal residence and (2) the property is not a vacant lot.

- Employ staff to do the bidding on behalf of the institution. Staff persons typically work a 9 to 5 workday and may not be present to increase the competition during lunch hours or extended bidding hours.

Chapter 7

Obtaining Investment Dollars

Unless an investor is independently wealthy with excess funds to invest in real estate tax liens, he or she will need to find ways of obtaining the necessary investment funds. One of the most widely used methods of obtaining money to fund tax lien certificate investments is to form a partnership or investment group. Partners work together to research and bid on valuable investment properties and then split the profits returned by the investment. Another good source of investment dollars is an individual's retirement plan. In the same manner as money held in a retirement plan is sheltered from taxation, investments made in the name of a retirement plan also are sheltered from taxation. Taxes play a vital role in the investment of tax lien certificates, as the return on investment is increased when the investor is capable of engaging methods of decreasing federal, state, and local income taxes.

Tax Considerations

A partnership or investment group needs to understand the tax laws applicable to tax liens and business operations. The best way to bring this type of knowledge to the partnership is to include an accountant or an attorney who is knowledgeable in tax liens and business taxes. An accountant is able to analyze business transactions and provide advice on how to best shelter income from taxes. As with any business entity that involves real estate, the tax lien investor needs the assistance of an accountant or attorney who is experienced in the specifics of real estate taxes and laws. The advertised returns on tax lien certificate investments never may be fully realized by a partnership because investment income is taxable income to the business entity and its individual partners. The true return on tax lien certificate investments or any type of investment is the amount of money that the investor or investment group is allowed to keep after satisfying any tax obligations. To assist in the planning and continuity of tax lien certificate investments, investors need expert knowledge and advice, not only in the laws that pertain to real estate taxes but also in the laws that pertain to investments, investment groups, business taxes, accounting, and contracts.

Attorneys and accountants need to have similar knowledge and skills to assist an investment partnership in making decisions that are in the best interests of the business entity. Though there are attorneys who are also competent accountants and accountants who are competent attorneys, the partnership is best served by having two separate and distinct individuals in the roles of attorney and accountant; however, it is not absolutely necessary. An accountant takes a more personable approach to the everyday aspects of the business functions. He or she will document and distribute a financial history of the business entity on a quarterly basis and periodically will perform checks and balances of the business entity to ensure that business practices are being followed and that documentation is being distributed to necessary parties, both internal and external to the business entity. Attorneys are overseers of the partners, as they engage in various contracts and agreements relative to real estate transactions and partnerships. The attorney assures that all rules, regulations, and transactions are being followed as dictated by contract and defends such actions in legal proceedings. Unless there is some dispute relative to business practices, an attorney does not need to be involved in the everyday aspects of the business in the same manner as the accountant. However, the attorney should be competent to analyze and interpret the financial descriptions of the business, as provided by the accountant.

An investor, for example, who is establishing a new investment venture, needs to consult with an accountant who understands the tax obligations of starting a new business. The IRS allows a $50,000 deduction on the startup costs associated with establishing a new business. However, the first $5,000 dollars may be deducted in the first year, and the remaining startup costs must be amortized over 15 years. Suppose an investor establishes a business to invest in tax lien certificates. He or she spends $11,000 to establish the business, and in the first year of operation, he or she receives a profit from redemptions that equals $6,500. The IRS allows the business to take an initial $5,000 deduction and an additional $400 deduction for the first year of amortization. A $400 deduction also is allowed over the next 14 years to account for the remaining startup cost of $5,600.

Startup cost	$11,000	
First-year startup deduction	$ 5,000	
Remaining startup amount	$ 6,000	$11,000 − $5,000
First year amortized deduction	$ 400	$6,000 ÷ 15
Total first year deductions	$ 5,400	$5,000 + $400

The $6,500 profit realized in the first year of business is offset partially by $5,400 (first year startup deduction plus first year amortized deduction) that also is allowed in the first year of the business operation. The investor has to be knowledgeable of such deductions in order to offset profits in such a manner. An accountant ensures the business entity makes such deductions, and a lawyer defends the right to make such deductions. If the same investor realizes a loss in the first year, the loss may be carried forward to offset gains that may be realized in future years. If, on the other hand, the business had been in existence for years and suffered a loss, the loss may be carried back, up to three years, to offset gains in those previous years. An amended tax return must be filed for the business in this situation in order to claim the loss.

In order to acquire lien certificates, most states require investors to travel to the taxing municipality to make a physical appearance at the tax sale or at the appropriate tax collector's office for the sale of over-the-counter tax lien certificates. Business tax laws allow individuals engaged in business to deduct business expenses, such as travel. However, an investor is not allowed to deduct travel expenses for the investigation of investment opportunities. Investors generally are not considered to be in the business of the entity in which they are investing. If an investor, for example, travels from Maryland to Chicago to investigate a restaurant for which he or she is considering purchasing a tax lien certificate, he or she is not considered to be in the restaurant business. Investors who hold substantial investments in tax lien certificates may make the argument that their profession is purchasing tax lien certificates, but generally, an investor who invests in lien certificates is not considered to be in the business of purchasing certificates. For tax purposes, the expenses of purchasing tax lien certificates are included in the cost of the tax lien certificate as the cost basis of the investment. However, once tax lien certificates are purchased and paid for, the expenses required to manage the certificates, such as travel expenses necessary to make court appearances to foreclose a property, are deductible. Such travel expenses must exceed 2 percent of the investor's adjusted gross income to qualify for a deduction, and the deduction may be reduced for high-income taxpayers.

Once foreclosure has taken place, the tax consequences of acquiring ownership to the property are not clearly defined. The IRS established policy for mortgaged or pledged properties makes the gain realized by foreclosure taxable when the property is acquired for an amount less than the fair market value. However, foreclosed tax lien certificates do not fall into the category of mortgaged or pledged properties. The ambiguity stems from the lack of statutes from the IRS. The IRS has not established whether a gain is realized when an investor completes the foreclosure of a tax lien certificate or when and if the foreclosed property is sold.

The tax law specifies mortgaged and pledged properties because mortgage companies are allowed to deduct a debt if a property is sold for less than the mortgage amount. As the complement, mortgage companies are required to report a gain if a property is sold for more than the mortgage amount. When the right to redeem a tax lien certificate is foreclosed, it is not likely that a property ever will sell for less than the cost of foreclosure. Unlike with mortgages, a loss rarely needs to be deducted for foreclosing a tax lien certificate. As such, the IRS's position of requiring mortgage lenders to report gains to offset losses does not apply to tax lien certificates. Investors are encouraged to consult with their accountants to determine how to best apply the law to their particular situations. An interesting analogy is: If an investor sells a vehicle valued at $25,000 for $15,000, does the new owner have a gain of $10,000 because of the sale? More important, is it a taxable event, such that the new owner should be required to pay tax on the gain? In most states, the answer is no. A taxable event does not occur unless a vehicle owner sells a vehicle for more than it is worth, not less than it is worth. The seller is taxed on the gain, and the buyer has no tax obligation to report.

To avoid the uncertainty in tax laws with regard to foreclosure of tax lien certificates, investors are encouraged to take advantage of their ability to schedule a foreclosure to occur at the beginning of the year. This gives the investor an opportunity to sell the property before the year ends. In such a case, the investor realizes a gain upon selling the property, and if any taxes are due, the investor has converted the investment to cash and is able to pay the tax. Investors also are encouraged to market the foreclosed property early and sell the property as quickly as possible. Given the relatively small amount invested in the foreclosure, the investor is in a position to offer a buyer a bargain in return for a quick sale. Quickly converting a foreclosed property to cash offers the benefit of allowing the proceeds to continue to be invested in buying tax lien certificates or other investments as well as avoiding the uncertainties of the tax law.

Retirement Programs

Investing money contributed to retirement programs in tax lien certificates may offer the benefit of increasing the amount of funds in the plan without incurring any additional tax obligations. Tax lien certificates are an investment that qualifies for inclusion in an Individual Retirement Account (IRA). However, the IRA must be a true self-directed IRA. A true self-directed IRA allows an individual to have control of the investments to include investments outside those established by the retirement program. Some mutual funds, for example, advertise that they offer self-directed IRAs. However, these types of IRAs are self-directed only in the sense that the individual may control investments between Fund A and Fund B, as predetermined by the plan. An individual may not include outside investments, such as tax lien certificates.

Retirement programs are commonplace in today's society, and caps on the amounts that may be contributed by individuals are steadily on the increase, providing individuals with more dollars to invest. Table 4 below shows the caps that have been established for some of the most common retirement programs.

Table 4
CAPS FOR RETIREMENT PLANS

PLAN	CAPS FOR CONTRIBUTIONS	
	Individuals born before 1962	Individuals born after 1961
401(k)	$22,500	$17,000
403(b)	$22,500	$17,000
457	$22,500	$17,000
Simple IRA	$14,000	$11,500
Keoghs		$50,000
Profit sharing		$50,000

Note: This table is necessarily a simplification, and values will be adjusted for cost of living increases, so check the current situation with your financial adviser.

Investors are allowed to use money secured by a retirement program to buy tax lien certificates in the name of the retirement program. When a property owner fails to redeem a lien certificate that is named in a retirement program, the retirement program may foreclose the right of redemption and obtain title and ownership of the property. Investing in tax lien certificates in the name of a retirement program protects the investment should the investor foreclose the property owner's right of redemption and then sell the property. When a property is titled to a retirement program and then sold in the name of the retirement program, the retirement program, not the individual enrolled in the program, secures the proceeds from the sale of the property. This shields all proceeds of the sale from tax obligations in the same manner as the retirement plan itself. The anomaly is that investments made through retirement programs cannot be converted to cash, without penalty and additional tax consequences, until the age requirement of the retirement program is met. The funds may, however, be used as a line of credit, though borrowing against funds held in a retirement program incurs interest. For these reasons, it would not be wise for an investor to make all of his or her investments within a retirement program. Retirement programs limit the investor's ability to liquidate the investment when cash is needed. Also, if through a retirement program, an investor is successful in foreclosing a property and the property is used to generate income under the retirement program, none of the tax benefits of business ownership are offered to the retirement program because it is already sheltered from taxes. The investor may find it more cost-effective to assign the property to himself or herself and take advantage of the tax benefits offered by business ownership, such as depreciation and deductions.

As a business entity, either as an individual investor or investment group, an investment in tax lien certificates that profits from redemption amounts also incurs tax obligations. Proceeds from redemption are profit to the business entity and, as such, they are taxable. If the investment is a capital investment, profits may be taxed at the rate established for capital gains, 15 percent. The IRS has established guidelines for determining when income may be classified as a capital gain. If the investment is not a capital investment, the profit is taxed as ordinary income. The IRS taxes ordinary income at a maximum of 35 percent at the time of writing. Again, consultation with an accountant will assist investors in determining the types of income that the investment business receives and the tax rate that is applicable to their redemption amounts.

Partnerships

A partnership among individuals provides a source of investment dollars that may be used to invest in tax lien certificates. The partnerships should include not only a collaboration of the money, but also a collaboration of knowledge, talent, skills, resources, and economic clout. Individual partners must be responsible for bringing one or more of these assets to the partnership. Partners may collaborate to create the following types of investment groups:

Corporations

Corporations have been in existence for more than a century and are incorporated business units with limits placed on the personal liability of the incorporated partners. Corporations are established as documented business entities that offer shares of the business unit to the public. The corporate partnership design is meant to limit lawsuits against the corporation to the assets of the corporation, not the personal assets of the incorporated members. However, some skilled attorneys have been successful in taking personal assets of partners under special circumstances. Another caveat of a corporate partnership is that its profits are taxed twice. When a corporation offers shares on the stock market, its shareholders are paid dividends on dollars invested in the corporation. The shareholders are personally taxed on the dividends distributed by the corporation. The corporation itself is taxed on its income at the corporate rate. When a sole proprietor establishes him or herself as an S corporation, no double taxation is assessed against the corporation. The individual proprietor is taxed only on the profits of the corporation.

Limited liability company

Two or more individuals may form a limited liability partnership. Unlike a corporation, no shares are offered for sale to investors and no double taxation is imposed on the partnership. Limited liability partnerships offer the protection of personal assets that is inherent in corporations, but the partners do not have the responsibility of record keeping and bookkeeping associated with selling shares like that of a corporate business structure.

General partnership

A general partnership is a contractual agreement formed between individuals, in which each individual has an equal role in the business relationship. The parties to a general partnership have unlimited liability. A legal suit against one of the partners extends to all of the partners. The general partnership must file taxes as a general partnership.

Real estate investment trust

A real estate investment trust is a trust offered for investment to the public. The trust produces income of which 90 percent is distributed to its shareholders. A real estate investment trust is free of double taxation, because the trust itself is not taxed. Only the investors that receive distributions from the trust are taxed. The partners have the responsibility of record keeping and bookkeeping associated with selling shares in the same manner as a corporation.

Limited partnership

A limited partnership must have at least two partners. One must be a general partner who is responsible for the decision making of the business. He or she decides when, where, and how to invest the money of the partnership and receives a fee for his or her services as the general partner. In addition, any expenses incurred to perform the duties of the general partner are paid by the partnership.

In a limited partnership, there must be at least one limited partner, who has limited liability equal to the amount he or she has invested in the partnership and has no say in how the partnership's money is invested. The limited partnership agreement should spell out the specific terms of the partnership, but in general, the limited partners are entitled to a return on their investment and a share of any profit. As stated above, the general partner usually is entitled to receive a fee or bonus for his or her services before any profit is divided among the remaining partners and is entitled to a return on dollars invested and a share of the profits.

Partnership Agreements

A partnership agreement should specify clearly a beginning and ending date of the partnership. Investors are encouraged to draft separate agreements for tax lien investment opportunities in different areas and for different investment years. A partnership agreement, at a minimum, should last throughout the redemption period of all tax lien certificates purchased by the partnership or until the partnership is otherwise dissolved. Other information that should be included in the partnership agreement is:

Purpose

The partnership agreement should indicate clearly that the purpose of the partnership is to make money investing in tax lien certificates. The purpose should be direct and to the point. In the event of a dispute, the purpose of entering into the contractual agreement should not be vague or ambiguous to the person arbitrating or judging the circumstances.

Goal

The business goals of the partnership should be defined clearly, and each partner must be in agreement with the overall goals of the partnership. Individual goals may be different based on the specific expertise of the individual, the amount of funds contributed to the partnership, or other contributions to the partnership, but the business goal should be to achieve a return on the dollars invested. Some investors may require a shorter time for receiving a return on their investments. The business entity should be capable of allowing these individuals to have their dollars invested in tax lien certificates with shorter redemption periods. Other investors may be willing to wait out the longer redemption periods, particularly if high rates of return are expected on the redemption amounts or the property is a valuable property for which research indicates a high potential to foreclose the right of redemption. The goal of the business should be to provide a return on dollars invested by both types of investors.

Contributions

No matter what form of partnership is chosen, the collaborating partners must be capable of contributing something to the partnership and must be in agreement with the role of the partners, as defined by the terms of the partnership agreement. Although it is expected that partners make a financial contribution to the business partnership, not all partners need to contribute financially. Partners may be sought who are capable of bringing physical assets and knowledge to the business. The partner or partners who are most skilled in tax lien certificates would be best suited to present such potential partners with the plan of action for the partnership and the terms for repayment of the funds invested. Expertise in tax lien certificates should be demonstrated with a presentation that focuses on the potential rates of interest and yields involved in tax lien certificate investing. The high rates of return for tax lien certificates, as compared to those achieved in other types of investment opportunities, will lure partners into the partnership.

Finances

It is wise to include partners who are capable of investing liquid capital in an investment partnership. Potential partners with liquid assets to invest may require that the partnership be secured. The language of a promissory agreement should specify that investment properties provide security for the promissory agreement in the same fashion as properties provide security for acquired tax lien certificates. Some potential partners may not have liquid capital to contribute to the partnership, but they may be in a position to provide other types of assistance in the area of finance. Partners may contribute by providing the following assets to the partnership:

- Strong financial statements that may be used to obtain loans for the partnership. Strong financial statements serve as a cosigner in applying for investment loans.

- Assets tied to other long-term investments, such as certificates of deposit. Partners may borrow against existing assets by using them as collateral for the loan. The contributing partners maintain their assets while also generating investment revenue for the partnership.

- Existing and open lines of credit that may be converted to cash for the purchase of tax lien certificates or used in negotiations with delinquent property owners to gain ownership before a property tax sale. The purchase of tax lien certificates usually requires payment in cash or certified funds. Investors need to have cash readily available for the purchase of tax lien certificates. Also, when investors attempt to negotiate with property owners who are delinquent in paying property taxes to acquire ownership of the property before the property is auctioned at tax sale, the property owners will require a cash equity offer.

- Credit card accounts where the creditor is willing to extend large lines of credit. These partners must be convinced that the rate of return offered by tax lien certificates will exceed the rate of interest charged by the credit card company. Since the purchase of tax lien certificates usually requires cash or some form of certified funds, the line of credit offered by credit card companies must be converted to cash. Most credit card companies charge relatively low interest rates on purchases to credit card holders in good standing. However, the interest rate for cash advances may be at a considerably higher rate, and cash withdrawals often attract an additional immediate fee of 3 percent to 5 percent. Rates may be as high as 18 percent to 24 percent. Some credit card companies allow cash advances to be made at the same interest rate as purchases. The partner may be able to secure an account with the latter.

Other Contributions

Partners may contribute other assets to the partnership outside of cash and financial contributions. A partnership requires office space, office equipment, legal counsel, bookkeeping, and a host of other services and skills. The contract agreement should specify the particular services, skills, or equipment contributed to the partnership by each partner. The contract also should specify how the proceeds from profits would be distributed among the partners who are responsible for providing physical assets, skills, and services as opposed to finances. The partners must be capable of determining the worth of partners that provide these types of assets. Having these assets provided by partners has the effect of reducing the operational costs of the partnership, which allows the individual partners to retain more of the profits.

Distribution of profits

The contract agreement should specify clearly how profits are to be distributed to each of the partners. It also should specify a time frame for the distribution of such proceeds. In addition to distributing profits, the contract agreement should spell out the procedure to use in the case of losses. The financial contributors are not necessarily also the partners who should absorb the whole of the financial loss. The partners who are paid for in-house skills and services, for example, may be required to accept a reduced fee for such services.

Account access

The contract agreement must stipulate when and how withdrawals are to be made from accounts of the partnership. The expense account, for example, should have specific and documented instructions with respect to who has access to the account, the types of activity to be funded by the account, when withdrawals are to be made, and the party responsible for tracking and managing the account. The terms of access and parties responsible for all other accounts of the partnership also must be specified. The contract agreement should stipulate that withdrawals from partnership accounts be capped at the amount of the individual partner's initial contribution to the partnership before any profits are disbursed to partners from the account. As another example, in-house services could be stipulated with a time frame for completion. The language of the contract agreement then could be structured such that withdrawals from the partnership account are disbursed to the servicing partner only upon the completion of such services. All funds brought into the partnership must be recorded and tracked. Likewise, all funds expended by the partnership must be recorded and tracked. Even when expenses are paid to partners for their in-house services, the payments must be recorded and tracked just as other expenses paid to outside parties are accounted for. Income and expenses should be documented in the partnership's balance sheet. Use of a software program designed to record assets, liabilities, income, capital, and expenses (ALICE) is recommended to balance the books and perform all other bookkeeping functions of the partnership.

General management

The duties and responsibilities of each partner should be defined clearly. The successful operation of the partnership is dependent upon an organized collaboration of thoughts, ideas, and procedures. The contract agreement should specify the parties responsible for each specific business function, the hierarchy of the partners, and the circumstances for which a vote or decision by all partners is needed.

Dispute resolution

Every partnership agreement should include language that defines the process for the resolution of disputes. It is recommended that the partners engage in methods of arbitration or binding arbitration as an alternative to judicial methods. Arbitration is a more cost-effective method of resolving disputes, and it prevents disputes from being made public. When disputes are argued and settled through judicial hearings, the process leaves the partnership as well as its partners vulnerable to public scrutiny.

Sale and assignment

The partnership agreement must include language that specifies the terms for selling or assigning a partner's interest in the partnership. Sometimes partnerships just do not work out, and one or more of the partners may want to separate from the partnership. The partnership agreement should indicate a mutually agreed-upon dollar value for each of its partners. It is recommended that existing partners be given first right of refusal in buying the interest of a departing partner.

Expulsion

It may become necessary to expel a partner against his or her will when he or she does not or cannot live up to the terms of the partnership. An expulsion is one the most unfavorable actions that must be executed in the best interests of a business entity. In addition, an expulsion can be costly, nasty, and difficult to carry out even when the procedures to implement such an action are defined in the language of the partnership agreement. To avoid the hassle and loss of productivity that expulsion may create for a partnership, it may be in the best interests of both the partners and the business unit to provide the unwanted partner with a financial incentive to leave the partnership. Though the partnership agreement clearly should define the terms of expulsion and the amount of money to be provided to the departing partner, the partners may decide to provide the departing partner with an amount in excess of that specified in the terms of the partnership agreement. The extra incentive is designed to reduce or avoid any disruptions to the operations and functions of the business entity.

Loss of a partner

The partnership agreement should specify the procedures in the case of a partner becoming severely ill, dying, or willfully withdrawing from the partnership. The partnership agreement should indicate a mutually agreed-upon dollar value to be paid to each of the partners under such conditions. The business still is expected to function under such adverse conditions. The partnership agreement should address the occurrence of common life issues and define the partnership's position in such circumstances. For example, a partnership interest may be willed to heirs in the case of a death of one of the partners, or a partner may file bankruptcy and have his or her assets frozen. A partner also may endure a long-term illness or just decide to abandon all interest in the partnership. The partnership agreement should address these types of situations.

Additional partners

Should it become necessary or desirable to include additional partners in an existing partnership, the existing partnership agreement should indicate the terms and procedures necessary to accommodate the additional partners. A new or modified partnership agreement may need to be established that clearly defines the role of the new partner and the modification of roles of the existing partners because of the addition.

Dissolution

At some point, the partnership will end. It is recommended that the partnership agreement specify and designate a time frame for starting and ending the partnership. Even when a successful partnership has acquired all of its initial goals and continues to thrive, the partnership should be ended. If agreeable, the partners always can establish a new partnership.

Chapter 8

Return on Investment Dollars

Usually, if an investor invests in tax lien certificates, he or she seeks one of three outcomes:

1. To profit from the return mandated for redemption amounts
2. To assign the certificate to another party for a fee
3. To take ownership of the property securing the certificate

The first outcome requires that the investor seek liens against properties that are likely to be redeemed. The second requires that he or she seek liens that present a favorable opportunity for other investors. The latter requires the investor to seek properties that are the least likely to be redeemed. It should be understood that this is a relatively low probability event that occurs in less than 10 percent of all cases. Although the first and second outcomes may produce a relatively lucrative return on investment dollars, the third presents a more favorable opportunity for some investors: property ownership at a fraction of its value.

Investors also may contact property owners who are delinquent in paying their property taxes before the property incurs a tax lien offered for sale at the annual tax sale. In this scenario, the investor attempts to engage the property owner in an equity-buying or equity-sharing agreement that would extinguish existing debts against the property in exchange for a quit-claim deed to the property or a share of the equity in the property. The investor, upon engaging in such a contract with the property owner, may assign or flip the contractual agreement to another investor for a profit. Though the investor seeks to engage in this type of activity before a tax lien certificate is sold for the securing property, he or she also may engage property owners in agreements to buy and share equity during the tax lien certificate redemption period, particularly when the property owner indicates an inability to pay the debts of the property. This type of contractual agreement offers the benefit of eliminating the time and expense required for obtaining deed and foreclosing on the property. A foreclosure through the normal tax sale process may not be executed until the redemption period has expired, but this type of contractual agreement provides the investor with the opportunity to acquire ownership earlier and, thus, the opportunity to rent and produce income or sell the property for profit much earlier.

Interest Rates

The investor seeking to profit from the return on redemption amounts measures two types of return: interest rate and rate of yield. State statutes require property owners to pay penalties, interest, or both in order to redeem a tax lien certificate. The interest rate on redemption amounts usually is assessed as a fixed rate. The dollar amount to be returned to the investor depends on the accumulated interest applicable at the time the tax lien certificate is redeemed. The penalty amount, however, usually is applied at the same rate, regardless of when the redemption takes place, and is usually a one-time payment to be applied at redemption. Some states allow the penalty to be staggered during the redemption period, such that the penalty rate is increased for additional years of delinquency. The penalty amount is established according to the statute devised for a particular state or municipality.

Indiana, for example, is a tax lien state that engages in premium bidding. The premium amount is the amount paid by a bidder that is in excess of the opening bid amount. Both the opening bid amount and the premium amount are subject to interest upon redemption. The interest assessed upon redemption depends on how long after the tax sale the redemption takes place as well as the premium amount necessary to win the bid. Indiana also imposes a penalty of 5 percent on the opening bid amount. If the redemption takes place soon after the tax sale, the interest amount may not offer much of a return, particularly for small tax liens. However, the 5 percent penalty assessed on the opening bid amount is guaranteed upon redemption, no matter when the redemption takes place.

As another example, the state of New Jersey engages in competitive bidding down of tax lien certificates. Bidding starts at 18 percent interest on the tax lien certificate amount and bid down to the lowest percentage a bidder is willing to accept. In addition, a penalty is imposed based on the cost of the certificate. Certificates that are sold for less than $5,000 incur a 2 percent penalty; those that cost from $5,000 to $9,999 incur a 4 percent penalty, while those in excess of $10,000 incur a 6 percent penalty. As such, a tax lien certificate purchased for $1,000 and bid down to 10 percent interest upon redemption would be redeemed for a maximum of 12 percent (10 percent + 2 percent) interest if the redemption occurs within the first year of the redemption period.

When working with interest rates, investors apply the Rule of 72 to determine how long funds need to be invested at a particular interest rate in order to double the amount invested. The time frame to double an investment under the Rule of 72 is calculated as follows:

$$72 \div \text{Interest rate} = \text{Time}$$

An interest rate of 12 percent per annum doubles the amount invested in 72 ÷ 12 percent = 6 years. The rule also may be used to do reverse calculations to determine what interest rate is needed to double an investment amount within a given time frame, as follows:

$$72 \div \text{Time} = \text{Interest rate}$$

The interest rate necessary to double an investment amount in five years is

$$72 \div 5 = 14.4 \text{ percent.}$$

Percentage Yield

In addition to interest rates, investors are concerned with maximizing the rate of return, also known as yield. As a rate of return, yield measures how quickly an investor receives a return on the investment amount. The faster he or she receives a return on an investment, the faster the acquired dollars may be used for more investment purposes. Investors use yield to determine the suitability of investment opportunities. When yield is positive, it represents the percentage of profitability of the investment. When yield is negative, it represents the percent of loss in the investment. Unlike interest rates, which are fixed, applied annually, or prorated for the portion of the year or month in which redemption takes place, yield is a calculated measure that takes considers the timeliness of the return from redemption.

In states where redemption requires that interest be applied to the redemption return on a tax lien certificate and the redemption amount is paid before the first year of redemption period expires, the value of yield is computed as an annual return. The percent of yield is always equal to the annual interest at the end of a one-year period. The percentage of yield is always greater than the interest rate when the redemption takes place before the end of one year. The increase in yield depends upon how soon the property owner redeems the tax lien certificate after an investor acquires the certificate. The yield for a $1,000 tax lien certificate that earns 12 percent interest upon redemption and is redeemed in one month is calculated as follows:

Cost of tax lien certificate:	$1,000
Annualized redemption interest:	12% = 1% per month
Tax lien redeemed after tax sale:	1 month
Actual interest paid after 1 month:	$10 = $1,000 x .01
Percentage return:	1% = $10 ÷ $1,000
Percentage yield:	12% = 1% x 12 months

States that also apply penalties to the redemption of tax lien certificates provide a method of increasing the yield on investments, which, in turn, provides investors with an incentive to purchase certificates. Using the state of New Jersey as an example, the interest to be applied to redemption is 18 percent per annum. The established bidding-down process reduces the interest rate on redemption to 1 percent for the winning bidder. No matter what interest rate is bid by the winning bidder, the property owner still is required to pay a statutory 4 percent penalty. For a tax lien certificate purchased at $10,000 and bid down to 1 percent interest upon redemption, the investor would receive a maximum of 5 percent interest on the investment if the tax certificate were redeemed in the first year. The penalty amount is the fixed amount that assures the investor of receiving a fair return on the purchase of the certificate. The more analytic value, yield, varies depending upon when the certificate is redeemed. If the certificate were redeemed within one month of the tax sale, the yield would be 60 percent, calculated as follows:

Cost of tax lien certificate:	$10,000
Annualized redemption interest:	1% = .083 % per month
Penalty on lien certificate:	4%
Tax lien redeemed after tax sale:	1 month
Actual interest paid after 1 month:	$83 = $10,000 x .083
Penalty paid after 1 month:	$400 = $10,000 x .04
Percentage return:	5% = $483 ÷ $10,000
Percentage yield:	60% = 4.8% x 12 months

Though the interest is fixed at 1 percent throughout the redemption period, the amount of interest paid by the property owner after one month is $83, and the amount increases by 1 percent (or $83) per month over the redemption period. The yield, however, is highest during the first month of redemption and is calculated as 60 percent at one month and continues to decrease throughout the redemption period.

As another example, statutes of Wyoming provide for interest and penalties to be applied to the redemption amount. State laws provide for the property owner to pay the following upon redemption:

- The amount paid for the tax lien at the annual tax sale
- 3 percent penalty on the amount paid at the tax sale
- 15 percent annual simple interest on the amount paid and calculated from the date of the sale

The property owner is given 4 years to redeem a tax lien certificate, and the annual interest is calculated and assessed from the date of the tax sale to the date of redemption. Table 5 below shows the yield returned to the investor for each month of the four-year redemption period.

Table 5
STATE OF WYOMING PERCENTAGE YIELDS FOR REDEEMED TAX LIENS

State of Wyoming Percentage Yields for Redeemed Tax Liens

Months Held	Percentage Yield	Months Held Past 1 Year	Percentage Yield	Months Held Past 2 Years	Percentage Yield	Months Held Past 3 Years	Percentage Yield
1	51.0	1	17.8	1	16.4	1	16.00
2	33.0	2	17.6	2	16.4	2	15.90
3	27.0	3	17.4	3	16.3	3	15.90
4	24.0	4	17.3	4	16.3	4	15.90
5	22.2	5	17.1	5	16.2	5	15.90
6	21.0	6	17.0	6	16.2	6	15.90
7	20.1	7	16.9	7	16.2	7	15.80
8	19.5	8	16.8	8	16.1	8	15.80
9	19.0	9	16.7	9	16.1	9	15.80
10	18.6	10	16.6	10	16.1	10	15.80
11	18.3	11	16.6	11	16.0	11	15.80
12	18.0	12	16.5	12	16.0	12	15.75

Note that the interest rate remains fixed at 15 percent throughout the redemption period. The yield, however, is calculated at 51 percent at the end of one month and decreases to equal the interest rate plus the penalty amount of 18 percent after one year. The yield continues to decrease for the remainder of the redemption period. If a tax lien certificate is for $10,000, the corresponding yields for one-month, one-year, and three-year redemption periods would be calculated as follows:

1-MONTH REDEMPTION

Cost of tax lien certificate:	$10,000	
Annualized redemption interest:	15%	= 1.25 % per month
Penalty on lien certificate:	3%	
Tax lien redeemed after tax sale:	1 month	
Actual interest paid after 1 month:	$125	= $10,000 x .0125
Penalty paid after 1 month:	$300	= $10,000 x .03
Percentage return:	4.25%	= $425 ÷ $10,000
Percentage yield:	51%	= 4.25% x 12 months

1-YEAR REDEMPTION

Cost of tax lien certificate:	$10,000	
Annualized redemption interest:	15%	= 1.25 % per month
Penalty on lien certificate:	3%	
Tax lien redeemed after tax sale:	1 year	
Actual interest paid after 1 year:	$1,500	= $10,000 x .15
Penalty paid after 1 year:	$300	= $10,000 x .03
Percentage return:	18%	= $1800 ÷ $10,000
Return per month:	1.5%	= $1800 ÷ 12
Percentage yield:	18%	= 1.5% x 12 months

The percentage return and percentage yield are equal.

3-YEAR REDEMPTION

Cost of tax lien certificate:	$10,000	
Annualized redemption interest:	15%	= 1.25 % per month
Penalty on lien certificate:	3%	
Tax lien redeemed after tax sale:	3 years	
Actual interest paid after 3 years:	$4500	= $10,000 x .0125
Penalty paid after 3 years:	$300	= $10,000 x .03
Percentage return:	48%	= $4800 ÷ $10,000

Return per month: 1.3% = $4800 ÷ 36

Percentage yield: 15.75% = 1.3% x 12 months

The percentage return exceeds the percentage yield.

Note that the percentage yield exceeds 51 percent of the cost of the tax lien certificate if the certificate is redeemed at any time before the end of one month. Also, the percentage yield is an analytical value that does not represent a dollar amount. In order for an investor to receive the dollar equivalent of the yield percentage, he or she immediately would have to reinvest the redemption amount at the same rate of interest with the same redemption period. This situation is not necessarily realistic. The percentage yield, therefore, represents the percentage of return that the investor would gain if he or she realistically were able to do so.

States that impose high interest rates as well as penalties, fees, assessments, and other costs on the redemption amount are in a position to provide the higher rates of yield. States that are positioned to provide rates of yield in excess of 10 percent include the following:

	STATE	YIELD POTENTIAL
1	Alabama	12
2	Arizona	16
3	Connecticut	18
4	D.C.	18
5	Delaware[1]	20
6	Florida	18
7	Georgia	20
8	Territory of Guam	12
9	Hawaii	12
10	Indiana	15
11	Iowa	24
12	Kentucky	12
13	Louisiana	17
14	Maryland[2]	10–24

	STATE	YIELD POTENTIAL
15	Massachusetts	16
16	Mississippi	18
17	Missouri	10
18	Montana	12
19	Nebraska	14
20	New Hampshire	18
21	New Jersey	18
22	Ohio	18
23	Commonwealth of Puerto Rico	20
24	Rhode Island	16
25	South Carolina	8–12
26	South Dakota	12
27	Tennessee	10
28	Vermont	12
29	Virgin Islands	12
30	West Virginia	12
31	Wyoming	18

[1]Includes the counties of Kent and Sussex

[2]Includes Baltimore City and the counties of Frederick, Worcester, Baltimore, Cecil, Charles, Harford, Queen Anne's, Somerset, Carroll, Allegany, Anne Arundel, Howard, Kent, Montgomery, and Prince George's

The yield potential shown represents the yield that would be achieved if a property owner redeemed a tax lien certificate at the end of one year. If the redemption occurs sooner, the yield increases exponentially. If the redemption occurs later, the yield decreases.

Flipping

Flipping is a transfer of ownership that may be applied to tax lien certificates and equity purchasing contracts. Investors that contract with property owners before the property tax sale to purchase their equity in a property in exchange for paying the delinquent property taxes may flip the contract to another party for a profit. Using the example from Chapter 6, a property owner has an outstanding mortgage of $80,000 and is delinquent in paying $4,200 worth of property taxes on a property valued at $200,000. The owner's equity is $115,800 (that is, $200,000 − $80,000 − $4,200). An investor offers to buy the owner's equity in the property for $50,000. In exchange for paying the outstanding mortgage loan, the delinquent property taxes, and $50,000 in cash, the property owner provides the investor with a quitclaim deed to the property. The property owner thus is relieved of the obligation to pay the outstanding mortgage, avoids having a tax lien placed against the property for the delinquent property tax, and receives $50,000 in cash. The investor purchases the property for an amount equal to the following:

Equity offer:	$ 50,000
Loan balance:	80,000
Delinquent property tax:	4,200
TOTAL PURCHASE PRICE	**$134,200**

Rather than following through on the contractual agreement with the property owner, the investor may flip the agreement to purchase the property to another investor. By flipping the property before the tax sale occurs, the initial investor is relieved of paying the delinquent property tax. The new investor would take on the tax debt. Continuing with the example above, the initial investor decides to flip the $200,000 property to another investor for $150,000. Because the initial investor is relieved of paying the delinquent property tax, the original purchase price is reduced by $4,200 to $130,000. The initial investor's return on investment dollars would be calculated as follows.

Flipped price	$150,000
Purchase price	$130,000
RETURN	$20,000

Assignment

If, instead of flipping the contract, the initial investor assigns the contract made with the property owner to another investor, the initial investor profits from the sale of the assignment without having to incur any of the expenses required by the contract. As the assignee of the contract, the new investor is held responsible for fulfilling the contractual obligation and paying the outstanding mortgage, delinquent property tax, and equity payment. Continuing with the example above, the initial investor decides to assign the equity contract that was made with the property owners to a new investor for a fee of $5,000. The new investor purchases the property owner's $115,800 equity in the $200,000 property and receives a quitclaim deed to the property just as the original investor would have. The new investor's cost of ownership is as follows:

Assignment fee:	$ 5,000
Equity offer:	50,000
Loan balance:	80,000
Delinquent property tax:	4,200
TOTAL PURCHASE PRICE	**$139,200**

The original investor's return is $5,000 on an investment for which he or she contributed nothing except the time and expense of engaging the property owners to enter into the equity contract.

Chapter 9

Steps To Purchasing Tax Lien Certificates

Investors can approach the purchase of tax lien certificates as a series of steps. Though it is more difficult for investors to purchase tax lien certificates at delinquent property tax sales than to purchase them over the counter, these steps allow investors to achieve success with either method of acquiring tax lien certificates.

Step 1: Understand state laws and procedures governing the taxing municipality.

Step 2: If a chosen state engages in over-the-counter offers of tax lien certificates, eliminate those states that are not likely to have certificates available for offer after the annual delinquent property tax sale has ended.

Step 3: Seek over-the-counter tax lien certificates in order of the oldest to newest.

Step 4: Determine the bidding system used by each state and within the various municipalities of the state.

Step 5: Bid for tax lien certificates in states where the bidding process does not affect the price significantly that would have to be paid should the property owner fail to redeem the tax certificate.

Step 6: Acquire the listing of delinquent properties that will secure tax lien certificates offered for sale.

Step 7: Determine those tax lien certificates that are less likely to be redeemed during the redemption period.

Step 1: Understand State Laws and Procedures Governing the Taxing Municipality

Each state has laws and statutes governing property tax delinquencies. Many states engage in an annual delinquent property tax sale where tax lien certificates, secured by the property, are offered for sale. Other states engage in the sale of tax deeds, which transfers ownership of the property from the delinquent property owner to the tax deed purchaser. Researching the laws and procedures governing the various states indicates those states that engage in the sale of tax lien certificates. When tax lien certificates are offered for sale, the sale usually is held annually. In many instances, states hold tax sales for the sale of tax lien certificates on the same day of the year for all municipalities of the state. This system makes it virtually impossible for an investor to participate in more than one tax sale. Research also indicates that in most tax lien states, tax certificates are sold or assigned to the state or participating municipality when they are not sold at the annual tax sale. They then are offered for sale to the public over the counter. An investor must be capable of identifying states that offer tax lien certificates for sale over the counter when the certificates are not sold at the tax sale. Those states that offer tax lien certificates for sale over the counter include the following:

Table 6
STATES THAT OFFER UNSOLD TAX LIEN CERTIFICATES FOR SALE OVER-THE-COUNTER

ALABAMA	
Holder of unsold tax lien certificates:	State of Alabama
Status of unsold tax lien certificates:	Judge of probate purchases tax liens for no less than the opening bid amount, on behalf of the state.

The jurisdiction's comptroller examines each tax lien certificate for the sufficiency of the sale. If the sale is found to be in error, the comptroller declares the tax lien certificate void and charges the officer who made the error an amount equal to the delinquent tax, interest, and costs involved in the sale. The county tax assessor is directed to assess the property as an escape for the years it was wrongfully assessed as delinquent. If the sale is rightfully engaged, the property may not be assessed until the tax lien is redeemed or sold.

State-held lien certificates are assignable in writing or by endorsement from the land commissioner upon payment of the bid amount; interest of 12 percent, calculated from the date of sale to the date of assignment; plus any taxes that have incurred since the tax sale; and 12 percent interest on the newly assessed taxes. The assignee is entitled to all rights and title that were held by the state. Certificates *may* also be offered over the counter to investors. The taxing authority is mandated to make notice of over-the-counter sales.

ARIZONA	
Holder of unsold tax lien certificates:	State of Arizona
Status of unsold tax lien certificates:	Assigned to the state by the county treasurer for no less than the opening bid amount

Annual tax sales commence on a specified and advertised date in February. Tax lien certificates are bid and rebid for a number of days until all tax liens are sold or until the county treasurer is satisfied that no more sales can be made. The treasurer assigns unsold tax lien certificates to the state for the tax, interest, and costs of the sale. The county treasurer is *mandated* to sell or assign state-held certificates to any purchaser who pays the amount of the certificate, subsequent taxes, and an assignment fee of one dollar. State liens have priority over tax liens.

COLORADO	
Holder of unsold tax lien certificates:	Colorado municipality governing the tax sale
Status of unsold tax lien certificates:	Assigned, sold, or transferred at the discretion of county commissioners

Tax lien certificates *may* be assigned, sold, or transferred, as determined by resolution of the particular county commissioners, for rights, title, and interest to the property held as security against the lien certificate. State laws do not mandate the sale of unsold tax lien certificates. The tax sale administrator must specifically approve certificates sold for property with delinquent taxes in excess of $10,000.

FLORIDA

Holder of unsold tax lien certificates:	State of Florida
Status of unsold tax lien certificates:	Assigned to the state by the county treasurer

Unsold tax lien certificates are offered over the counter; however, state laws do not provide for the property to be held as security against the lien certificate. If the property owner does not redeem the property, the tax lien certificate holder has no vested interest in the property. The property is auctioned to the highest bidder in a subsequent public oral bid auction.

KENTUCKY

Holder of unsold tax lien certificates:	State of Kentucky
Status of unsold tax lien certificates:	Assigned to the state by the county treasurer

Unsold tax lien certificates are offered over the counter; however, state laws do not provide for the property to be held as security against the lien certificate. If the property owner does not redeem the property, the tax lien certificate holder has no vested interest in the property. The property is auctioned to the highest bidder in a subsequent "deed with right of redemption" auction. The investor must engage in legal actions to recover the cost of the lien or to foreclose the property. If the property is not sold at the "deed with right of redemption" auction, the state commissioner may make deed to the tax lien certificate holder.

MARYLAND

Holder of unsold tax lien certificates:	Maryland municipality governing the tax sale.
Status of unsold tax lien certificates:	Issued by the tax collector to the mayor and city council of Baltimore City or the governing body of a particular county

Unsold lien certificates may be sold or assigned, but there is no mandate governing the sale of such certificates. The investor or governing body is given the right to foreclose the right of redemption.

MONTANA

Holder of unsold tax lien certificates:	Montana municipality governing the tax sale
Status of unsold tax lien certificates:	Assigned to the county by the county treasurer for no less than the opening bid amount

Unsold tax lien certificates are assigned to the county. Certificates *must* be sold to any purchaser upon payment of all delinquent taxes, interest, and other costs

NEBRASKA

Holder of unsold tax lien certificates:	Nebraska municipality governing the tax sale
Status of unsold tax lien certificates:	Assigned to the county by the county treasurer

Unsold tax lien certificates are assigned to the county. Certificates *may* be sold to any purchaser upon payment of all delinquent taxes, interest, and other costs.

NORTH DAKOTA

Holder of unsold tax lien certificates:	North Dakota municipality governing the tax sale
Status of unsold tax lien certificates:	Assigned to the state by the county treasurer

The county treasurer, on behalf of the county, bids unsold tax lien certificates. The county acquires all legal and equitable rights to the property that secures the lien. Certificates *may* be sold to any purchaser upon payment of all delinquent taxes, interest, and other costs.

OKLAHOMA

Holder of unsold tax lien certificates:	State of Oklahoma
Status of unsold tax lien certificates:	Assigned to the state by the county treasurer

Unsold tax liens are *mandated* to be offered for sale to the first purchaser willing to pay the taxes, interest, costs of the sale, and transfer as calculated up to the day of sale.

SOUTH CAROLINA

Holder of unsold tax lien certificates:	South Carolina municipality governing the tax sale
Status of unsold tax lien certificates:	Assigned to the forfeited land commission

The state of South Carolina does not engage in the offer of tax lien certificates but offers to sell "receipts for the purchase money" to be used in the purchase of the property itself. The receipt acts as a tax lien certificate and requires that the property owner be allowed a one-year redemption period before the receipt holder may make deed. A forfeited land commission is established in each county of South Carolina. This commission is entitled to assign title of unsold receipts for an amount no less than the cost of taxes, interest, and costs of the sale at its discretion.

SOUTH DAKOTA

Holder of unsold tax lien certificates:	South Dakota county treasurer
Status of unsold tax lien certificates:	Held for sale by the county treasurer

The county treasurer is *mandated* to sell unsold tax lien certificates at a private sale to any person willing to pay the taxes, interest, and costs of the sale. The treasurer may make bid in the name of the county for the sale of properties, which secure unsold lien certificates. The treasurer is mandated to sell properties for which delinquent taxes have not been paid in the preceding one or more years. In short, the county treasurer may make bid to purchase the property at minimal cost or to sell the property if the county holds it for more than one year.

WYOMING	
Holder of unsold tax lien certificates:	Wyoming municipality governing the tax sale
Status of unsold tax lien certificates:	Purchased in the name of the county by the county treasurer
The county *may* sell or assign unsold tax lien certificates at either a public or private sale to any person willing to pay the taxes, interest, and costs of the sale.	

Step 2: Eliminate States That Are Not Likely to Have Certificates Available for Offer

Having identified those states that offer tax lien certificates for sale when they are not sold at the annual delinquent property tax sale, the investor must be capable of identifying those states that are most likely to have a significant number of tax lien certificates to offer over the counter. As with all investment opportunities, adequate research is necessary for good investing. Understanding state laws and procedures governing a taxing municipality should be part of the initial step in the tax lien certificate investment process. This will allow the investor to identify and eliminate those states not likely to have certificates available to offer over the counter. States that are not likely to have certificates available for sale after the tax sale include the following:

- States that allow for attractive rates of return for redemption.

    Tax liens sold by states that allow investors to collect the most attractive rates of return on redemption amounts have high turnover rates at their municipal tax sales. Investors usually purchase most or all available tax lien certificates at the annual tax sale in an effort to profit from the high rates of return.

- States that have laws that prevent the sale of over-the-counter certificates following the tax sale.

    Laws that permit the purchase of tax liens over-the-counter do not govern all states. Seven states have laws and statutes that do not provide an opportunity for the purchase of tax lien certificates over the counter. Currently, Illinois, Indiana, Iowa*, Mississippi, Missouri, New Jersey, and Vermont do not offer over-the-counter sales of tax lien certificates. The investor should be sure to check into the laws applicable to a particular state, since such laws are subject to change or modification from year to year. The seven tax lien states that do not offer over-the-counter sales of tax lien certificates are listed below:

Table 7
STATES THAT PROHIBIT OVER-THE-COUNTER OPPORTUNITIES

ILLINOIS
The state holds an annual tax sale for the sale of tax lien certificates. Tax lien certificates that are not sold at the annual tax sale are forfeited to the state and offered for public sale again at an Illinois **collector's scavenger sale**. The collector's scavenger sale is mandatory for counties with more than 3 million residents and must be ordered by resolution in the remaining counties. The collector's scavenger sale is held for properties with two or more years of tax delinquency, including the tax year in which the collector's scavenger sale is advertised and held. If a property tax lien certificate is not sold at the collector's scavenger sale or confirmed by a court, the lien certificate is offered annually at the collector's scavenger tax sale until sold. An exception to Illinois state laws applies to mineral rights. If the lien certificate to mineral rights is not confirmed by a court or sold at the collector's scavenger tax sale for ten consecutive years, it is no longer offered for sale.
INDIANA
The state does not engage in over-the-counter sales of tax lien certificates. Tax lien certificates that are unsold at the annual tax sale or bid for an amount that is less than the opening bid amount, are either offered for sale at the next annual tax sale or offered for sale at a special sale. A special sale is held between January 1 and March 31 of the year following the annual tax sale. The annual tax sale usually is held during the month of August or September. The particular county treasurer and county auditor must agree to hold the special tax sale, and this sale must be held, at a minimum, 90 days after the initial tax sale. If a tax lien certificate is not sold at the special tax sale or the offered price is not sufficient to cover the minimum amount established as the opening bid amount, the tax lien certificate is bought and held by the county for the opening bid amount. The county may hold unsold tax lien certificates for acquisition by a metropolitan development commission in a consolidated city or for use by a nonprofit corporation.
IOWA
If tax sale certificates are not sold in the state during the annual tax sale, the certificates are offered for sale at subsequent adjournments of the tax sale. The first adjourned sale is held within two months of the tax sale. Subsequent adjournments are held, at a maximum, within two months of previous adjourned sales. These adjourned sales are continued until all properties have been sold or until the next annual tax sale is held. State laws dictate that notice of adjourned sales be posted

in a conspicuous place in the county treasurer's office. Iowa state laws do not dictate a need for any other type of public notice. As such, investors must contact the particular treasurer's office of interest to obtain information about adjourned sales. The state has 99 such county treasurers. State laws provide for the various counties to engage in three basic systems of adjourned sales, including:

1. Daily adjourned sales
2. Monthly adjourned sales
3. Bimonthly adjourned sales

*When a municipality engages in the daily sales method, it has the same effect as allowing investors to buy tax lien certificates over the counter.

Tax lien certificates that are not sold at adjourned sales before the next annual tax sale are offered for sale at a public bidders sale. The public bidders sale is advertised and conducted in the same manner and on the same date as the annual tax sale. If a tax lien certificate is not sold at the public bidders sale or the bid amount is not sufficient to cover the amount due as predetermined by the treasurer, the board of supervisors of the particular municipality decides the disposition of the tax lien certificate. The board either may allow the particular county to bid the property for the opening bid amount, or the board may make a written compromise and assignment of the certificate to the county. In most instances, tax certificates that are unsold and bid or assigned to the county are secured by properties that are the least attractive of the county's base of real properties.

MISSISSIPPI

In Mississippi, tax liens that are not sold at the annual delinquent property tax sale are struck off to the state. The tax collector is responsible for striking off tax liens to the county, which provides the county with title to the property without right of possession. Property owners are entitled to redeem tax lien certificates. The tax collector also may assign a certificate to any assignee as named and specified by written approval of the property owner. Upon payment of the tax lien certificate and all associated costs, the assignee is given first lien against the property. The assignee may sell the property to satisfy the lien. If the property is neither redeemed nor assigned within a specified time, the state land commissioner may sell the property itself, not the tax lien certificate. The property **must** be sold for a minimum of $2 per acre, unless otherwise specified and approved by the land commissioner and the state governor.

MISSOURI

The state records properties held as security for tax lien certificates in the state's back-tax book when tax lien certificates are not sold at the annual delinquent property tax sale. If the delinquent property taxes are not paid or any subsequent taxes become delinquent by the next annual tax sale, tax lien certificates for the securing properties are offered for sale again at the next annual delinquent property tax sale.

NEW JERSEY

The state provides for tax lien certificates that are not sold at annual delinquent property tax sales to be struck off and sold to the particular municipality offering tax lien certificates for sale. State laws provide for striking off properties only in the case that the particular municipality has not received 15 percent of the total revenue that should be realized by the municipality through tax sales. Tax lien certificates may be purchased by bid that is sufficient to cover the cost of the tax lien, or they may be purchased at 18 percent of the property's value. The tax lien certificate is then subject to redemption. If the property owner fails to redeem the tax lien certificate, the lien-holding city or county may exercise the right to make deed to the property and foreclose the property. State law prohibits tax liens held by municipalities from being assigned or sold over the counter. Government-held tax lien certificates are offered at subsequent tax sales, as directed by a resolution of the municipality's governing body. Existing and newly assessed taxes, interest, and other costs are added as additional lien amounts before the tax lien certificate is offered at the subsequent tax sale. The property owner must pay existent and newly assessed amounts before the tax lien certificate can be redeemed. Interest is calculated on the newly assessed amounts from the date of the new tax sale. Amounts are recalculated and assessed in the name of the property owner as if the original delinquent property tax sale had never taken place.

VERMONT
The state laws of Vermont permit the tax collector to collect on delinquent taxes by seizing and selling the property. The property owner, mortgage holder, or assignee is given a one-year period of right of redemption. If the property is not redeemed within the one year allowed, the tax collector may make title to the property. Vermont laws do not make mention of or provide for the assignment of tax lien certificates.

Counties in the state of Wyoming are examples of municipalities that offer few, if any, over-the-counter sales of tax lien certificates because the rate of return is so attractive to investors that investors buy all or most tax lien certificates offered at the annual delinquent property tax sale.

In contrast to Wyoming, the state of Oklahoma offers a low rate of return on redemption amounts to be paid by property owners. Counties in Oklahoma offer all or most of their lien certificates for sale over the counter because the rate of return on redemption is not attractive enough for investors to bid on tax liens at the annual tax sale. The redemption amount to be paid by the property owner includes the following:

- The amount paid for the tax lien at the annual tax sale or the amount paid for the over-the-counter tax liens
- All subsequent taxes assessed
- Annual simple interest of 8 percent calculated from the date of the tax sale or purchase of the over-the-counter certificate
- Costs of the sale and transfer

Oklahoma state laws do not permit competitive bidding, which means the cost of a tax lien certificate is simply the delinquent tax amount, interest, and any associated costs. No additional penalties assessed, and the cost cannot be bid up. The property owner is given two years to redeem the tax lien certificate, and the annual interest is calculated and assessed from the date of the tax sale to the date of redemption.

State statutes dictate the rate of return to be assessed by states that offer over-the-counter certificates. Those rates are summarized in Table 8 below. States are listed in order of lowest annualized interest rate to the highest:

Table 8
ANNUALIZED REDEMPTION RATES FOR OVER-THE-COUNTER TAX LIEN CERTIFICATES DICTATED BY STATE STATUTE

	State	Interest Rate on Redemption
1	Maryland	6 percent per annum, except as "fixed" by the municipality's governing body
2	Oklahoma	8 percent per annum
3	South Carolina	8 to 12 pecent per annum dependent on when the property is redeemed and whether the property is the legal residence of the property owner. The redemption period is 1 year, and the annual interest is computed at 8% within the first 6 months and 12 percent in the last six months. The state also classifies real property. Redemption statutes apply to property that is less than five acres and occupied by owners or family members of the owners. Owners may hold title to the property in whole or in part.
4	North Dakota	9 percent per annum
5	Montana	10 percent per annum
6	Alabama	12 percent per annum
7	South Dakota	12 percent per annum
8	Colorado	9% above the discount rate, as established on September 1 of the year in which the tax sale is held. The discount rate is defined as the rate of interest that commercial banks pay to the Federal Reserve Bank of Kansas City using government bonds or other securities. The amount is rounded to the nearest percent.
9	Nebraska	14 percent per annum
10	Michigan	15 to 50 percent per annum depending upon the date of redemption. If redemption occurs within 1 year of the tax sale, the redemption rate is 15%. After a 1 year, an additional 50% penalty is assessed.
11	Arizona	16 percent per annum

	State	Interest Rate on Redemption
12	Wyoming	18 to 51 percent per annum depending upon the date of redemption. If the redemption occurs within 1 year of the tax sale, the annualized rate ranges from 18% to 51%. The minimum annualized rate is computed as 15% per annum interest plus 3 percent penalty. If redemption occurs after the first year, but before the 4th year, the rate may range from 15.75 to 17.8 percent per year.
13	Iowa	24 percent per annum

Municipalities in the state of Maryland offer some of the lowest annual interest rates on redemption. However, the rates vary depending upon the taxing municipality. As Table 9 below shows, most municipalities have statutes that dictate a 6 percent rate; a few have statutory 10 percent rates, while only one has a 14 percent statutory rate. However, with the exception of St. Mary's county, that rate may be "fixed" by the governing body or ordinances enacted by the governing body. As such, the fixed per annum interest rates for Maryland may range from 6 to 24 percent, making Maryland a state that offers some of the lowest as well as some of the highest interest rates on redemption. Interest rates established by statute and those fixed by governing authorities, for each of Maryland's taxing municipalities, are shown in Table 9 listed by fixed interest rates.

Table 9
PER ANNUM INTEREST RATES FOR MUNICIPALITIES IN THE STATE OF MARYLAND

Municipality	Per Annum Interest Established by Statute	"Fixed" Interest Rate
Baltimore City	6 percent a year or as fixed by a law of the city council	24 percent per annum computed from the date of the sale
Montgomery County	6 percent a year or as fixed by a law of the county council	20 percent per annum computed from the date of the sale to the date of redemption
Prince George's County	6 percent a year or as fixed by a law of the county council	20 percent per annum computed from the date of the sale
Allegheny County	6 percent a year or as fixed by the county commissioners	18 percent per annum computed from the date of the sale
Anne Arundel County	6 percent a year or as fixed by a law of the county council	18 percent per annum computed from the date of the sale
Howard County	6 percent a year or as fixed by a law of the county council	18 percent per annum computed from the date of the sale

Municipality	Per Annum Interest Established by Statute	"Fixed" Interest Rate
Kent County	6 percent a year or as fixed by the county commissioners	18 percent per annum or 1 1/2 percent per month or fraction thereof, calculated from the date of sale
Cecil County	6 percent a year or as fixed by the county commissioners	12 percent per annum or 1 percent per month or fraction thereof
Baltimore County	6 percent a year or as fixed by a law of the county council	12 percent per annum or 1 percent per month or fraction thereof
Queen Anne's County	6 percent a year or as fixed by a law of the county council	12 percent per annum or 1 percent per month or fraction thereof
Somerset County	6 percent a year or as fixed by the county commissioners or by a law of the county council	12 percent per annum
Charles County	6 percent a year or as fixed by the county commissioners or by a law of the county council	12 percent per annum
Harford County	6 percent a year or as fixed by a law of the county council	12 percent per annum
Worcester County	6 percent a year or as fixed by the county commissioners or by a law of the county council	10 percent per month or fraction thereof
Frederick County	6 percent a year or as fixed by the county commissioners	10 percent computed daily
Wicomico County	6 percent a year or as fixed by the county commissioners or by a law of the county council	8 percent per annum
Washington County	6 percent a year or as fixed by the county commissioners	Same
Talbot County	6 percent a year or as fixed by a law of the county council	Same
Calvert County	10 percent a year or as fixed by the county commissioners	Same
Caroline County	10 percent a year or as fixed by the county commissioners	Same
Dorchester County	10 percent a year or as fixed by the county commissioners	Same
Garrett County	10 percent a year or as fixed by the county commissioners	Same
Carroll County	14 percent a year or as fixed by the county commissioners	Same
St. Mary's County	6 percent a year	Same

Step 3: Seek Over-the-Counter Lien Certificates in Order of the Oldest to Newest

One of the objectives of investors in purchasing over-the-counter tax lien certificates is to reduce the amount of time that investment dollars are vested in tax lien certificates. States provide property owners with an opportunity to redeem tax lien certificates, and the redemption period may range from months to years. If an investor purchases tax lien certificates at annual state tax sales, the investor may be required to wait anywhere from six to 60 months before receiving a return from the redemption of the tax lien certificate. The investor who seeks older lien certificates, which have been held by the state for the longest time, benefits from a more immediate return on investment dollars.

Statutory redemption periods for over-the-counter tax lien certificates are listed in Table 10, in order of shortest to longest possible redemption period.

Table 10
REDEMPTION PERIODS ESTABLISHED BY STATE STATUTES FOR OVER-THE-COUNTER TAX LIEN CERTIFICATES

	State	Redemption Period	Position After Redemption Period
1	Maryland	6 months Exception: The property is certified as needing substantial repairs to comply with building codes. The investor may file a complaint to foreclose the right of redemption within 60 days of the sale of the tax lien certificate.	File complaint to foreclose the right of redemption
2	Michigan	1 year	Initiate processes to obtain a tax deed
3	Iowa	1 year following annual tax sale 9 months following public bidders' sale	Held by the county for offer at the next year's public bidders sale
4	Mississippi	2 years Exception: The property owner is an infant who inherited the property or an individual of unsound mind. The property may be	18% per annum computed from the date of the sale

	State	Redemption Period	Position After Redemption Period
		redeemed within 2 years of attaining legal age or being restored to sanity. The redemption amount includes the cost of any permanent improvements made in the 2 years following the tax sale.	
5	New Jersey	6 months, if the municipality makes purchase at the annual tax sale 2 years, if an investor makes purchase at the annual tax sale or otherwise	
6	Oklahoma	2 years	County treasurer issues a deed for unredeemed land upon the property owner's failure to respond to a lien holder's final notice requesting redemption within 60 days.
7	Alabama	3 years	
8	Colorado	3 years	
9	Montana	3 years	Lien holder is issued a deed upon the property owner's not responding to the lien holder's final notice to the property owner requesting redemption within 60 days of the final notice.
10	Nebraska	3 years	The lien holder has 6 months to initiate the process of obtaining a deed.
11	North Dakota	3 years	
12	South Dakota	3 years, if the property is located within the limits of any municipality	Initiate the process of obtaining a deed
13		4 years, if the property is located outside the limits of any municipality	Initiate the process of obtaining deed
14	Wyoming	4 years	Foreclose the right to redemption.
15	Arizona	3 years	Same

When redemption periods have expired, the investor is required, in most states, to follow some prescribed procedure for foreclosing the property owner's right to redemption and making deed to the securing property. Some states, however, offer more immediate methods of getting title to a property that secures a tax lien certificate.

Arizona, for example, is a state that allows unsold tax lien certificates to be sold or assigned to the state, rather than the particular municipality (see Table 7 on pages 115-117). Following a three-year redemption period, an investor may judicially foreclose the right to redemption and obtain a deed to the property. An investor who purchases an over-the-counter tax lien certificate that has been held by the state for more than three years immediately may put processes in place to gain a deed to the property. If an investor has taken no action to foreclose ten years after the sale, the lien expires and is voided, with no payment to the purchaser. Although these certificates offer an investor the opportunity to quickly realize a return on investment dollars, other state laws reduce the likelihood that the state will have any unsold tax lien certificates to offer. Arizona offers an attractive 16 percent interest on redemption amounts. The high redemption rate ensures that interested investors will make bids at the annual tax sale, particularly for improved properties. When tax lien certificates are available for over-the-counter sales, the offer of sale is not always immediate, but depends on the workload of the particular county treasurer's office. Interested investors must contact the treasurer of individual municipalities to find out when, if any, sales of state-held over-the-counter tax lien certificates are being made.

Step 4: Determine the Bidding Systems Used

An investor needs to determine the bidding system used by the state or a municipality before bidding on tax lien certificates. The investor wishing to gain ownership should buy tax lien certificates in those states that engage in noncompetitive bidding, which does not adversely affect the price that must be paid for the property if the property owner fails to redeem the tax lien certificate. States that engage in the competitive premium bidding of tax lien certificates are not likely to provide an opportunity for an investor to purchase liens for the minimum of tax, interest, and cost of the sale. States that engage in this type of competitive premium bidding include Alabama, Maryland, Missouri, South Carolina, and Vermont.

Because an investor or investment group is not likely to be able to attend all annual delinquent property tax sales to bid on available tax lien certificates, the investor or investment group is left to engage in the purchase of leftover certificates offered over the counter by the taxing authority. Properties purchased over the counter offer the benefit of being acquired at minimum cost, particularly in states that engage in the competitive bidding down of ownership in the securing property. In these states, no competitive bidding is used when tax lien certificates are offered over the counter, and the investor bids for 100 percent ownership of the property. An investor may purchase tax lien certificates for an amount equal to the delinquent tax amount, interest, penalty, and any associated fees and costs. Over-the-counter sales offer the investor the benefit of receiving tax lien certificates secured by 100 percent of the property for the minimum cost.

The state of Maryland allows competitive bidding and offers its tax lien certificates to the highest bidder. The system ensures no investor may acquire a lien certificate unless no one else is willing to bid a higher price. The state, however, does not require that the full amount of the bid be paid initially. Only the opening bid amount is paid to the tax collector, and the balance of the bid amount (the premium amount) is considered a credit. If the property owner fails to redeem the tax lien certificate, the premium amount and all newly assessed taxes, interest, penalties, and costs must be paid before the lien holder may obtain a deed. Maryland statutes provide for a redemption interest of 6 percent but also provide for the governing body of a jurisdiction to increase the amount at will. Most jurisdictions, particularly Baltimore City, have opted to impose substantially higher rates, which has attracted investors wishing to profit from the high rate of return. The Maryland system offers investors the benefit of having a vested interest in a tax lien certificate without ever having to invest more than the minimum opening bid amount if the tax lien certificate is redeemed. The ability of the governing body to override the interest rate established by state statute also provides the benefit of a lucrative rate on return for redeemed tax lien certificates. Maryland municipalities with the highest interest rates on redemption include the following, listed in order of highest to lowest rates:

Table 11
MARYLAND'S HIGHEST REDEMPTION RATES

Municipality	Per Annum Simple Interest Computed From the Date of Sale
Baltimore City	24%
Montgomery County	20%
Prince George's County	20%
Allegany County	18%
Anne Arundel County	18%
Howard County	18%
Kent County	18%

Although these municipalities present opportunities for the investor interested in profiting from the high yield required for redemption, these municipalities are not cost-effective for investors seeking to gain property ownership. The high yield expected from redemption is converted to high costs for the investor who wishes to foreclose the property owner's right of redemption. In order to begin the process of obtaining a deed and foreclosure, the investor is required to pay the premium amount bid to acquire the tax lien certificate as well as any newly incurred taxes, penalties, and interest. The interest is paid at the "fixed" interest rate established by the taxing municipality.

Statutes established for the state put Maryland in the unique position of offering some of the highest and lowest interest rates for redemption. Investors interested in gaining home ownership should concentrate on the Maryland municipalities that offer low redemption interest rates. Municipalities with the lowest interest rates include those shown in Table 12 below.

Table 12
MARYLAND'S LOWEST REDEMPTION RATES

Municipality	Per Annum Simple Interest Computed From the Date of Sale
St. Mary's County	6%
Talbot County	6%
Washington County	6%
Wicomico County	8%

Step 5: Bid Where the Bidding Process Does Not Significantly Affect Price

Some states are governed by statutes that provide for bidding up of premiums on tax lien certificates if more than one individual is interested in purchasing the certificate. However, the implementation of such statutes does not necessarily mean that the price paid by investors to foreclose the right of redemption and acquire ownership of the property is significantly increased. States where this bidding process does not significantly drive up the cost of obtaining title and possession of foreclosed properties include Colorado, Mississippi, and Indiana. These states engage in desirable methods of bidding when ownership of a property is the objective.

Desirable competitive premium bidding

The state of Colorado engages in the competitive bidding up of premiums. The winner among one or more bidders is the bidder willing to pay the largest premium amount, in cash, above the opening bid. Upon redemption, the property owner is required to pay the opening bid amount plus interest from the date of sale. The redemption interest rate is set at 9 percent plus the federal discount rate established for a particular year. The tax lien certificate holder is not reimbursed for the premium amount used to win the bid, nor does the certificate holder receive interest on the premium amount invested. If a property owner is quick to redeem a tax lien certificate after the tax sale or if the premium amount bid and paid by the investor is significantly more than the amount received from interest on the redemption amount, the investor takes a loss. As an example, an investor bids $1,200 for a tax lien certificate. The opening bid amount is $1,000, but the investor bids up the premium to $200.

Opening bid	$1,000
Premium bid	200
Total cost of tax lien certificate	$1,200

The property owner redeems the tax lien certificate with a 12 percent interest rate one month after the tax sale. Upon redemption, the investor receives the following:

Tax lien cost	$1,000	Opening bid does not include the premium amount
Interest on opening bid	10	12% per annum (1% per month)
Total returned	$1,010	
Total loss	−$ 190	$1,010 − $1,200

Because the premium amount and interest on the premium amount are excluded from the redemption amount, and the premium ($200) does not exceed the amount paid in interest ($10), the investor takes a loss. If, on the other hand, the property owner fails to redeem the tax lien certificate, the investor would obtain the deed to the property for the opening bid amount plus the premium amount and any newly accrued taxes, which is substantially cheaper than purchasing the property in the real estate market.

The state of Mississippi also engages in the competitive bidding up of premiums. The winning bidder among one or more bidders is the bidder willing to pay the largest premium amount, in cash, above the opening bid amount. Upon redemption, the premium amount is refunded to the tax lien certificate holder, but no interest is paid on the premium amount. The property owner is required to pay the following:

- The opening bid amount
- Interest at 18 percent of the opening bid amount computed at 1.5 percent per month or any fractional part thereof, calculated from the date of the tax sale
- Any taxes that have accrued since the date of the sale
- Interest on the newly accrued taxes computed at 1 percent per month or any fractional part thereof calculated from the date of the tax sale

If a $1,000 tax lien certificate were bid up in premium to $1,200, the investor would receive the following from redemption 1 month after the tax sale:

Tax lien cost	$1,000	Opening bid	
Refund of premium	200		
Interest on opening bid	15	18% per annum (1.5% per month)	
Total returned	$1,215		
Total gain	$ 15	$1,215 – $1,200	

If the property is redeemed quickly, no new taxes are likely to accrue, as in the example above. However, if the redemption occurs after subsequent taxes are assessed, the investor may not receive much return on the investment or may even take a loss. If, on the other hand, the property owner fails to redeem the tax lien certificate, the investor may obtain deed to property for the minimum of the opening bid amount, the premium amount, and any newly accrued taxes, which is still significantly cheaper than purchasing property through normal real estate channels.

Bidders in Colorado and Mississippi realize that early redemptions may create low gains or losses, so they make an effort to keep premiums low. Not only does this type of premium bidding have the potential to create a loss when tax lien certificates are redeemed early, control of the premium bid amount may offer a benefit should the property owner fail to redeem the tax lien certificate. Should the tax lien certificate investment lead to property ownership, ownership would be acquired at substantially lower costs than would be required to purchase property through normal real estate channels.

The state of Indiana engages in the competitive bidding up of premiums much like that of Mississippi, except that the tax lien investor must file a verified claim with the county auditor to recover the premium amount from the county's tax sale surplus fund. Also, Indiana does not require property owners to pay any interest on redemption amounts, but requires that they pay a penalty on both the opening bid and premium. Upon redemption, the property owner is required to pay the following:

- The opening bid amount
- A 10 percent penalty on the opening bid amount if the redemption occurs in the first 6 months
- A 15 percent penalty on the opening bid amount if the redemption occurs after 6 months
- A 10 percent penalty on the premium amount
- Any taxes that have accrued since the date of the sale

If a $1,000 tax lien certificate were bid up in premium to $1,200, the investor would receive the following from redemption one month after the tax sale:

Tax lien cost	$1,000	Opening bid
Refund of premium	200	
Penalty on opening bid	100	10%
Penalty on premium	2	10% per annum (0.83% per month)
Total returned	$1,302	
Total gain	$ 102	($1,302 – $1,200)

Not only does the tax sale process provide for the investor to profit from the redemption amount paid, it also provides for the investor to acquire property without substantially increasing the cost of ownership. If the tax lien certificate is not redeemed, the investor may obtain a deed to property for the minimum tax, interest, penalty, sale costs, and any newly accrued taxes, which is substantially cheaper than if he or she bought the property in the real estate market.

Desirable bidding down of interest rates

Some states assign tax lien certificates to the bidder who purchases the certificate at the opening bid and also bids down the lowest percentage of interest to be paid upon redemption. The states of Arizona, Illinois, and New Jersey engage in this type of bidding process. Arizona and Illinois sell tax lien certificates at the exact amount of the opening bid. When there is more than one bidder for a particular property, the successful bidder is the one who bids down the lowest redemption interest to be paid when the tax lien certificate is redeemed. In New Jersey, a successful bidder of the competitive bidding-down process is decided by bidding down the redemption interest and then engaging in a competitive bidding up of premium amounts.

Both Arizona and Illinois have been identified as states that are not likely to have worthwhile tax lien certificates available to offer over the counter. Investors wishing to profit from the high-yielding redemption rates of 16 and 18 percent, respectively, usually attend the tax sales held in these states. Bidders in these states are not likely to bid down too far because it would defeat the purpose of receiving the high rates of interest. The average rate received in Arizona is about 10 percent. Statutes governing the state of Arizona provide for a 16 percent per annum redemption interest. A bidder may bid down to accept an interest rate that is less than the statutory 16 percent, but not too much more. If, however, the property owner fails to redeem the tax lien certificate, the investor's cost to obtain deed to the property is, at a minimum, an amount equal to the opening bid and any newly accrued taxes. The same holds true for the state of Illinois, except that the interest rate is 18 percent.

New Jersey uses a similar process, except that limits are established for redemption rates. State statutes dictate that redemption rates may not exceed 18 percent. Also, should more than one bidder offer to purchase a tax lien certificate and the bid-down process results in a redemption rate that is less than 1 percent, the successful bidder is the one who pays the highest premium over the opening bid. If, however, the property owner fails to redeem the tax lien certificate, the investor's cost to obtain a deed to the property is, at a minimum, an amount equal to the opening bid, the premium bid, and any newly accrued taxes.

Desirable first-come, first-served bidding

The states of Kentucky, Montana, and Oklahoma engage in first-come, first-served methods of offering tax lien certificates for sale. No premium amounts are paid, and the opening bids may not be bid up or bid down. The opening bid is the final bid.

In Kentucky, tax lien certificates are not secured by real property. If a tax lien certificate is not redeemed within the redemption period, the tax lien certificate is offered for sale again at a subsequent auction. The successful bidder at the subsequent tax sale is the bidder who, based upon the judgment of the sheriff, makes the first offer to pay cash for the lien certificate. However, the initial lien holder is given preference in the subsequent tax sales.

Statutes governing the state of Montana dictate that tax lien certificates be sold to any purchaser willing to pay the opening bid amount. Most municipalities engage in a first-come, first-served method of offering tax lien certificates for sale.

In Oklahoma, the successful bidder is the bidder who, based upon the decision of the county treasurer, makes the first offer to purchase a tax lien certificate. The county treasurer, using his or her own discretion, is required to implement fair and impartial methods of determining the successful bidder when multiple bidders wish to purchase the same tax lien certificate.

Undesirable bidding down of ownership

Some states engage in competitive bidding that results in investors having to bid down the percentage of ownership in property used as security for tax lien certificates. The investor does not obtain 100 percent ownership in the property should the property owner fail to redeem the tax lien certificate. The states of Iowa, Michigan, Louisiana, Massachusetts, New Hampshire, and Rhode Island engage in this type of competitive bidding.

In Iowa, the tax lien certificate purchaser is the bidder who offers to pay the lien for the smallest portion of ownership in the property used to secure the tax lien certificate. This portion of ownership is designated an undivided portion. The remaining portion of ownership in the property belongs to the property owner. When two or more investors wish to bid on the same tax lien certificate, the percentage of ownership in the securing property is bid down until no other bidder wishes to bid. Iowa state statutes provide for a 24 percent per annum redemption rate. If a tax lien certificate is not redeemed within the one-year, nine-month redemption period, the investor may foreclose the owner's right to redemption. The lien holder is granted a treasurer's deed for the percentage of interest that was bid to obtain the tax lien certificate. Because a treasurer's deed entitles both the investor and the property owner to a percentage of tenancy-in-common, an investor is not likely to obtain full ownership. Specific and time-consuming processes must be followed in order to sell the property and receive a return on the investment.

Undesirable random selection bidding

Some states implement a system of randomly selecting bidders to purchase tax lien certificates. The state of Wyoming and certain municipalities of Colorado and Iowa engage in a random selection process. First-come, first-served methods that allow each purchaser to bid on all available tax lien certificates that have not been purchased are more desirable than selection processes in which bidders are randomly chosen to purchase a particular tax lien certificate. Random selection bidding offers investors low or no odds of being able to invest in specific or valuable properties. The random selection process reduces the odds of being able to bid on a particular property to one out of the number of total bidders participating in the tax sale. If the tax sale, for example, draws 150 bidders, the chance of being offered the opportunity to bid on any one property is 1 out of 150 or .007 percent. An investor has virtually no chance of being able to bid on a property of choice.

Though Iowa is not governed by statutes that allow for random selection, many municipal treasurers are favorable to, and choose to engage in, such a process rather than engage in the mandatory system of bidding down ownership established by the state. Likewise, the statutes established for Wyoming provide for bidding down the percentage of interest in tax lien certificates. However, all 15 municipalities of Wyoming choose to engage in a random selection process. The state of Wyoming also provides bidders with an opportunity to purchase tax lien certificates over the counter. When tax lien certificates are available for over-the-counter sales, the bid-down process and the random selection process are eliminated.

Step 6: Acquire the Listing of Delinquent Properties

Most delinquent property tax sales are mandated to be held on a particular date or within a particular time frame. Other states allow tax sale dates to be determined by the governing body responsible for the sale. Statutory dates established by states are as shown in Table 13 below. Investors must contact those states and municipalities that do not have laws or statutes governing delinquent property tax sales to determine when the particular taxing municipality holds its annual tax sale.

Table 13
STATUTORY TAX SALE DATES

	State	Statutory Date of Sale
1	Arizona	Month of February. Each municipality establishes its own day in February. Most municipalities choose dates near the end of the month.
2	Colorado	Before the second Monday in December. Sales typically are held during November.
3	Illinois	No date is specified in the statutes; sales typically are held during November.
4	Indiana	Between August 1 and October 31, but must not extend beyond October 31
5	Iowa	Third Monday in June
6	Maryland	As specified by the particular municipality
	• Baltimore County	Within four months of the first Monday in February
8	• Cecil County	First Monday in June
9	• Harford County	Third Monday in June, after 10 a.m.
10	• Montgomery County	Second Monday in June
11	• Prince George's County	Second Monday in May, after 10 a.m.
12	• Queen Anne's County	Third Tuesday in May
7	Michigan	First Tuesday in May, after 10 a.m.
8	Missouri	Fourth Monday in August
9	Mississippi	Last Monday in August or, at the discretion of the tax collector, the first Monday in April
10	Montana	No date is specified in the statutes; sales typically are held during July. Notice of a pending sale must be published once a week, beginning before the last Tuesday in June and continue, once a week, for three consecutive weeks. The tax sale must occur within 21 to 28 days of publication.

	State	Statutory Date of Sale
11	North Dakota	Second Tuesday in December, after 10 a.m.
12	Oklahoma	First Monday in October, 9 a.m. to 4 p.m.
13	South Dakota	Third Monday in December, 9 a.m. to 4 p.m.
14	Wyoming	No date is specified in the statutes; sales typically are held during July. A listing of unpaid and delinquent taxes must be certified before the May 22. Notice of a pending sale must be published once a week, at least four weeks before the sale and before the first week of September. Publication must continue, once a week, for three consecutive weeks. Real property must be sold between 9 a.m. and 5 p.m., exclusive of Sundays.

All tax lien certificates offered for sale in a given municipality must be published in a local newspaper of general circulation in the particular municipality where the tax sale is held. The treasurer's office of each municipality decides which newspaper to use for the publication of tax lien certificates. An investor may request that the treasurer indicate which newspaper it intends to use by addressing a letter to the treasurer's office. A prepaid and self-addressed envelope should be included with the letter to cover the expense of mailing a response. Once the newspaper and date of publication have been determined, the investor may order the particular issue of the newspaper directly from the publisher to begin research.

January 16, 2012
Treasurer's Office
123 Street Address
Anytown, USA 00000

Dear Treasurer,

I am requesting information regarding the upcoming 2012 annual property tax sale. Would you please provide the name, address, and phone number of the newspaper that will be used by your office to publish the

> listing of certificates for offer? In addition, would you please provide the dates for which your office plans to list certificates in the publication? I have enclosed a self-addressed, stamped envelope for your response.
>
> Thank you for your assistance.
>
> > Sincerely,
> >
> > Your Name

Step 7: Determine Properties Less Likely to Be Redeemed

Though redemption offers the investor the benefit of profiting from the redemption interest and penalties applied to tax lien certificates, the ultimate goal of some investors is acquire ownership of a property that secures a tax lien certificate. Having acquired a listing of all tax lien certificates for offer at the delinquent property tax sale, the investor must identify those tax lien certificates that he or she would like to pursue in an attempt to gain ownership. In order to gain ownership, an investor needs to identify those properties less likely to be redeemed by the property owner, and the investor should attempt to buy tax lien certificates from those municipalities that engage in desirable bidding processes. Tax lien certificates document a priority lien, which means they are given priority over all other liens except liens held by the state in which the property is located and certain liens held by the federal government. When tax lien certificates are not redeemed, the investor must obtain a tax deed to the securing property and foreclose to gain ownership. Because most states provide for two- to three-year redemption periods, property ownership may be acquired for an amount equal to the real property taxes and costs assessed during the redemption period (typically, three years), the expenses of applying for a deed, and the expenses required for foreclosure. Typical real property taxes are assessed in the range of 1 to 4 percent of the real property's market value. Accumulated interest, penalties, costs, and fees over a three-year redemption lien, could increase the cost of ownership from as little as 4 percent to as much as 15 percent of the market value of a property.

When a tax lien is sold for delinquent taxes, the property may be redeemed by anyone having any type of secured interest in the property. This is inclusive of anyone having ownership interest or security interest in the property. Ownership interest is the interest of any party named on the deed to the property. Security interest is the interest of any party having a lien against the property, such as a mortgage company.

States such as Oklahoma require that the tax lien holder make notice of the intent to foreclose, not only to property owners, but also to any lenders with outstanding loans against the property, before making application for a deed to the property. Thus, the investor seeking to gain property ownership is reliant upon both the owner and lender to fail to respond to the notice and abandon responsibility for the property. The investor must be skillful in identifying those tax lien certificates not likely to be redeemed. Few property owners will allow their valuable properties to be foreclosed because of delinquent taxes, and lenders are not likely to forfeit security on their loans for the relatively small cost of redeeming a tax lien certificate. Usually, when a seemingly valuable property is not redeemed, the owner or lender with security interest in the property has intentionally or unintentionally abandoned the property. If the property is intentionally abandoned, it is likely to have some peculiarities that are not cost-effective or time-effective to deal with. A property may be assessed with the same value as other similar properties in an area, but research indicates that the property contains some environmental hazard or the property may have been damaged severely by fire, and the property owner had no insurance to cover the loss. Valuable properties rarely are abandoned intentionally. Unintentional abandonment, on the other hand, may be caused by a number of factors. The property owner could have passed away and left no will that would indicate the disposition of the property. The party responsible to pay property taxes could have moved and not provided the tax collector with a forwarding address. The property owner could be facing a long-term illness, and relatives are irresponsible in paying bills on his or her behalf. Any number of reasons could cause unintentional abandonment.

In general, the investor attempting to gain ownership should seek properties that are:

- High in market value
- Free of any lender liens
- Abandoned by the owner

Whether tax lien certificates are purchased at annual tax sales or purchased over the counter, the investor is required to engage in research to determine whether properties are likely or not likely to be redeemed. That research should indicate the following:

1. If the tax lien certificate is secured by a valuable parcel of real estate

The amount of taxes due and delinquent, as published in the tax sale listing, may provide some indication of the market value of a property. Evidence from an inspection, as outlined in Step 11 below, also will help determine market value. In general, taxes are higher on more valuable real property. The published annual tax sale listing indicates an amount of delinquent taxes, but that amount also may include the associated penalties, interest, and other costs due. Listings also may include a single amount with no indication as to the number of years of delinquency. An investor must be sure to interpret the listed values according to the tax sale laws and procedures of the given municipality. To be more precise in determining market value, the investor may examine the tax assessor's records, which indicate a property's appraised market value. In addition, records held by the municipality's tax assessor indicate the owner's name and legal description or account number, which can be queried against the owner and legal description identified in the tax sale listing. A computer-generated output of the assessor's information pertaining to a tax lien certificate may contain information similar to the following:

Market/Use		
Assessed land	[9,234]	[876]
Improvements	[38,831]	[5,042]
Mobile home	[]	[]
Total ------>	48,065	5,918

The output indicates a valuation of fair market value equal to $48,065, land valued at $9,234, improvements valued at $38,831, and the property does not include a mobile home. An improvement can be a house or other structure. As a rule, if the assessed value of the land is more than 40 percent of the total assessed value, the property may offer no value. The output shows that the assessed value of the land, relative to the total property value is 19 percent ($9,234 + $48,065). The output, therefore, represents a property where most of the worth is in the structure. This type of property is likely to be of value to an investor. If the output is reversed and the structure is assessed at 19 percent of the total property's worth, the land would hold the greater percentage of worth. The property is likely to be a parcel of land with a small structure, such as a shed or a larger structure that is below par. Only a visual inspection of the property will determine the suitability of such a property for investment purposes. Other records available from the assessor's office may be used to determine the use of a property as well as other specific characteristics of the property. The property file may indicate all or some subset of the following:

- Use of the property, for example, single family home
- Lot size
- Size of additions to the land
- Composition of the exterior, foundation, roof, fireplace, and utilities
- Composition of the foundation
- Photographs of the property

Clearly, if records indicate that a property represents a single family home, but the property assessment assigns 80 percent of the worth to the land, there likely are problems with the structure identified as a single family home, or there was some error in the recording of the assessment values. Investors must remember that assessors are not immune from making mistakes in their assessments or in recording assessment data.

2. If the real property is owned free of any lender liens

The investor must be capable of researching the title to the property as held by the registrar of deeds, recorder's office, or county clerk of the municipality. Properties used as security against lender loans are most likely to be redeemed because a tax lien has priority over a lender's loan. In order for a lender to move its loan into highest priority and prevent it from being discarded, the lender must extinguish any outstanding tax lien certificates by redeeming them. In order to research the outstanding debt held against a parcel of property, the investor must be capable of using the property description and other information provided in the tax sale listing to locate information contained and recorded in public records. The investor must be capable of researching properties using the particular state's method of indexing properties. States index properties using either a tract indexing system or a grantor-grantee indexing system.

Tract indexing

In states like Oklahoma, a tract indexing method is used to index mortgages by the legal property description of the property for which they are held. Tax sale listings may provide a legal description of a property in one of two different formats. Either the state subdivision name is listed along with the block and lot number, or a government survey description is provided. The county clerk of each municipality maintains a book or database of all mortgages held against each parcel of real property in the particular municipality. Mortgages are indexed by the property's legal description. The legal description provided in a tax sale listing may used to query against the legal descriptions used to index mortgaged properties. If the property specified in the tax sale listing has an existing mortgage, it will be documented in the records held by the county clerk. An example of a government survey legal description for a parcel of real property, as published in a tax sale listing, is as follows:

> SMITH, JOHN Q. ET OX. 10 21N 03E, E2 NW4 LESS N 466 FT of E 466 FT ...

The actual legal description is the series of numbers and characters, "10 21N 03E, E2 NW4 LESS N 466 FT of E 466 FT," that follows the named party to the mortgage note. The legal description signifies the location of the property as Section 10, Township 21 North, and Range 3 East. The party to the mortgage (grantee) is named as John Q. Smith and his wife (ET OX).

Other information that may be contained in the file or record for a particular property includes the following:

- The named lender or grantor
- The type of instrument recorded, that is, mortgage
  The entry indicates "Mtg" if a mortgage was ever held against the property. The entries "Mtg Rel" or "Rel Mtg" are used to signify that the mortgage was paid off or released.
- The location of the copy of the mortgage note, that is, book and page number. For a computerized system, the location may be a link to a stored file position in a database.

The following states make use of a tract indexing system:

- Nebraska
- North Dakota,
- Oklahoma
- South Dakota
- Wyoming

Grantor-grantee indexing

With the exception of Ohio, states that use grantor-grantee indexing are able to identify properties by the names of the grantor (borrower), grantee (lender), or their equivalents. A legal description of the property is not used as the index. Instruments documented and recorded under this system are indexed under the names of individuals associated with the document.

The state of Arizona, for example, maintains an indexed record of instruments for each property in each of its municipalities. The record contains, as a minimum, the following indices for each instrument recorded:

- Date of recording
- Page number
- Grantor (borrower)
- Grantee (lender)

Records may be indexed by either single or multiple indices. The identifying names used to index official records are stored and arranged in alphabetical order using some form of storage and retrieval system. Indices must be accessible to the public, yet protected from compromise when electronic storage and retrieval systems are used. Both the grantor and grantee or their equivalents must have indexed instruments for each of the following categories:

- Transference of real property
- Mortgage
- Mortgage release
- Miscellaneous
- Lease
- Secured transactions
- Assignments of mortgages
- Leases
- Governmental liens
- Nongovernmental liens
- Attachments
- Judgments
- Agreements

Instruments may also be categorized according to the following optional categories:

- Powers of attorney
- Official bonds
- Executions
- Lis pendens

- Mine location notices
- Partnerships
- A description or code indicating the type of instrument recorded

Arizona uses two types of grantor/grantee indexes, as follows:

- A combined general grantor/grantee index in which all documents of a specific type are indexed under the grantor and grantee in one separate volume

- Separate indexes for each type of recorded document. All documents of a specific type that pertain to a particular grantor are indexed in one volume, while documents of a specific type that pertain to a particular grantee are indexed in another volume.

Instruments are categorized according to the type of instrument. Documents indexed as miscellaneous do not fall into the established types of instruments. In Arizona, lenders are likely to hold deeds of trust as well as mortgages as security interest in a property. The investor seeking to invest in tax lien certificates in Arizona must be sure to research both types of documents. As an example, if an investor wants to determine whether a deed of trust or mortgage is being held as a lien against a property, the investor would need to research the grantor-grantee indexing system using the name of the property owner, as published in the tax sale listing. If an entry is found for the grantor, grantee, or both, the investor may use the indicated document number or book and page number to locate the specified document. The document indicates a legal description for the property that should be identical to the legal description of the property published in the tax sale listing. If the legal descriptions match, an outstanding lien is being held against the property.

3. If outstanding liens against the property are discharged by tax sale process

In general, a real property tax lien is the first lien against a property, with the exception of states that allow liens assessed by the state to be given higher priority and certain liens held by the federal government. Before an investor purchases a tax lien certificate, he or she must research the title to the property to determine if any other liens are senior to the tax lien.

In Oklahoma and Arizona, for example, state-held liens are senior to tax liens. State-held liens include liens assessed by commissions, boards, and officers with the power to make loan of public funds or any funds held as security for real estate and under the control of the state. Should an investor obtain ownership of real estate through the tax sale process, he or she also would assume any outstanding liens held by the state. The property would not be acquired free and clear. This is in contrast to a lien held by a private institution, such as a mortgage lender. Tax lien certificates are senior to lender liens, and in all likelihood, the lender would redeem the property before the investor exercised his or her right to foreclose the right of redemption. In the case that the lender, for whatever reason, fails to redeem the tax lien certificate, the investor obtains ownership, free and clear of the lender's lien against the property.

4. Liens that indicate abandonment, such as violations of building codes or liens for services performed

Some municipalities are governed by statutes that allow them to abate properties that are not maintained, such as vacant lots, vacant houses, and transient housing. In general, the process of abatement involves notifying the property owner to correct the situation and assessing liens against the property for the cost of correcting the situation when the property owner fails to comply. This type of lien instrument generally is indexed, classified, and recorded as a "notice of lien" in the municipality's public records. Any such recorded entries are potential indicators of an abandoned property. In other states, the abatement is not recorded, but the amount is added to the real property tax bill as part of the delinquent tax amount.

5. Whether the property was inherited or given as a gift

Oftentimes, properties are inherited or given away to individuals, free and clear, but the individuals do not pay the property tax or other costs that may be assessed by the municipality against the property. An investor may research the method in which title was acquired. If a property is given by a gift of deed or inherited, a decree of distribution is recorded with the taxing municipality.

6. Whether tax bills and notices have been returned undeliverable

When tax bills are returned to the treasurer's office by the postal system as undeliverable, the property may have been abandoned. Returned postage usually includes some type of endorsement, such as moved, left no address, vacant, or deceased. If available, these endorsements will help in the research identify abandoned properties. If certified mailings, with return receipts are not deliverable, the party serving the notice may be required to publish his or her notice, depending upon the type of correspondence being delivered. If a public notice is required to advertise the correspondence, it is likely that property ownership will be obtainable. Most notices that must be published by statute generally are not published with widespread circulation to the general public, which means that the property owner is not likely to see the notice or respond to it.

7. Whether the property owners have out-of-state or out-of-country mailing addresses

If mail is delivered out of state or out of country to the property owner and the mail is returned undeliverable, the likelihood of ownership increases, particularly when a tax lien certificate is purchased near the end of the redemption period.

8. Whether mailings to the property address are forwarded to another

If mail is addressed in care of another, it is likely that the other party may not get the mail, or the mail will be returned undelivered.

9. Whether the property owners are a named defunct corporation, LLC, limited partnership, or entity of trust

Corporations, LLCs, limited partnerships, or investment trusts that hold property usually are required to register with some agency of the state. When the particular entity fails to register, it may be an indication that the entity is defunct, which means it is no longer a legal entity. In this situation, the property or properties held by the entity may be abandoned.

10. Information provided about the owners from the treasurer's or collector's office

In less populated municipalities, it may be advantageous to speak with personnel at the treasurer's office to try to gain information about specific properties. In more populated municipalities, especially large cities, the effort may be wasted.

11. Evidence obtained from inspecting the property for market value

The investor must be responsible for inspecting a chosen property before attempting to purchase a tax lien certificate that is secured by it. Sometimes records are incorrect or out-of-date. An assessed value may be the result of an old assessment that was completed before the roof of the property was blown away and the garage caught fire. If possible, an investor should attempt to gain entry to the property or talk to the occupants of the property. If access to the occupants is not possible, the investor may try to talk to others who have examined the inside of the property, such as neighbors or persons who have made repairs. The investor should be sure to examine the front, sides, and rear of the property. Many times, curb appeal can be deceiving. While examining a property in an unfamiliar neighborhood, the investor should note advertised real estate postings and make contact with such realtors to gain a better understanding of the market potential of the area.

12. Evidence obtained from inspecting the property for abandonment, usually a report of curb appeal

The investor must be responsible for inspecting a chosen property rather than relying on public records. Sometimes, records are incorrect or out-of-date. It is not unusual for a property to be listed as an improved property, but a visual inspection proves the property to be just a vacant lot. Some properties, particularly raw land, have no street address, are landlocked, and are difficult, if not impossible, to locate. The investor should acquire a parcel map from the assessor's office to assist in locating properties.

13. The availability of tax lien certificates for other neighboring and vacant or improved properties

While inspecting a chosen property location, the investor should take note of any neighboring vacant, valuable, and improved properties and then determine the availability of a tax lien certificate for purchase.

14. Whether an estate has been opened when the owner is deceased

Probate records should indicate whether an estate has been established for a vacant property. If an estate has been established, the owner is deceased and the heirs of the owner are likely to redeem the tax lien certificate.

15. Whether the listed owner has any other abandoned properties

If research indicates that an owner has, in fact, vacated a property, the investor should check with the assessor to determine if the owner has abandoned any other properties for which tax lien certificates are available.

Chapter 10

Making Use of
Tax Lien Certificates

Purchasing tax sale certificates at annual tax sales, purchasing tax lien certificates over the counter at some time after the annual tax sale, or making assignment of tax lien certificates are just parts of the process necessary to make money from tax lien certificates. In order to profit from the purchase of tax lien certificates, the investor must be capable of understanding and following procedures established by the municipalities of each state. The investor must understand how to assign, redeem, and foreclose tax lien certificates such that the return on investment is maximized.

Tax Lien Certificate Assignments

Tax lien certificates are a form of real estate contract, and like all real estate contracts, they may be assigned to another party for a fee. An assignment transfers all rights to purchase real estate under a real estate contract from the assignor to the assignee. Assignments represent an easy and quick method of flipping a parcel of real estate. A tax lien certificate holder may assign his or her rights, responsibilities, and interest in a tax lien certificate to another investor. The tax lien certificate holder assigns the certificate by making a contractual agreement with another party to receive the assigned lien certificate. The other party, the assignee, contractually obligates himself or herself to pay the cost of the lien certificate plus a fee for the tax lien certificate assignment. Like tax lien certificates, tax lien certificate assignments are also a form of real estate contract. The assignment and reassignment of tax lien certificates must be recorded by the taxing municipality to become valid. The taxing authority in the property that secures the tax lien certificate usually will record an assignment for a nominal fee of a couple of dollars. When the taxing authority sells a tax lien certificate, it assigns the tax lien certificate to the purchaser for a fee. In most instances, the fee includes the delinquent tax amount, penalty, interest, and costs. That assignment then can be reassigned to another party for a fee. In situations where an investor engages in a contract with a property owner to buy equity, share equity, or lease the property before the tax sale, the established contract represents a real estate contract, and this may also be assigned to another party for a fee.

Tax lien certificates may be assigned during the redemption period, and the assignment entitles the assignee to all rights and responsibilities with regard to redemptions, initiating processes to obtain a deed, and foreclosing the property held as security for the tax lien certificate. Upon redemption, the assignee receives the penalty, interest, and other costs that accrue during the redemption period. If the property owner fails to redeem the lien certificate, the assignee is entitled to foreclose the right of redemption just as the original lien holder would have. The newly established property owner may make use of the property to provide living space, rental income, appreciation, or whatever purpose he or she deems appropriate.

If the assignment is made after issuance of a tax deed, the tax deed holder may assign the property at foreclosure. The assignee is issued an assignment deed (or quitclaim deed) for a fee.

Collecting Redemption Amounts

When tax lien certificates are acquired for delinquent property taxes, the investor is assigned a lien certificate, which indicates that the named lien holder holds indebtedness against the property that secures the tax lien certificate. Depending on the tax sale system used in a particular municipality, the investor has to allow time for the delinquent property owner to redeem the tax lien certificate. The redemption period may range from 60 days to four years. Some municipalities provide investors with a physical tax lien certificate to be held as evidence of the purchase and assignment of the certificate. Other states record the paid assignment, but do not provide the actual certificate. This works in the best interests of the investor in the event that a property owner decides to redeem the tax lien certificate.

When tax lien certificates are redeemed, the tax collector is responsible for collecting the payment from the property owner and recording the assignment in his or her records. In most states, the tax collector notifies the tax lien certificate holder of the redemption and requests that the certificate is returned to the collector. Following receipt of the tax lien certificate, the tax collector issues the tax lien certificate holder a check for the proceeds received for redemption. The period from which the property owner redeems the tax lien certificate and the time in which the tax collector issues a check to the investor may be a matter of days or weeks, depending on the workload of the tax collector's office. During this period, no interest is earned. In states where the tax lien is recorded, but the actual certificate is held by the tax collector, the time frame from redemption to reimbursement may be shortened severely. This shortened time frame provides investors with a faster turnover rate, which increases the rate of return for the investment and allows the investor to reinvest redeemed dollars quicker. Investors are cautioned to notify tax collectors of any address change. Some states have a time limit in which a tax lien certificate holder may respond to the request to return a tax lien certificate in return for the redemption amount. If the notice is delivered to the wrong address or returned undeliverable, the investor risks exceeding the time limit imposed and may suffer a loss of the redemption amount.

When the redemption period associated with a lien certificate extends one year and the property owner fails to redeem the property, new real estate taxes are assessed against the property in subsequent years. Some municipalities require the tax lien certificate holder to pay subsequent taxes that accrue over the redemption period if the property owner fails to do so. In other states, it is optional for the tax lien certificate holder to pay subsequent taxes. If the newly assessed property taxes are not paid, the property may go to tax sale again. In this situation, a second investor may acquire the tax lien certificate offered for sale for newly assessed and delinquent tax amounts. As such, the delinquent property becomes security for two distinct and separate tax liens. In order to maintain ownership of the property, the property owner would have to satisfy the redemption amounts associated with both tax liens. This process will continue to manifest itself until the redemption period has expired. The redemption period for the first tax lien certificate will expire before any subsequent tax lien certificates. The owner of the first tax lien certificate will have the first opportunity to foreclose the property owner's right of redemption in accordance with the laws of the particular municipality. In order to foreclose, however, the first tax lien certificate holder must redeem the second tax lien certificate as well as any subsequent tax lien certificates. This process insures that dollars invested in any tax lien certificates always are protected. Second and subsequent tax lien certificate holders may never get an opportunity to gain ownership of the securing property unless the previously held tax lien certificate fails to engage in a foreclosure. Investors that engage in the purchase of tax lien certificates subsequent to previously held tax lien certificates are guaranteed of having the redemption amount satisfied by the previous tax lien certificate holder, or they will be given the opportunity to foreclose.

Lien priorities

Tax lien certificates are but one type of indebtedness for which a property may be held as security. Liens against the real estate title may be held by federal, state, or local government entities. Liens also may be placed against the title to a property if the property owner is the losing party in a civil lawsuit. Real estate cannot be sold free and clear until all liens against the property are satisfied. The IRS may place tax liens against real estate owned by individuals who fail to pay required federal income taxes. State tax liens may be placed by state taxing authorities for unpaid state income taxes. Local taxing authorities may place liens against real estate for unpaid property taxes or the nonpayment of services performed by the local government. Liens against a parcel of property are set in priority, and tax liens are generally in first position against a property. This is because real property taxes are used to pay for local services. Tax rates are set and assessed against real property to fund budgets that pay the expenses of the local municipality. Without such funds, the municipality would not be capable of funding its share of police protection, emergency services, public schools, public libraries, court systems, local roadways, or salaries for the jurisdiction's local employees. When a property owner loses a civil lawsuit to another party, the other party may file a lien against the property owner's property and everything else that he or she owns. If the property owner fails to redeem a tax lien certificate secured by the property, this type of lien, which is junior to a tax lien, is wiped out by the foreclosure of a tax lien certificate.

In New Mexico and Arizona, state-held liens against a property are given priority over tax liens. One of several reasons for engaging in the research of properties before acquiring tax lien certificates is to discover if any outstanding debts are in place against a chosen parcel of property. When a lien exists and is in excess of the market value of a property, the property is considered to be overencumbered. If a property is overencumbered by a state-held lien and the state's lien is given priority over tax liens, then the security of the tax lien certificate is nonexistent. As an example, an investor, without researching a particular property, purchases a $3,000 tax lien secured by a property valued at $46,000 in Arizona. At foreclosure, the investor learns that the state of Arizona also has a lien against the property for $45,000. If the investor pays the state lien, he or she would have $1,000 worth of security in a property that was purchased for $3,000. The property is overencumbered by $2,000. Rather than acquiring free and clear title to the property, the investor would be required to pay for the property at $2,000 above its fair market value to gain title to it. This scenario very different from one in which ownership is obtained for pennies on the dollar.

Fair market value	$46,000
State lien	$45,000
Tax lien	$ 3,000

Total required for foreclosure $48,000 = $45,000 + $3,000
Overencumbered $ 2,000 = $48,000 – $46,000

State lien priority

With the exception of certain government liens, tax liens have first priority over other liens, such as those assessed for the nonpayment of mortgage or other instruments in which the property is held as security for the instrument. Other liens are prioritized according to their recording dates. As an example, a property in Arizona is valued at $100,000, with property taxes equal to $1,600. The property has several other liens against it: a first mortgage with a balance of $50,000, a second mortgage with a balance of $20,000, and a $300 lien assessed by the state for the nonpayment of state income taxes. The state of Arizona offers a three-year redemption period when neither the first tax lien certificate holder nor the property owner pays the property taxes for subsequent tax years. As such, two other certificates are sold to recoup the loss to the municipality for the delinquent property taxes in subsequent years. In Arizona, state-held liens are given priority over tax liens. Following the expiration of the three-year redemption period for the first tax lien certificate, the order of precedence for liens against the property is as follows:

1   State lien $300 plus interest
2   First tax lien: $1,600 plus interest and costs
3   Second tax lien: $1,600 plus interest and costs
4   Third tax lien: $1,600 plus interest and costs
5   First mortgage: $50,000
6   Second mortgage: $20,000

- If the second mortgage company forecloses the property for nonpayment of the mortgage note, all other liens must be paid before the foreclosure can be completed.

- If the first mortgage company forecloses, the state lien and the three tax liens must be paid before the mortgage company can complete its foreclosure. The second mortgage is wiped out and not paid.

- If the first tax lien holder forecloses, the second tax lien, third tax lien, and the state lien must be paid. Both mortgages are wiped out and neither is paid.

The second and third tax lien holders are not in a position to foreclose because the period of redemption has not expired for their lien certificates. If the state forecloses, no other liens will be paid; however, it is not likely that the state will foreclose because the state of Arizona mandates that individual county treasurers sell tax lien certificates. The attractive 16 percent interest rate applied to redemption amounts ensures that the certificates will be sold.

If, by rare circumstance, neither of the mortgage companies forecloses and the first tax lien certificate holder fails to foreclose within one year of the expiration of the redemption period, the second tax lien holder is put in a position of being able to foreclose. When the redemption period of the second tax lien certificate has expired, the second certificate holder is put a position of being able to foreclose by paying the first tax lien, third tax lien, and the state lien. Neither mortgage lien would have to be paid. The second lien holder then would acquire ownership of the property, free and clear.

Given that tax liens are given first priority over mortgage liens, a foreclosure by a tax lien certificate holder wipes out any mortgage liens. Mortgage companies will redeem tax liens should the delinquency of the property owner lead to such a circumstance. This is because the amount necessary to redeem a tax sale certificate is relatively small compared to the loss of the mortgage amount. In this example, the first mortgage company would have paid the required redemption amount rather than have the mortgage wiped out. In fact, unless some bizarre occurrence of events prevents the mortgage company from becoming aware of the delinquent tax amount, the situation in this example probably never would present itself.

Federal lien priority

The federal government also may assess liens against real property for the nonpayment of a government debt by the property owner. An IRS lien has priority immediately following the expiration of the first redemption period. Once the redemption period has expired and a deed sale has been completed, the IRS is given 120 days from the date of the deed sale to redeem all lien certificates. If the IRS redeems a property, it must pay all tax lien amounts. However, the IRS only is required to pay interest on the redemption amount at 6 percent per annum from the date of the tax sale. The IRS also is required to pay expenses of the tax sale and any expenses to maintain or provide protection for the property if those expenses exceed any income that may be generated by the property. If the IRS does not redeem during this 120-day period, its lien is extinguished. An IRS lien has no ability to wipe out tax liens.

Bankruptcy and lien priorities

Bankruptcies affect the process of redeeming and foreclosing tax lien certificates by increasing the time line to receive a return on the investment. Federal bankruptcy laws allow judges to order a stay of claims against the individual who has filed for bankruptcy as well as a stay of claims against property owned by such individuals. A stay order halts all claims by creditors, including tax lien certificate holders. For the purposes of bankruptcy, tax lien certificate holders are considered secured creditors. As such, any processes initiated because of the sale, purchase, or assignment of tax lien certificates are stayed. Even during bankruptcy, property tax liens have the highest priority of liens against real property of bankrupt property owners. The tax lien will remain in first position throughout the bankruptcy proceedings unless a bankruptcy judge orders that all property of the bankrupt individual be sold. In this situation, all secured creditors will receive a prorated amount of their claims, based upon the proceeds from the sale of the property. The judge also may require creditors to file an "answer" in response to requests for information about their claims. The answer requires lien holders to acquire legal services and present their positions during bankruptcy court proceedings. The tax lien certificate holder must consider whether a prorated redemption amount plus the cost of engaging necessary legal services is cost-effective in pursuing the return offered by a particular tax lien certificate, when the certificate is secured by the property of a bankrupt party.

Chapter 11

Foreclosing Unredeemed Properties

Tax lien states extend to property owners an opportunity to redeem tax lien certificates. Some deed states also offer property owners an opportunity to redeem properties sold at tax deed sales. When the property owner or other vested party fails to redeem a tax lien certificate, the investor may foreclose the right to redemption of the certificate and obtain title to the property. Before an investor is able to foreclose the right of redemption, the foreclosing investor must pay all delinquent taxes, penalties, interest, and costs. The longer the redemption period on a tax lien certificate, the greater the amount that must be paid. The state of Arizona offers the longest redemption period of four to five years. The accumulated taxes, interest, and other costs will far exceed those required for a foreclosure in some municipalities of Maryland. Certain Maryland municipalities offer the shortest redemption period of just six months. The right to foreclose a property owner's right of redemption does not guarantee that the investor will gain title to the property. Some states may limit the investor's return by ensuring that the cost of the tax lien certificate and any interest, penalties, costs, and fees are reimbursed to the tax lien certificate holder as a result of a foreclosure sale but allow any remaining equity in the property to be returned to the property owner.

In general, there are two types of foreclosures. The first type provides for the investor to obtain title to the property free and clear, that is, without payment of any additional liens or consequences. This type of foreclosure is considered an administrative filing of foreclosure. The second type of foreclosure requires the tax lien certificate holder to force a sale of the property at a tax deed sale. This type of foreclosure is known as a force of sale foreclosure. The fees associated with both types of foreclosures may include the following:

- Attorney's fees when court proceedings are necessary
- Filling fees
- Court costs
- Fees required of the taxing authority
- Title expenses

Administrative Filing of Foreclosure

An administrative filing of foreclosure is the process used by most tax lien states to foreclose the right of redemption of a tax lien certificate. This type of foreclosure is considered a nonjudicial foreclosure, as no court proceedings are required to foreclose. The investor must be diligent in following the processes defined by public notices and other state requirements established for foreclosure or risk forfeiting rights to the property. The process usually involves the following steps, once the redemption period of a tax lien certificate has expired.

- Notify the municipality of the desire to foreclose

In some states, an investor need only apply to the taxing authority for a tax deed once the redemption period has expired. Upon receiving and verifying the application, the tax collector will issue a tax deed in the name of the party on record as holder of the tax lien certificate.

- Pay any administrative fees required to file for foreclosure.

Foreclosure is not immediate or without costs. Most states that provide investors with the capability to foreclose administratively the right of redemption also charge a fee to administer the tax deed.

- Complete necessary paperwork required by the municipality.

The investor usually is required to complete certain paperwork before the issuance of a tax deed.

- Send a notice of intent to the property owner or publish legal notice in a local paper.

The various states have differing requirements for making notice of a foreclosure. Meeting the requirements may require that the investor provide the taxing authority or court with specific details of the information included in the notice, who was notified by the notice, and how those parties were notified. Some states require that only the persons named on the property record as property owners be notified. Other states insist that the documented owners be notified as well as occupants of the property and mortgage holders. In addition, heirs of the property owner and other lien certificate holders may need to be notified. Some states require that notice be posted on the particular property or posted at a public location or both. In most states, if the property owner can be located, the state may require that the he or she be notified by "personal service." The investor is expected to bear the expense of hiring a process server to make delivery of the notice. The particular state statute indicates whether personal service, certified mail, or registered mail is an acceptable form of delivering notice. All states accept service by publication when the property owner cannot be located. Some states may require both personal service and service by publication to make the notice available to any other person who may have an interest in the property. The courts do not look favorably on investors who resort to trickery in making notice of a foreclosure. Tactics such as placing notice in a foreign paper will cause the notice to be thrown out of court. The requirements for foreclosure can be restrictive and might require, for example, that the full name, as specified on the property deed, be used and not an individual's initials. At a minimum, the notice of foreclosure must detail the following:

- An adequate description of the property to be foreclosed
- When the foreclosure proceedings are to be held
- Where the foreclosure proceedings are to be held
- The name of the property owner
- The types of taxes due

When the notice is determined to be inadequate, the courts lack jurisdiction, which allows the property owner or mortgage holder to contest the deed, even if they are not present at the court proceedings. If, on the other hand, a party to the foreclosure is not properly notified, yet appears in court for the proceedings, that party is considered to have been properly notified.

- Pay all other tax liens and government liens, if required.

In order for a tax lien certificate holder to foreclose the right of redemption, the investor must pay all other tax liens held against the property. In addition, if any liens are superior to the investor's tax lien, the investor must satisfy those liens as well. Such liens may include state-held liens and federal liens held against the property.

Even when states allow an investor to engage in an administrative foreclosure process, he or she still may have to engage the services of an attorney. Title companies are not always willing to insure a property title acquired through a judicial foreclosure process. Some title companies wait one year after foreclosure to see if any claims are filed against the property before issuing a title policy. Most investors are not willing to wait. In such instances, the investor may have to engage the services of an attorney to bring the matter before a judge and obtain a court order of foreclosure through a quiet title action, explained in a future section. When a court order is necessary to foreclose a tax lien certificate, the foreclosure is considered a judicial foreclosure.

Force of Sale Foreclosure

A foreclosure that requires a tax lien certificate holder to force a sale of the securing property is used in most tax deed states. The lien holder must follow the same process as outlined above for an administrative filing of foreclosure. However, the participating municipality, not the lien holder, is responsible for handling the issuance of all notices. The municipality also establishes and sets the date for the sale. The property owner is given additional time, up to the date of the deed sale, to redeem the property. If the property owner fails to redeem, the property is auctioned on the specified and published date. The party named on the tax deed receives preference at the sale and is given a credit for holding the first position lien. The credit is an amount equal to the following:

- First position lien, plus interest
- Costs to buy out subsequent liens, plus interest
- Filing fees
- Other administrative costs

A winning bid at the tax sale auction is the bid that exceeds the credit amount established for the party named on the tax deed. If no one bids above the lien credit amount, the named party to the tax deed acquires the property free and clear. If a bidder bids in excess of the lien credit amount, the named party to the tax deed may compete in bidding up the cost of the property. The winning bidder acquires the property, free and clear. If the winning bidder is someone other than the named party to the tax deed, the named party to the tax deed is paid the credit amount, and the winning bidder acquires ownership of the property, free and clear. For this reason many investors choose to engage primarily in the sale of tax deeds. The investor does not have to vest dollars in the investment throughout a redemption period, and any money invested at the deed sale receives either an immediate return of the money invested or property ownership.

Quiet Title

A force of sale foreclosure, like an administrative foreclosure, may be non-judicially processed in some states and judicially processed in others. It is recommended that investors bear the expense of hiring legal representation to ensure that the specific procedures required for a foreclosure are followed and complied with, even when states do not require it. Investors are encouraged to file a legal claim against any potential claimants of the foreclosed property. By doing so, the investor engages in what is known as a quiet title action. Such an action, when successfully pursued, provides the investor with a court declaration that the title to the property is good. The courts will determine whether documents are properly completed, whether they include all required information, and whether the proper notices of foreclosure were put into place. Given that all procedures are followed and all paperwork is complete, claimants, including the former property owner, can do little to disrupt the foreclosure. Should the investor choose to sell the foreclosed property, the court declaration protects the investor against any challenges to the foreclosure process and assures any potential buyer that the title was properly and legally acquired. Some title companies require such a declaration from the courts before they will insure the title to a foreclosed property.

Hindrance to Foreclosure

Although a successful foreclosure to gain ownership of valuable property is a goal of investors, situations may arise that will hinder and delay efforts to foreclose on valuable properties. In most instances, judicial foreclosures are default proceedings, which means that the foreclosure proceeds with no one opposing the foreclosure action. The governing tax authority issues a deed in the name of the investor only after the court is satisfied that all procedures have been followed and that the foreclosure should have taken place. Occasionally, a property owner may halt a foreclosure action successfully when it is determined that he or she paid the required property tax or properly redeemed the tax lien certificate but was not given credit for such actions. Attempts to challenge the tax assessment, property tax amount, or foreclosure procedures usually are dismissed by the courts during this phase of the tax sale process. However, when property owners are able to provide proof that some form of fraud made cause for a foreclosure, they may be successful in stopping foreclosure actions.

Bankruptcies, destruction, and environmental issues may adversely affect the property used to secure a tax lien certificate. Bankruptcy may have the effect of delaying the foreclosure process and significantly reducing the yield on a tax lien certificate investment. Environmental issues and property destruction may reduce the value of the securing property significantly and, in some cases, render it worthless.

Bankruptcy

When a property owner files a petition for bankruptcy, the bankruptcy may delay or eliminate any effort to foreclose a tax lien certificate. There are two categories of bankruptcy: liquidation under Chapter 7 of the U.S. Bankruptcy Code and reorganization under Chapters 11 and 13 of the U.S. Bankruptcy Code.

Chapter 7 bankruptcies provide for the property owner to turn over all nonexempt assets to a court-appointed trustee of the bankruptcy court. The trustee is required to liquidate all nonexempt assets of the property owner. The bankruptcy court first freezes the nonexempt assets of the property owner and then liquidates them. Proceeds gained from liquidation of the property owner's assets are used to pay creditors. For the purpose of bankruptcy, tax lien certificate holders are considered creditors. As creditors, tax lien certificate holders hold first lien priority and are paid all costs associated with acquiring the tax lien certificate. Liquidation by the bankruptcy court eliminates any opportunity for an investor to foreclose the right to redeem a tax lien certificate and gain ownership of the property. Once an individual files a petition for bankruptcy under Chapter 7, a new petition cannot be filed for seven years.

Chapters 11 and 13 provide for the property owner to reorganize his or her financial obligations by continuing to make payments to creditors. The property owner also is required to make up any back payments with interest through a modified and extended payment schedule. Chapter 13 is intended for individuals, while Chapter 11 is intended for corporations and partnerships. As such, court proceedings under Chapter 11 are the most complex, time consuming, and costly. Unlike bankruptcy under Chapter 7 liquidation, bankruptcies under Chapters 11 and 13 have no time limits for subsequent petitions to be filed. When the property owner files a petition for bankruptcy, the bankruptcy court enacts a legal moratorium called an automatic stay. The stay prevents a tax lien certificate holder and all other creditors from engaging in any legal actions against the property owner to satisfy a debt. The mere act of filing a petition for bankruptcy creates an automatic stay, and many property owners have been known to file such petitions continuously under Chapters 11 or 13 in an effort to delay foreclosure. Although this process has proven successful in delaying foreclosures in the past, in recent years, courts have tended to lift recurring stays.

Relief of stay

If a foreclosure sale occurs after the property owner has filed a bankruptcy petition, the bankruptcy court will order the foreclosure null and void. As a creditor, the lien certificate holder may file a petition to seek relief from the automatic stay imposed by the bankruptcy court. The bankruptcy court has a legal obligation to hear the relief case within 30 days; otherwise, the stay is lifted and the tax lien certificate holder is allowed to continue with the foreclosure. This, however, is not likely to happen. In all likelihood, the bankruptcy court will hear all requests for relief from stay. The court usually considers the amount of equity in a property in making a decision as to granting a relief from stay. When the property has significant value and the owners have significant equity in the property, the court is more likely to deny a relief of stay. It is anticipated that all creditors will be better served if the property is sold and the proceeds are used to satisfy creditors. If, on the other hand, the property owners have little equity in the property, the court is more likely to grant a relief from stay to the foreclosing creditor. Because the tax lien certificate holder holds a first priority lien against the property does not necessarily mean the tax lien certificate holder will be the creditor that the bankruptcy court allows to foreclose.

In many instances, there is at least one mortgage lender involved in the bankruptcy proceedings of a property owner. The courts may order that a cram-down or short sale provision be imposed on the mortgage lender to assist the property owner with reorganization under Chapters 11 and 13 of the U.S. Bankruptcy Code. Under such circumstances, the court orders a modification of terms of the mortgage or trust deed, which may include a modification of the payment schedule or a reduction of the principal amount to be paid to the mortgage lender. The tax lien certificate holder is reimbursed for the costs associated with the tax lien certificate, but any plan to acquire deed to the property and foreclose is voided. If a petition for bankruptcy is filed after a foreclosure sale, the court may order the foreclosure null and void if it is determined that the equity in the property could have been more wisely used to pay the debts of creditors. The petition initiates an automatic stay of any foreclosure proceedings. If the stay is lifted, the foreclosure process continues from the point at which the creditor was frozen by the stay.

In instances where the tax lien certificate holder is seeking a relief of stay and no mortgage lenders are seeking foreclosure, the court may declare that the relatively small amount invested in a tax lien certificate provides too much equity for the tax lien certificate holder when there other creditors with claims against the property owner. The court may order a bankruptcy liquidation sale of the owner's assets, as specified under Chapter 7 of the U.S. Bankruptcy Code. Assets, including the property that secures a tax lien certificate, are auctioned to the highest bidder. The highest bidder for the property receives title to the property, free and clear. The proceeds from the sale of assets then are used to reimburse the tax lien certificate holder for the cost of the tax lien certificate, interest, penalties, fees, costs, and expenses associated with the tax lien. Because the tax lien certificate holder holds the first priority lien against the property, he or she is reimbursed for his or her investment. The remaining proceeds are prorated and distributed to the other creditors. No foreclosure of the right to redeem a tax lien certificate may take place.

Destruction

After having acquired a tax lien certificate, but before redemption takes place, there is a possibility that any structures located on the property may be destroyed by fire, vandalism, or a natural disaster, such as a tornado or hurricane. If the property owner holds casualty insurance on the property, the cost of repairs will be covered by the insurance. If the loss results in a total destruction, the insurance company may pay all outstanding liens against the property on behalf of the property owner. In the absence of casualty insurance, the equity in a tax lien certificate may be reduced accordingly. There are some instances, however, where the tax lien certificate still may be secured. The property tax bill issued to property owners by the tax collector indicates assessment amounts allocated for land and improvements on the property. When the land on an improved property is more valuable than the improvements, the value of the land may be sufficient to provide security for the tax lien certificate even though the structures are damaged or destroyed. In instances where the structure is the most valuable part of the property, destruction in the absence of casualty insurance may render the securing property worth less than the tax lien certificate held.

Environmental issues

One of the issues surrounding the availability of tax lien certificates for commercial and industrial properties is the potential for the existence of environmental issues. The Superfund Act enacted by the U.S. Congress makes all property owners and operators responsible for contamination on their property whether or not they are the party that caused the contamination. Commercial and industrial properties are the most likely properties to suffer contamination from hazardous chemicals. Properties such as gas stations, chemical plants, and other businesses that may be contaminated, used to produce contaminants, or that make use of contaminants, such as gas, toxic wastes, mold, lead paint, and radon, often are cited by government entities for the exposure or release of contaminants. If a property is cited for environmental problems, the property owner or operator becomes responsible for any necessary environmental analyses and cleanup efforts. Property owners are forced to incur large expenses for the detection, removal, or containment of contaminants. In some instances, property owners default on paying the property tax associated with such a property to avoid the expense of an environmental cleanup. It is their intent to rid themselves of the property and its associated expenses and allow the tax lien certificate investor to inherit the problems. A property listing for a property that presents a potential environmental issue is shown in Form 5 on the next page.

```
ITEM            LEGAL   LATEST                                          MB  PG  PCL
 NO    NSB#     DESC    ASSESSEE    LOCATION        MIN BID.    IMPS  LASTEST PARCEL
                                                                      EARLIEST PARCEL

3719    176     E J  BALDWIN'S  FIFTH   $87,553       Y         8741 011 002
                SUBDIVISION  OF  A  PORTION  OF                 81/8741 011 002
                RANCHO LA PUENTE LOT  COM  AT  S
                TERMINUS OF A COURSE IN  W  LINE
                OF VALINDA AVE  PER  MB533-48-49
                HAVING A BEARING OF S 0¢39'50" W
                AND A LENGTH OF 473.38 FT   TH  N
                0¢39'50" E TO A PT N 0¢39'50"   E
                150 FT FROM E PROLONGATION OF  N
                LINE OF MAPLEGROVE ST PER CSB119
                TH N 86¢02'49"  W   150  FT  TH  S    THIS PROPERTY MAY BE CONTAMINATED
                0¢39'50" W TO SD   N  LINE   TH  E    INVESTIGATE BEFORE YOU PURCHASE
                THEREON TO A PT  S  47¢18'35"   W
                23.44 FT FROM BEG TH N 47¢18'35"
                E TO BEG    PART   OF   LOT    349
                ASSESSED     TO
                LOCATION COUNTY OF LOS ANGELES
```

Form 5: Property description that indicates a potential environmental issue

Investors are encouraged to invest in residential properties to avoid the potential loss and complications that environmental issues may add to commercial and industrial properties. Though residential properties are not exempt from environmental contamination, the likelihood of contamination is far less probable for residential properties than commercial and industrial properties. As stated previously, properties under consideration for tax lien certificate investment should be properly researched and evaluated. Some residential properties, for example, located in rural communities or communities that were once considered rural may have gasoline tanks or underground heating oil tanks installed on or the near the property. Over time, these storage units may leak contaminants. Also, properties developed on farmland may be candidates for contamination, particularly when the land has a history of being treated with pesticides or other chemical contaminants. In most instances, farmland must be graded for development, and the process of grading is usually sufficient to dilute contaminants below detectable levels. Time also contributes to the breakdown of contaminants such as pesticides. Properties developed on industrial land present more risk of contamination, particularly when the developer has failed to record an environmental report for the property. An environmental report indicates the results of an environmental inspection of the land. Investors are encouraged to check the previous history of properties under consideration to determine whether any such inspection reports exist. In the absence of an inspection report, the investor should check public records to determine the use of the property before making an investment decision. Although commercial properties present a high risk of contamination, they also provide a good investment when they are usable and free of contaminants.

Phase I environmental evaluations

A Phase I environmental evaluation is designed to confirm whether hazardous substances ever existed on a property. The process of the evaluation is such that an environmental consultant requests that property owners provide information about the environmental history of the property. The consultant then engages in a walk-through inspection of the property to seek any visible indications of contamination. Such visible indicators include sticky vegetation, soil discoloration, and vent pipes that may be attached to underground storage units. A search of government records also may be performed to determine if the property is listed in one of its many lists of contaminated properties or whether a permit ever has been issued for the installation of underground storage units. A search of government records also may be performed to locate any existing aerial photographs that may indicate the previous uses of the property. As helpful as an environmental inspection is in confirming the existence of contaminants, it is not likely that a tax lien certificate holder will be given access to a property to perform such an inspection. As a tax lien certificate holder, the investor has no right of possession to the securing property. Unless the property is open to the public, an inspection is not feasible. The investor will have to rely on the historical public records of the property to confirm the existence of environmental contaminants.

Phase II environmental evaluations

A Phase II evaluation involves a more scientific approach to evaluating the property. Samples are taken from the property and sent to a laboratory for evaluation. This process is necessary for high-risk properties that indicate some potential for contamination. This phase of evaluation is much more expensive, as the consultant first must determine where to sample and then what to sample. As with a Phase I evaluation, access to property to perform such an evaluation is likely to be denied by the owners or operators, and a tax lien certificate holder has no authority to override the property owner's decision.

Although the Superfund Act holds property owners and operators responsible for environmental contamination, the U.S. Congress exempts lien holders from such a liability. Specifically, the exemption indicates that a lien holder is not an owner or operator as long as he or she is acting in a capacity to protect a security interest in the property and not participating in the management of the property. A tax lien certificate documents such a lien and, by definition, only serves the purpose of protecting the security interest of a property. The certificate does not give an investor any right to participate in the management of a property. The exemption, however, may not carry forward should the property owner fail to redeem a tax lien certificate and the investor forecloses the right of redemption. The EPA requires foreclosing tax lien certificate holders to auction or sell the property or make a good faith effort to sell the property in order to maintain the exemption. If a lien holder outbids, rejects, or fails to accept a cash offer for the property, the exemption may be lost. Furthermore, if within 90 days of a written, legally binding, and reasonable offer of cash, the investor refuses the offer, he or she loses the exemption and becomes the responsible owner of the property. The property must be offered for sale by either listing it through a broker within one year of foreclosure or listing it monthly in an appropriate publication. If the property has an existing business that the investor continues after foreclosure, he or she may retain the exemption as long as no contamination continues under the new ownership.

Unlawful detainer

Once title to a foreclosed property is acquired, the investor still may have problems gaining possession of the property. When an investor forecloses an occupied property, he or she may find that existing occupants are reluctant to leave the property. Occupants that are not owner-occupants may not be aware that a foreclosure has taken place and a change of ownership has been granted. When occupants refuse to leave a foreclosed property, the investor is put in the same position as a landlord whose tenants refuse to leave. The investor must seek a court order to force an eviction and gain possession of the property. Rather than seeking an eviction, such as that used by landlords, the foreclosing investor must engage an unlawful detainer action. Such an action, when successfully pursued, provides the investor with a court declaration granting him or her possession of the property. The order may then be presented to local law enforcement officials who will assist in removing the occupants and their possessions from the property.

When an investor is given reason to believe that the occupants are posed to challenge the newly established title and ownership of the property (usually owner-occupants), the investor is encouraged to engage in the process of both a quiet title action and an unlawful detainer action. An unlawful detainer judgment can be acquired within weeks. A quiet title action, on the other hand, or a combination of both actions takes much longer.

Adverse possession (Squatter's rights)

In some states, if an individual or group of individuals makes an otherwise unoccupied property their personal living space, the inhabitants may make claim to the property. States have statutes for what is known as adverse possession or squatter's rights. The investor should seek legal advice as to the application of such laws to a particular parcel of property. He or she is encouraged to act upon the rights granted through the tax sale and tax lien foreclosure processes within the time allocated to do so, particularly as most states impose statutes of limitation with regard to foreclosure and possession of a property. State and local governments have supported individuals in their claims for adverse possession when their occupancy has been established for a period of years.

After Foreclosure

Foreclosure gives the investor title to the foreclosed property as well as all of the responsibility of home ownership. Upon foreclosure, the investor should acquire hazard insurance to cover any losses that may occur on the property. As the newly established property owner, the investor needs to protect his or her investment against natural disasters, fire, and other causes of damage. Insurance also will prove useful for foreclosed properties that have existing occupants. Occupants of the property may decide to cause damage and destruction to the property if they are requested or forced to leave.

The investor must consider all costs that may be required before he or she is able to take possession of the property. Those costs may include any or all of the following:

- Other tax liens held against the property
- Federal liens
- State liens
- Municipal liens
- Quiet title fees
- Fees for issuance of a deed
- Attorney's fees for judicial foreclosures
- Environmental inspection
- Environmental cleanup
- Hazard insurance
- Eviction of existing occupants

Chapter 12

What Next?

By now, you should be seeing the possibilities and be keen to try your first tax lien or tax deed purchase. Until you know what you are doing, it probably is best to concentrate on residential properties and particularly three-bed, two-bath suburban homes, which seem to be in the greatest demand. This recommendation should not prevent you from looking for agricultural, commercial, or industrial properties if you have specialized knowledge or feel particularly drawn to them. However, there are pitfalls in nonresidential property, such as EPA issues for industrial buildings, and you need to take extra care when going outside your familiar area.

This is not to say all residential properties are desirable. Bear in mind that some areas of towns are "no-go" areas, with street violence and vandalism. Make every effort to ensure that you are not buying yourself into trouble, particularly as these areas are ones where the properties are most likely to have been abandoned and taxes not paid.

Use this chapter as the basis of an action list, but modify it as necessary to account for the particular regulations of the jurisdiction you are interested in.

Choose the State

The first decision that you will want to make is which state to look in. If you refer to the tables following, you will get a better idea of which ones may be worthwhile from a financial standpoint. For tax lien states, you may be interested in the rate of return you can achieve if the property is redeemed, and in all cases, you will be interested in the time that must pass before you can foreclose legally and get possession of the property, if that is your primary aim. Given that you do not want to carry out the whole process remotely, the areas you look at should be ones you are prepared to visit, even if not your home or bordering states.

Another factor that may influence your choice is the amount of paperwork involved, for example, if you have to employ an attorney to progress a tax deed and possession, and to what extent the authorities assist you in this. You can get a good idea of the state's attitude to the process from studying the details of the laws on the Internet. States that concentrate on online bidding may appeal to you, although this should never be used as a reason not to physically see the property. Other states that require your presence at the auction may have to be ruled out. The halfway solution of bidding by mail may appeal, and undoubtedly the amount of deposit and terms of payment if you are successful will have to be factored into your selection.

Pick Your County

As mentioned in the introduction, there are more than 3,000 counties in the U.S., and many states have more than 100. If you do not live close to the area, you will find it easiest if you look for a county with friendly and helpful staff when you call. Often, these will be the more rural areas where the staff may be less busy. You can learn a lot from talking with the county employees. Another feature to look for is a county that has put many records and maps online, which will facilitate your search.

If you are lucky, you will be able to use the local knowledge of the county workers to form an initial impression of the areas to concentrate on. You can obtain a list of delinquent properties online, in many cases, or by mail, and it is helpful to discuss the generalities of the county with this in hand. For instance, you will be able to find out which areas are residential, commercial, agricultural, or simply rural and undeveloped.

Research Properties

Now you have a list and can see which properties fit your price range. Going through likely candidates in turn, examine the assessed value of the land and the improvements, which is the assessors' term for any buildings. Whether the property is redeemed, or you end up owning it, properties where the improvements are much more valuable than the land are usually a better choice.

Whether you are looking in a town or in the rural county area, you may find that the planning department also can assist you. They will know if there are any planned municipal improvements to roads, give you the comparative zoning of the local area, and even advise if you are looking in a designated floodplain. By looking in the area on www.realtor.com you will be able to see any local houses for sale and get a better feel for the properties of interest.

An important part of your research is looking into other liens or mortgages on the property. The laws in many municipalities mean that the tax lien or tax deed purchaser can get a "clean title," with any other debts counted as junior liens by the process, but the county recorder or county clerk should be able to advise you of any possible difficulties.

Inspect the Properties

Once you have gleaned all the information you can on the telephone and the Internet, it is time for you to make a visit to the area. This will allow you to find out firsthand whether these are properties you would want to put money into and possibly own and allow you to clear up any errors or omissions that may be in the county records. You may need several days to visit with the county officials and tour the properties, but bear in mind that you frequently will be unable to inspect inside the buildings.

Your first stop may well be the county office, as you want to be sure you locate the correct properties. Frequently, the legal description may be confusing and made up of metes and bounds or lot numbers that have nothing to do with the street address. This is also your chance to work further on developing a good working relationship with the staff. If you have not been able to find information online, you also may wish to visit the county assessor's office to look up the assessed value of the properties.

Your goal in doing this research is to make sure you are not stuck with a property that is not worth your investment. You even could check with the EPA to see if there are any environmental issues or Superfund sites involved.

After looking at the properties, ideally, you will have found some you want to bid on. You then can go back to the county offices to make sure you take the steps necessary to become registered as an eligible bidder in the auction. This information will be specific to the county and state and may involve filling out a W-9 form for the IRS. You can clarify any deposit and payment requirements and make sure that you have all your questions answered before you return home.

The Auction

If required by the county, you may have to return to attend the actual auction if you are not allowed to bid online or by mail. Many people are concerned about attending live auctions, but as long as you pay attention to the auctioneer, you should not have a problem. In many cases, the auction will proceed smartly, and you must make sure you bid on the lot that you want, rather than being too slow and bidding on the one following. To get an idea of what these auctions are like, you will find several videos posted on YouTube™ if you search on "tax lien auction," "tax deed auction," or simply "tax auctions." Before bidding, make sure you are able to comply with any funding requirements if you are successful, as failure to do so could result in legal action against you.

Conclusion

There are many benefits to investing in tax liens and tax deeds, and also some challenges, such as the fact that many municipalities only have one auction a year. Armed with the information in this book, you now are well placed to start taking part in what can be a lucrative investment for your money. You may find that you need some perseverance, particularly at the outset when you are becoming familiar with the municipalities' requirements and way of working. Expect few or none of your bids to win while you get a feel for the market, but prepare yourself for all of them to be successful so you do not risk being overwhelmed. Your success rate will vary wildly depending on the part of the country you are concentrating on, and you can research previous sales to get a better idea of the sales to expect.

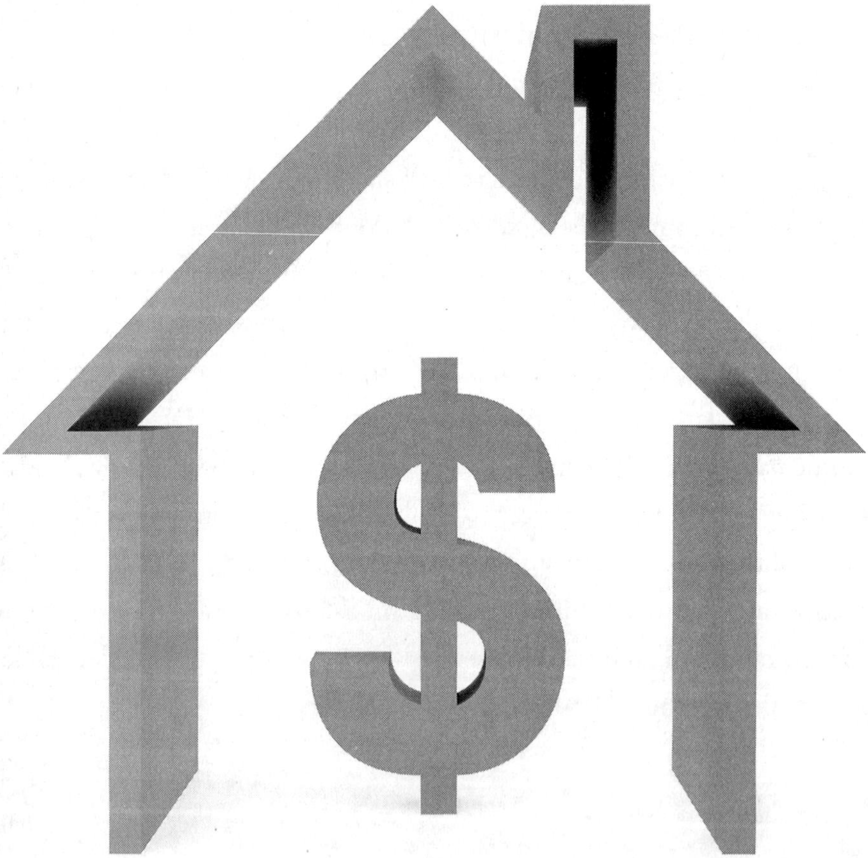

Appendix 1

State Laws

The following list details the laws and anomalies that apply to each of the 50 continental states as well as the District of Columbia (Washington, D.C.), the territory of Guam, the commonwealth of Puerto Rico, and the U.S. Virgin Islands. The websites for the counties are included where known and have been checked in 2012. Not all county websites include online access to tax lien or deed information, but at a minimum, this list will give you a means to contact the revenue department.

The information given is current at the time of going to press but should, of course, be checked when you decide to go forward with purchasing liens or deeds.

	STATE		
	Alabama		
1	Type of sale	Tax lien	Certificate of sale or certificate of purchase
	Sale date	May	Property taxes are due in October and delinquent on January 1. The tax sale listing is published after the month of April.
	Bid method	Premium	The premium amount is paid to the property owner or added to the municipality's general fund. Property owners may request that amounts placed in the general fund be paid to them.

STATE		
Payment method	Cash or certified funds	
Interest rate	12% per annum	
Subsequent taxes	Optional	The tax lien certificate holder must present the tax lien certificate before paying delinquent taxes for subsequent years. The additional amount earns interest at the same rate as the original lien certificate.
Redemption period	3 years	If the tax lien certificate is not redeemed, a tax deed is delivered to the lien holder who must, in turn, return the lien certificate to the judge of probate.
Over the counter	Yes	Over-the-counter sales are handled by the state commissioner of revenue.
Municipalities	67	Autauga – no website Baldwin – **www.co.baldwin.al.us/PageView.asp?PageType=R&edit_id=595** Barbour – no website Bibb – no website Blount – **www.blountrevenue.com** Bullock – no website Butler – no website Calhoun – **www.calhouncounty.org/revenue/collection.html** Chambers – **www.chamberscounty.com** Chilton – **www.chiltoncounty.org** Choctaw – no website Clarke – **www.clarkecountyal.com/revenue_commissioner.htm** Clay – no website Cleburne – no website Coffee – **www.coffeecounty.us/RevenueDepartment.html** Colbert – **www.revenuecommissioner.com** Conecuh – no website Coosa – no website Covington – no website Crenshaw – no website Cullman – **www.co.cullman.al.us** Dale – **http://dalecountyrevenuecommissioner.com/Default.aspx** Dallas – no website Dekalb – **www.revenue-dekalbco-al.us** Elmore – **www.elmoreco.org/Default.asp?ID=2&pg=Home** Escambia – **www.co.escambia.al.us** Etowah – **www.etowahcounty.org** Fayette – no website Franklin – no website

	STATE		
			Geneva – **www.genevacounty.net**
			Greene – no website
			Hale – no website
			Henry – no website
			Houston – **www.houstoncounty.org/dept.php?id=12**
			Jackson – **www.jacksoncountyrevenue.com**
			Jefferson – **http://jeffconline.jccal.org**
			Lamar – no website
			Lauderdale – **http://lauderdalecountyonline.com**
			Lawrence – no website
			Lee – **www.leeco.us**
			Limestone – **www.limestonecounty.net**
			Lowndes – no website
			Macon – no website
			Madison – **http://madisoncountyal.gov**
			Marengo – no website
			Marion – **http://marioncountyalabama.or**g
			Marshall – **www.marshallco.org/index.php**
			Mobile – **www.mobilecopropertytax.com**
			Monroe – no website
			Montgomery – **www.mc-ala.org/Pages/Default.aspx**
			Morgan – **www.co.morgan.al.us**
			Perry – no website
			Pickens – no website
			Pike – no website
			Randolph – no website
			Russell – **www.rcala.com**
			Shelby – **www.shelbyal.com**
			St. Clair – **www.stclairco.com**
			Sumter – no website
			Talladega – **www.talladegacountyal.org**
			Tallapoosa – no website
			Tuscaloosa – **www.tuscco.com**
			Walker – **www.walkercounty.com**
			Washington – no website
			Wilcox no website
			Winston – no website
	Statutes	Code of Alabama	Sections 40-10-15, 20,120,121,187
	Alaska		
2	Type of sale	Tax deed	
	Sale date	Various	
	Bid method	Determined by the municipality	Only municipalities are present at the tax sale. Properties are transferred to the municipality. The municipality may sell the property after the expiration of the one-year redemption period. Properties usually are sold according to local ordinances and usually are sold at fair market value.

	STATE		
	Payment method		
	Interest rate	N/A	
	Redemption period	Up to 1 year	
	Over the counter	No	
	Municipalities	18 municipalities are termed *boroughs* **(B)**, 11 unorganized areas are called census areas **(C)**	Aleutian Islands East(B) – www.aleutianseast.org Aleutian Islands West(C) Anchorage(B) – www.muni.org/pages/default.aspx Bethel(C) Bristol Bay(B) – www.bristolbayboroughak.us Denali (B) – www.denaliborough.govoffice.com Dillingham (C) Fairbanks North Star (B) – www.co.fairbanks.ak.us Haines(B) – www.hainesborough.us Hoonah-Angoon (C) Juneau(B) – www.juneau.lib.ak.us Kenai Peninsula (B) – www.borough.kenai.ak.us Ketchikan Gateway (B) – www.borough.ketchikan.ak.us Kodiak Island (B) – www.kodiakak.us Lake & Peninsula (B) – www.lakeandpen.com Matanuska-Susitna (B) – www.matsugov.us Nome(C) North Slope (B) – www.co.north-slope.ak.us North West Arctic (B) – www.northwestarcticborough.org Petersburg (C) Prince of Wales-Outer Ketchikan (C) Sitka(B) – www.cityofsitka.com Skagway (B) – www.skagway.org Southeast Fairbanks(C) Valdez-Cordova (C) Wade-Hampton(C) Wrangell(B) – www.wrangell.com Yukon-Koyukuk (C) Yakutat(B) – www.yakutatak.govoffice2.com
	Statute	Alaska Statutes	Chapter 48
	Arizona		
3	Type of sale	Tax lien	Tax lien or certificate of purchase
	Sale date	February	The tax sale listing must be compiled by December 31 and published at least two weeks before the tax sale. The listing of delinquent properties must be published in an officially designated county newspaper. Additional notices are to be posted near the door to the county treasurer's office.

Appendix 1: State Laws

STATE		
Bid method	Bid down interest	
Payment method	Cash	Payment is due on the date of the tax sale.
Interest rate	16% per annum	Any fraction of the month is counted as a whole month.
Redemption period	3 years	Property owners may redeem after foreclosure has been initiated and before the foreclosure judgment is made. The redemption amount includes additional costs for "reasonable" attorney's fees.
Over the counter	Yes	Tax lien certificates not purchased at the tax sale are offered for sale every day until all tax liens are sold or the treasurer is convinced that no more liens can be sold. The remaining tax lien certificates are assigned to the state and reassigned to the buyer willing to pay the delinquent tax, interest, penalties, and charges.
Subsequent taxes	Optional	The tax lien certificate holder must present the tax lien certificate before paying delinquent taxes for subsequent years. The additional amount earns interest at the same rate as the original lien certificate.
Foreclosure	Within 10 years	A judicial foreclosure must be initiated within ten years.
Municipalities	15	Apache – www.co.apache.az.us/Departments/Treasurer/Treasurer.htm Cochise – http://cochise.az.gov/cochise_treasurer.aspx?id=52 Coconino – www.coconino.az.gov/treasurer.aspx?id=548 Gila – www.gilacountyaz.gov/treasurer/default.html Graham – www.graham.az.gov/Graham_CMS/Treasurer.aspx?id=800 Greenlee – www.co.greenlee.az.us/treasurer La Paz – www.co.la-paz.az.us/CoLaPazAzUs/Main_Pages/Dept_Assessor/assessor.htm Maricopa – http://treasurer.maricopa.gov/research.htm Mohave – www.co.mohave.az.us/ContentPage.aspx?id=132&cid=223 Navajo – www.navajocountyaz.gov/treasurer/inqnotice.aspx Pima – www.to.pima.gov/tax-information/tax-lien-sale-information Pinal – www.pinaltaxsale.com/?redirected=1 Santa Cruz – www.co.santa-cruz.az.us/treasurer/index.html Yavapai – www.yavapaitaxsale.com/?redirected=1 Yuma – www.yumacountyaz.gov/index.aspx?page=86
Statute	Arizona Revised Statutes	Sections 42-312, 390, 393, 410, 451, 462

	STATE		
	Arkansas		
4	Type of sale	Tax deed	
	Sale date	May 1	The tax sale, called a *tax-delinquent sale*, is a public oral-bid foreclosure auction of real estate.
	Bid method	Premium bid	The opening bid amount includes the tax lien amount plus the assessed value of the property. The assessed value is calculated as 20 percent of the market value.
	Payment method		
	Interest rate	N/A	
	Redemption period	30 days from date of auction	
	Over the counter	No	
	Municipalities	75	Arkansas – no website Ashley – no website Baxter – **www.baxtercounty.org** Benton – **www.co.benton.ar.us** Boone – no website Bradley – no website Calhoun – no website Carroll – no website Chicot – no website Clark – **www.clarkcountyarkansas.com/index.html** Clay – no website Cleburne – no website Cleveland – no website Columbia – no website Conway – no website Craighead – **www.craigheadcounty.org** Crawford – **www.crawford-county.org/default.aspx** Crittenden – **www.crittendencountywebsite.com** Cross – no website Dallas – no website Desha – no website Drew – no website Faulkner – no website Franklin – no website Fulton – no website Garland – **www.garlandcounty.org** Grant – no website Greene – no website Hempstead – no website Hot Spring – no website Howard – no website0

STATE			
			Independence – no website
			Izard – no website
			Jackson – **www.jacksoncountyar.org**
			Jefferson – no website
			Johnson – no website
			Lafayette – no website
			Lawrence – no website
			Lee – no website
			Lincoln – no website
			Little River – no website
			Logan – no website
			Lonoke – no website
			Madison – no website
			Marion – no website
			Miller – no website
			Mississippi – **www.mcagov.com**
			Monroe – no website
			Montgomery – no website
			Nevada – no website
			Newton – no website
			Ouachita – no website
			Perry – no website
			Phillips – no website
			Pike – no website
			Poinsett – **www.poinsettcounty.us**
			Polk – no website
			Pope – no website
			Prairie – no website
			Pulaski – **www.co.pulaski.ar.us**
			Randolph – no website
			Saline – **www.salinecounty.org**
			Scott – no website
			Searcy – no website
			Sebastian – **www.sebastiancountyonline.com**
			Sevier – **www.seviercountyar.com**
			Sharp – **www.sharpcounty.org**
			St. Francis – no website
			Stone – no website
			Union – no website
			Van Buren – no website
			Washington – **www.co.washington.ar.us**
			White – **www.whitecountyar.org**
			Woodruff – no website
			Yell – no website
	Statute	Arkansas Code	Chapter 38

STATE		
California		
5	Type of sale	Tax deed	Tax certificate
	Sale date	Varies by municipality	The tax sale, called a *tax-defaulted land sale*, is a public oral-bid foreclosure of real estate. Though state statutes provide for the sale of tax lien certificates, local municipalities have never made use of the statutes. Property owners are allowed to incur five years of delinquent property taxes before the local government intervenes and offers the property at a foreclosure sale.
	Bid method	Premium bid	Many California counties use **www.bid4assets.com** to conduct their auctions.
	Payment method		The tax sale is free of all liens and encumbrances except that special assessments, easements, and IRS liens must be paid.
	Interest rate	N/A	Tax deed
		18%	When tax lien certificates are offered for sale (none of the counties currently offer tax liens)
	Redemption period	N/A	
		2 years	When tax lien certificates are offered for sale
	Over the counter	No	
	Municipalities	58	Alameda – **www.acgov.org/treasurer/index.htm** Alpine – **www.alpinecountyca.gov/assessor** Amador – **www.co.amador.ca.us/index.aspx?page=132** Butte – **www.buttecounty.net/Treasurer%20-%20Tax%20Collector.aspx** Calaveras – **www.co.calaveras.ca.us/cc/Departments/TaxCollector.aspx** Colusa – **www.countyofcolusa.com/index.aspx?NID=184** Contra Costa – **www.contracosta.ca.gov/index.aspx?nid=199** Del Norte – **www.dnco.org/index.php?option=com_content&view=category&layout=blog&id=144&Itemid=150** El Dorado – **www.edcgov.us/Government/TaxCollector/Public_Auction_Tax_Sale.aspx** Fresno – **www.co.fresno.ca.us/DepartmentPage.aspx?id=15105** Glenn – **www.countyofglenn.net/govt/departments/tax_collector/contact.aspx** Humboldt – **http://co.humboldt.ca.us/taxcollt/auction-info.html** Imperial – **www.co.imperial.ca.us/TaxCollectorTreasurer/Treasurer/PdfDoc/PropertyTaxAuction.pdf** Inyo – **www.inyocounty.us/taxcollector/tax_auction.htm** Kern – **www.kcttc.co.kern.ca.us** Kings – **www.countyofkings.com/finance/index.html**

STATE	
	Lake – **www.co.lake.ca.us/Government/Directory/tax.htm**
	Lassen – **www.co.lassen.ca.us/govt/dept/treasurer/default.asp**
	Los Angeles – **http://ttc.lacounty.gov**
	Madera – **www.madera-county.com/treasurer/default_taxsale.html**
	Marin – **www.co.marin.ca.us/depts/TC/main/taxes/pages/auctioninfo.cfm**
	Mariposa – **www.mariposacounty.org/index.aspx?NID=317**
	Mendocino – **www.co.mendocino.ca.us/tax/auction.htm**
	Merced – **www.mercedtaxcollector.org/tax_defaulted_tax_sale.html**
	Modoc – **http://modoc.taxcess.com/screens/tax_sales.php**
	Mono – **www.monocounty.ca.gov/departments/treasurer/treasurer.html**
	Monterey – **www.co.monterey.ca.us/taxcollector/Auction_Internet.html**
	Napa – **www.countyofnapa.org/Pages/DepartmentContent.aspx?id=4294970826&linkidentifier=id&itemid=4294970826**
	Nevada – **www.mynevadacounty.com/ttc/index.cfm?ccs=1730**
	Orange – **http://egov.ocgov.com/ocgov/Residents/Taxes%20&%20Assessments**
	Placer – **www.placer.ca.gov/Departments/Tax/LandSale.aspx**
	Plumas – **www.countyofplumas.com/index.aspx?NID=95**
	Riverside – **www.countytreasurer.org/tax_sale_information2.aspx**
	Sacramento – **www.finance.saccounty.net/tax/TaxSale.asp**
	San Benito – **www.cosb.us/county-departments/ttcpa**
	San Bernardino – **www.mytaxcollector.com**
	San Diego – **www.sdtreastax.com/property-tax-sales.html**
	San Francisco – **www.sftreasurer.org/index.aspx?page=129**
	San Joaquin – **www.sjgov.org/Treasurer/dynamic.aspx?id=9511**
	San Luis Obispo – **www.slocounty.ca.gov/tax/taxsaleinfo.htm**
	San Mateo – **www.sanmateocountytaxcollector.org/index.html**
	Santa Barbara – **www.countyofsb.org/ttcpapg/taxsale.asp**

	STATE		
			Santa Clara – www.sccgov.org/portal/site/tax/agencyarticle?path=%252Fv7%252FTax%2520Collector%2520%2528DEP%2529&contentId=34245121d22b5210VgnVCM10000048dc4a92____
Santa Cruz – www.co.santa-cruz.ca.us/ttc/Frequently%20asked%20questions.htm
Shasta – www.co.shasta.ca.us/index/tc_index/tax_auction.aspx
Sierra – www.sierracounty.ws/index.php?module=pagemaster&PAGE_user_op=view_page&PAGE_id=24&MMN_position=47:46
Siskiyou – www.co.siskiyou.ca.us/tax/auction.aspx
Solano – www.co.solano.ca.us/depts/ttcc/tax_collector/tax_sale/sales_information.asp
Sonoma – www.sonoma-county.org/tax/property_taxes.htm
Stanislaus – www.stancounty.com/tr-tax/auction/index.htm
Sutter – www.suttercounty.org/doc/government/depts/ttc/ttchome
Tehama – www.co.tehama.ca.us/index.php?option=com_content&task=view&id=64&Itemid=114
Trinity – www.trinitycounty.org/Departments/taxtreas/auction.htm
Tulare – www.co.tulare.ca.us/government/treasurertax/tax_auction/default.asp
Tuolumne – http://portal.co.tuolumne.ca.us/psp/ps/TUP_TREASURER/ENTP/c/TU_DEPT_MENU.TUOCM_HTML_COMP.GBL?action=U&CONTENT_PNM=EMPLOYEE&CATGID=2417&FolderPath=PORTAL_ROOT_OBJECT.ADMN_TUOCM_MENUREF_2417&IsFolder=false&IgnoreParamTempl=FolderPath%2cIsFolder
Ventura – http://portal.countyofventura.org/portal/page/portal/tax_collector/public_auction
Yolo – www.yolocounty.org/Index.aspx?page=852
Yuba – www.co.yuba.ca.us/Departments/Treasurer/auction
	Statute	California Revenue and Taxation Code	Chapter 7, Sections: 3691, 3698, 3712
	Colorado		
6	Type of sale	Tax lien	Tax lien, tax certificate, tax sale certificate, or certificate of purchase

Appendix 1: State Laws

STATE		
Sale date	November, first Thursday	The tax sale must be held on or before the second Monday in December. Notice of the sale must be published beginning four weeks before the sale. The tax sale must be published in a local newspaper or, in the absence of a local newspaper, at the treasurer's office.
Bid method	Premium bid	The premium amount is not returned, and no interest is applied to the premium amount upon redemption.
Payment method	Cash	The purchaser receives a certificate of purchase that indicates the Interest rate.
Interest rate	9% plus FDR	FDR is the federal discount rate, which is set in September and rounded to the nearest full percent.
Redemption period	3 years	A fee charged by the taxing authority must be paid before a tax deed is requested. Any outstanding property taxes must be paid by the tax lien certificate holder before a tax deed is acquired.
Over the counter	Yes, with exceptions	Over-the-counter sales are optional, and the jurisdiction of Denver does not offer liens over the counter.
Subsequent taxes	Optional	The tax lien certificate holder must present the tax lien certificate before paying delinquent taxes for subsequent years. The additional amount earns interest at the same rate as the original tax lien certificate.
Foreclosure	Within 5 years	Property owners may dispute the foreclosure up to five years after its issuance. Under certain circumstances, the period can be extended to nine years if a quiet title judgment has not been made.
Municipalities	63	Adams – **http://co-adamscounty.civicplus.com/index.aspx?NID=829** Alamosa – **www.alamosacounty.org/index.php?option=com_content&view=article&id=60&Itemid=90** Arapahoe – **www.arapahoetaxsale.com/?redirected=1** Archuleta – **www.archuletataxsale.com./?redirected=1** Baca – **www.springfieldcolorado.com/bacacountygov.html** Bent – no website Boulder – **www.bouldercounty.org/government/dept/pages/treasurer.aspx** Broomfield – **www.broomfield.org/treasurer/taxsale.shtml** Chaffee – **http://chaffee.visualgov.com** Cheyenne – **www.co.cheyenne.co.us/countydepartments/treasurer.htm** Clear Creek – **www.co.clear-creek.co.us/index.aspx?nid=193** Conejos – **www.conejoscounty.org/Webpages/treasurer.html**

STATE	
	Costilla – www.colorado.gov/cs/Satellite/CNTY-Costilla/CBON/1251595035177
Crowley – www.crowleycounty.net/treasurer.htm
Custer – www.custercountygov.com/index.php?pg=treasurer
Delta – www.deltacounty.com/index.aspx?nid=141
Denver – www.denvertaxsale.com/view_bids.cfm
Dolores – www.dolorescounty.org/gov_treasurer.shtml
Douglas – www.douglas.co.us/treasurer/Tax_Lien_Sale_Information.html
Eagle – www.eaglecounty.us/Treasurer/Tax_Lien_Sale/Overview
El Paso – http://trs.elpasoco.com/Pages/TaxLienSale.aspx
Elbert – www.elbertcounty-co.gov/dept_treasurer.php
Fremont – www.fremontco.com/treasurer/index.shtml
Garfield – www.garfield-county.com/treasurer/tax-lien-sale.aspx
Gilpin – www.co.gilpin.co.us/Treasurer/TaxLienSale.htm
Grand – http://co.grand.co.us/treasurer/treasurer.html
Gunnison – www.gunnisoncounty.org/treasurer_tax_lien_sales.html
Hinsdale – www.hinsdalecountycolorado.us
Huerfano – www.huerfano.us/Treasurer_s_Office.html
Jackson – no website
Jefferson – http://jeffco.us/treasurer/treasurer_T68_R9.htm
Kiowa – www.kiowacountycolo.com/treasurer.htm
Kit Carson – http://www.kitcarsoncounty.org/Treasurer.html
La Plata – http://co.laplata.co.us.staging.frii.com/departments_officials/treasurer
Lake – http://lake.visualgov.com/TaxLienInfo.aspx
Larimer – www.co.larimer.co.us/treasurer/taxsale.htm
Las Animas – no website
Lincoln – www.lincolncountyco.us/treasurer/treasurer.html
Logan – www.logancountyco.gov/?page_id=461
Mesa – www.mesataxsale.com/?redirected=1
Mineral – http://mineralcountycolorado.com/treasurer.html
Moffat – http://moffat.visualgov.com/TaxLienInfo.aspx
Montezuma – www.co.montezuma.co.us/newsite/treasurerhome.html
Montrose – www.co.montrose.co.us/index.aspx?NID=217
Morgan – www.co.morgan.co.us

Appendix 1: State Laws

	STATE		
			Otero – www.oterogov.com/index.php?option=com_content&view=section&layout=blog&id=16&Itemid=137
Ouray – http://ouraycountyco.gov/treasurer.html
Park – www.parkco.us/DocumentView.aspx?DID=198
Phillips – no website
Pitkin – http://www.aspenpitkin.com/Departments/Treasurer/Tax-Information/Tax-Lien-
Prowers – www.prowerscounty.net
Pueblo – http://county.pueblo.org/government/county/treasurer
Rio Blanco – www.co.rio-blanco.co.us/treasurer/tax_sale.php
Rio Grande – www.riograndecounty.org/index.php?option=com_content&view=article&id=36&Itemid=70
Routt – www.co.routt.co.us/sections.php?op=viewarticle&artid=80655
Saguache – www.saguachecounty.net/index.php?option=com_content&view=category&layout=blog&id=42&Itemid=119
San Juan – www.sanjuancountycolorado.us/treasurer.html
San Miguel – www.sanmiguelcounty.org/departments/treasurer/index.html
Sedgwick – www.sedgwickcountygov.net/index.php?option=com_content&view=category&layout=blog&id=21&Itemid=38
Summit – www.co.summit.co.us/Treasurer/TaxLienSale/tax_lien_info.htm
Teller – www.co.teller.co.us/pt/TaxSaleProc.aspx
Washington – http://co.washington.co.us/txpmntlien.htm
Weld – www.co.weld.co.us/Departments/Treasurer/TaxLienInformation/index.html
Yuma – www.yumacounty.net/treasurer.html#top
	Statute	Colorado Revised Statutes	Sections 39-123-103, 39-11-120,122
	Connecticut		
7	Type of sale	Hybrid tax deed	Collector's deed
	Sale date	June	Real property is sold at public auction to the highest bidder. A tax deed is executed and delivered to the purchaser within two weeks of the tax sale. The deed is not recorded until a one-year redemption period has expired. The town of New Haven only sells deeds in bulk to qualified buyers.

	STATE		
	Bid method	Premium bid	The premium amount receives 18% interest upon redemption.
	Payment method		
	Interest rate	18% annually	
	Redemption period	6 months	
	Over the counter	No	
	Municipalities	8	Fairfield, Hartford, Litchfield, Middlesex, New Haven, New London, Tolland, Windham
	Statute	General Statutes of Connecticut	Section 12-157
	Delaware		
8	Type of sale	Hybrid tax deed	Deed
	Sale date	Varies by municipality	The tax sale is a public oral-bid foreclosure sale of real estate.
	Bid method	Premium bid	
	Payment method		
	Interest rate	15% penalty	
	Redemption period	60 days	
	Over the counter	No	
	Municipalities	3	Kent – www.co.kent.de.us/Departments/RowOffices/Sheriff/ssprocedures.htm New Castle – www2.nccde.org/home/default.aspx Sussex – www.sussexcountyde.gov/e-service/propertytaxes
	Statute	9 Del. Code	Sections 8721, 8728, 8749, 87650, 8758
	Florida		
9	Type of sale	Tax lien	The sale of tax lien certificates is an offer to invest. If a tax lien certificate is not redeemed during the redemption period, no foreclosure will take place. A tax deed for the associated property is offered for sale at another auction.
		Tax deed	The tax deed sale is a public oral-bid foreclosure of real estate.

Appendix 1: State Laws **191**

STATE		
Sale date	Tax lien: on or before June 1	The tax lien certificate sale must be published in a local newspaper beginning three weeks before the sale.
	Tax deed	The tax deed sale must be held at least 30 days following the first publication of the sale. Publication is required for four consecutive weeks.
Bid method	Bid down interest	Bids must be placed in increments of 1/4 of 1%.
Payment method	Cash, certified check, bank draft, money order	A deposit of at least 10% is required before bidding, and the balance of all purchases must be received within 48 hours of the sale or within 48 hours of notification from the tax collector that the tax lien has been prepared. Failure to pay within 48 hours results in a forfeiture of the deposit.
Interest rate	Tax lien: 18% per annum with a 5% minimum	If the sale of a tax lien certificate is voided due to error, the cost of the tax lien certificate is refunded to the purchaser by the municipality, with 8% interest.
	Tax deed: 18% per annum	If the tax certificate holder does not win the subsequent tax deed bid, he or she is, instead, refunded the value of the tax lien certificate, application fees, and interest at 18% per annum from the date of the application for a tax deed. The Interest rate is fixed during this period, irrespective of the bid-down Interest rate.
Redemption period	2 years	Tax lien redemption periods are calculated from April 1 of the year in which the lien certificate was purchased. The cost of the tax lien certificate and a minimum 5% penalty are paid upon redemption.
Over the counter	Yes, for liens	Tax lien certificates are offered for sale with an 18% redemption rate; the interest rate is not bid down.
	No, for deeds	
Subsequent taxes	Optional	
Foreclosure	Within 7 years	Tax lien certificates expire after seven years. Application for a tax deed must occur within the seven-year expiration period. Making application for a tax deed causes the particular municipality to initiate a sale of the tax deed. The winning bidder must offer a bid in excess of the amount that the tax lien certificate holder invested in the property. If the property is a homestead property, the cost of the tax deed will include half of the appraised value of the property. A four-year statute of limitations exists for anyone challenging the tax deed after foreclosure and also for the investor to engage an adverse possession action.

STATE		
Municipalities	67	Alachua – www.alachuaclerk.org/civil/taxsale.cfm
Baker – http://bakercountyfl.org/taxcollector/TAXSALEI.htm
Bay – http://tc.co.bay.fl.us
Bradford – http://bradfordtaxcollector.com
Brevard – www.brevardtaxcollector.com/taxcol2.htm
Broward – www.bidbroward.com
Calhoun – www.calhouncountytaxcollector.com/TaxCertificates.aspx
Charlotte – www.cctaxcol.com/#
Citrus – www.bidcitrus.com
Clay – www.claycountytax.com/Property%20Tax/TaxCertificates.html
Collier – www.colliertax.com
Columbia – www.columbiataxcollector.com/PropertyTaxes/TaxDeedTaxCertificateInfo/tabid/410/Default.aspx
Desoto – www.desotocountytaxcollector.com/TaxCertificates.aspx
Dixie – www.dixiecountytaxcollector.com
Duval – www.duvaltaxsale.com
Escambia – www.escambiataxsale.com
Flagler – www.flaglertaxsale.com
Franklin – http://franklincountytaxcollector.com/TaxCertificates.aspx
Gadsden – www.gadsdentaxsale.com
Gilchrist – www.gilchristtaxsale.com
Glades – www.mygladescountytaxcollector.com/TaxCertificates.aspx
Gulf – www.gulfcountytaxcollector.com/TaxCertificates.aspx
Hamilton – www.hamiltoncountytaxcollector.com/TaxCertificates.aspx
Hardee – www.hardeecountytaxcollector.com/TaxCertificates.aspx
Hendry – http://fl-hendry-taxcollector.manatron.com/RealEstateTaxes/DelinquentTaxes/tabid/798/Default.aspx
Hernando – www.hernandotaxsale.com
Highlands – www.hctaxcollector.com/taxes/tax-certificate-sale.html
Hillsborough – www.hillstax.org/tax/proptaxcert.asp
Holmes – www.holmescountytaxcollector.com/TaxCertificates.aspx
Indian River – www.bidindianriver.com
Jackson – www.jacksoncountytaxcollector.com/TaxCertificates.aspx

STATE	
	Jefferson – **www.jeffersoncountytaxcollector.com/Tax-Certificates.aspx** Lafayette – **www.lafayettetc.com** Lake – **www.bidlaketax.com** Lee – **www.leetc.com** Leon – **www.leontaxcollector.net/TaxSale.html** Levy – **www.levytaxcollector.com** Liberty – **www.libertycountytaxcollector.com/TaxCertificates.aspx** Madison – **www.madisoncountytaxcollector.com/Tax-Certificates.aspx** Manatee – **www.taxcollector.com/index_news_detail.asp?id=420** Marion – **www.mariontax.com** Martin – **http://taxcol.martin.fl.us/ws/index.aspx** Miami-Dade – **www.bidmiamidade.com** Monroe – **www.bidmonroe.com** Nassau – **www.nassauclerk.com/officialrecords/official-records.taxdeeds.cfm** Okaloosa – **www.bidokaloosa.com** Okeechobee – **www.okeechobeecountytaxcollector.com/TaxCertificates.aspx** Orange – **www.orangetaxsale.com** Osceola – **www.bidosceola.com** Palm Beach – **www.taxcollectorpbc.com/i&p_taxcert.shtml** Pasco – **www.pascotaxes.com** Pinellas – **www.bidpinellas.com** Polk – **www.polktaxsale.com/faq.cfm?redirected=1** Putnam – **www.putnam-fl.com/txc/index.php?option=com_content&view=article&id=107&Itemid=82** Santa Rosa – **www.srctc.com** Sarasota – **www.sarasotataxcollector.com/PROPERTY-TAX_PAGES/PT_TaxSale_offseason.htm** Seminole – **www.seminoletaxsale.com** St. Johns – **www.sjctax.us/TaxSales.aspx** St. Lucie – **www.bidstlucie.com** Sumter – **www.sumtertaxsale.com** Suwannee – **www.suwanneetaxsale.com** Taylor – **www.taylortaxsale.com** Union – **www.unioncountytaxcollector.com** Volusia – **www.bidvolusia.com** Wakulla – **www.wakullacountytaxcollector.com/TaxCertificates.aspx** Walton – **www.waltontaxcollector.com/subpage.asp?pageID=107** Washington – **www.washcofl.com/tc**

	STATE		
	Statute	Florida Statutes Annotated	Section 197
	Georgia		
10	Type of sale	Hybrid tax deed	Sheriff's deed or deed
	Sale date	First Tuesday of selected month	The tax sale is a public oral-bid foreclosure sale of real estate. Tax sales are advertised for four consecutive weeks before the tax sale.
	Bid method	Premium bid	
	Payment method	Cash, certified check, cashier's check, money order	Payment is required by the end of the tax sale day.
	Interest rate	10%–20% penalty	The redemption amount is equal to the amount that was paid by the high bidder plus a penalty of 10% per annum of the bid amount. An investor is required to serve notice of the intent to foreclose the right of redemption within the six months before the end of the redemption period. Notice is issued to the property owner and other parties with interest in the property, as shown in public records. If the redemption takes place after the notice to foreclose has been issued, an additional 10% penalty is added to the redemption amount.
	Redemption period	1 year	If a tax lien certificate is redeemed, the investor must issue the property owner a quitclaim deed to the property. If a creditor or other person with interest in the property redeems the property, that party is given first lien to the property for the redemption amount expended.
	Subsequent taxes	Optional	Subsequent tax bills are sent to the property owner of record as well as the tax deed purchaser. The first tax deed purchaser is the superior lien holder. Subsequent tax deed purchasers become lien holders and are listed as owners along with the prior tax deed holders.
	Foreclosure	Within 7 years	Tax deeds purchased before July 1, 1989, ripen to a fee simple title in seven years. No notice of intent to foreclose the right of redemption needs to be sent to the property owner or persons with interest in the property, as found in public records.
		Within 4 years	Tax deeds purchased after July 1, 1989, ripen to a fee simple title in four years. No notice of intent to foreclose the right of redemption needs to be sent to the property owner or persons with interest in the property, as found in public records. An administrative and nonjudicial process is followed to foreclose the right to redemption. The tax deed is recorded upon following the established process; however, the deed cannot be executed for four years from the date of recording.

STATE		
Over the counter	No	
Municipalities	159	Appling – www.baxley.org
Athens-Clarke – http://athensclarkecounty.com/index.aspx?NID=1719
Atkinson – www.atkinson-ga.org/index.html
Augusta – www.augustaga.gov/index.aspx?NID=843
Bacon – no website
Baker – no website
Baldwin – www.baldwincountygatax.com/default.aspx
Banks – www.co.banks.ga.us
Barrow – www.barrowga.org/taxcommissioner/?id=28
Bartow – www.bartowga.org
Ben Hill – www.benhillcounty.com
Berrien – no website
Bibb – www.co.bibb.ga.us
Bleckley – www.bleckley.org
Brantley – www.brantleycountyga.blogspot.com
Brooks – no website
Bryan – www.bryancountyga.org
Bulloch – http://bullochcounty.net
Burke – www.burkecounty-ga.gov/burke-county/department-profile.php?Department_ID=57
Butts – no website
Calhoun – no website
Camden – www.co.camden.ga.us
Candler – www.metter-candler.com
Carroll – www.carrollcountyga.com
Catoosa – www.catoosa.com
Charlton – no website
Chatham – www.chathamcounty.org
Chattahoochee – no website
Chattooga – www.chattoogacountyga.com
Cherokee – www.cherokeega.com
Clay – www.claycountyga.org
Clayton – www.claytoncountyga.gov
Clinch – no website
Cobb – http://portal.cobbcountyga.gov/index.php
Coffee – no website
Colquitt – no website
Columbia – www.columbiacountyga.gov
Columbus-Muscogee – www.columbusga.org
Cook – www.cookcountyga.us/index2.html
Coweta – www.coweta.ga.us
Crawford – no website
Crisp – no website
Dade – no website
Dawson – www.dawsoncounty.org

	STATE		
			DeKalb – www.co.dekalb.ga.us
			Decatur – no website
			Dodge – www.eastman-georgia.com
			Dooly – no website
			Dougherty – www.dougherty.ga.us
			Douglas – www.celebratedouglascounty.com
			Early – no website
			Echols – no website
			Effingham – www.effinghamcounty.org
			Elbert – no website
			Emanuel – no website
			Evans – no website
			Fannin – no website
			Fayette – no website
			Floyd – www.romefloyd.com
			Forsyth – www.forsythco.com
			Franklin – no website
			Fulton – www.co.fulton.ga.us
			Gilmer – www.gilmercounty-ga.gov
			Glascock – no website
			Glynn – www.glynncounty.org
			Gordon – www.gordoncounty.org
			Grady – no website
			Greene – www.greenecountyga.gov
			Gwinnett – www.gwinnettcounty.com
			Habersham – www.habershamga.com
			Hall – www.hallcounty.org
			Hancock – no website
			Haralson – no website
			Harris – no website
			Hart – www.hartcountyga.org
			Heard – no website
			Henry – www.co.henry.ga.us
			Houston – www.houstoncountyga.com
			Irwin – no website
			Jackson – www.jacksoncountygov.com
			Jasper – no website
			Jeff Davis – no website
			Jefferson – www.jeffersoncounty.org
			Jenkins – www.jenkinscountyga.com
			Johnson – no website
			Jones – www.jonescounty.org
			Lamar – no website
			Lanier – no website
			Laurens – www.laurenscoga.org
			Lee – www.lee.ga.us
			Liberty – www.libertycountyga.com
			Lincoln – no website

STATE	
	Long – no website
Lowndes – www.lowndescounty.com
Lumpkin – www.lumpkincounty.gov
Macon – no website
Madison – www.madisoncountyga.us
Marion – no website
McDuffie – no website
McIntosh – no website
Meriwether – no website
Miller – no website
Mitchell – no website
Monroe – no website
Montgomery – no website
Morgan – www.morganga.org
Murray – no website
Newton – www.co.newton.ga.us
Oconee – www.oconeecounty.com
Oglethorpe – www.onlineoglethorpe.com
Paulding – www.paulding.gov
Peach – www.peachcounty.net
Pickens – http://pickenscountyga.gov/government
Pierce – no website
Pike – http://pikecounty.ga.gov
Polk – no website
Pulaski – www.pulaskico.com
Putnam – www.putnamcountyga.us
Quitman – no website
Rabun – no website
Randolph – no website
Richmond – www.augustaga.gov
Rockdale – www.rockdalecounty.org
Schley – no website
Screven – no website
Seminole – no website
Spalding – www.spaldingcounty.com
Stephens – no website
Stewart – no website
Sumter – no website
Talbot – no website
Taliaferro – no website
Tattnall – www.tattnall.com
Taylor – no website
Telfair – no website
Terrell – no website
Thomas – www.thomascountyboc.org
Tift – www.tiftcounty.org
Toombs – no website
Towns – no website

	STATE		
			Treutlen – no website Troup – www.troupcountyga.org Turner – no website Twiggs – www.twiggscounty.us Union – www.unioncountyga.gov Upson – no website Walker – no website Walton – www.waltoncountyga.gov Ware – no website Warren – no website Washington – www.washingtoncounty-ga.com Wayne – www.co.wayne.ga.us/home Webster – no website Wheeler – no website White – www.whitecounty.net Whitfield – www.whitfieldcountyga.com Wilcox – no website Wilkes – no website Wilkinson – no website Worth – no website
	Statute	Official Code of Georgia Annotated	Annotated Sections 48-240; 48-319, 20; 48-4-42,45
	Hawaii		
11	Type of sale	Hybrid tax deed	Conveyance deed or tax deed
	Sale date	June and November or December	The tax sale is a public oral-bid foreclosure sale of real estate. Tax sales are held twice a year. The county of Hawaii has both an east and west office. The east office is responsible for handling the more remote locations of the island. The west office handles the more populated areas.
	Bid method	Premium bid	
	Payment method		
	Interest rate	12% per annum	
	Redemption period	1 year	The redemption period is one year, provided the tax deed is recorded within 60 days of the tax sale. The redemption amount includes all costs incurred by the deed purchaser to acquire the deed. If the deed is not recorded within the 60-day time frame, the redemption period may be extended to one year beyond the date on which the tax deed is recorded. Interest is not applied to the redemption amount during the period that the redemption is extended.
	Over the counter	No	

	STATE		
	Municipalities	4	Hawaii – **www.hawaiipropertytax.com/Forms/Html-Frame.aspx?mode=Content/Tax_Sales_FAQ.htm** Honolulu – **www.realpropertyhonolulu.com** Kauai – **www.kauai.gov/Government/Departments/Finance/RealProperty/tabid/178/Default.aspx** Maui – **www.co.maui.hi.us/index.aspx?NID=576**
	Statute	Hawaii Revised Statutes	Section 246-60
	Idaho		
12	Type of sale	Pure tax deed	Real property with delinquent taxes is foreclosed and acquired by the municipality in which the property is located. The municipality then is authorized to offer for sale any property that is not necessary for use by the municipality.
	Sale date	May	
	Bid method	Premium bid	The particular municipality determines opening bid amounts. Some municipalities include the lien amount plus any pending issue fees, certifications, special assessments, recording fees, and cost of publication of the sale notice. Other municipalities also may include the current market value, as determined by the tax assessor.
	Payment method		
	Interest rate	N/A	
	Redemption period	N/A	
	Over the counter	No	
	Municipalities	44	Ada – **www.adaweb.net/Treasurer/PropertyTaxInformation/TaxDeedSales.aspx** Adams – **www.co.adams.id.us/treasurer.html** Bannock – **www.co.bannock.id.us/treasurer** Bear Lake – **www.bearlakecounty.info** Benewah – no website Bingham – **www.co.bingham.id.us/treasurer/treasurer_tax_deed.html** Blaine – **www.co.blaine.id.us** Boise – **www.boisecounty.us/Treasurer.aspx** Bonner – **http://co.bonner.id.us/treasurer/index.html** Bonneville – **www.co.bonneville.id.us/index.php/treasurer/treasurer-faq** Boundary – **http://boundarycountyid.org/treasurer** Butte – **www.buttecounty.net** Camas – no website Canyon – **www.canyonco.org/Treasurer/Tax_Deed_Information**

STATE		
		Caribou – www.co.caribou.id.us/departments/342/TreasurerTaxCollector.aspx
		Cassia – www.cassiacounty.org/treasurer
		Clark – www.clark-co.id.gov
		Clearwater – www.clearwatercounty.org/departments/treasurer
		Custer – www.co.custer.id.us/treasurer
		Elmore – www.elmorecounty.org/offices/treasurer/tax-sales.htm
		Franklin – www.franklincountyidaho.org/County1/Treasurer.html
		Fremont – www.co.fremont.id.us/departments/treasurer
		Gem – www.co.gem.id.us/treasurer
		Gooding – www.goodingcounty.org/Treasurer.htm
		Idaho – www.idahocounty.org/treasurer.html
		Jefferson – no website
		Jerome – www.jeromecountyid.us/index.asp?Type=B_BASIC&SEC={22F1C5EF-8DEE-4D04-B380-CCF09059AF53}
		Kootenai – www.kcgov.us/departments/treasurer/propertytaxsale.asp
		Latah – www.latah.id.us/treasurer
		Lemhi – www.lemhicountyidaho.org
		Lewis – http://lewiscountyid.us/Treasurer/Treasurer.htm
		Lincoln – http://lincolncountyid.us/page7.php
		Madison – www.co.madison.id.us/index.php/depts/treasurer
		Minidoka – www.minidoka.id.us/treasurer/default.htm
		Nez Perce – www.co.nezperce.id.us/ElectedOfficials/Treasurer.aspx
		Oneida – www.co.oneida.id.us
		Owyhee – http://owyheecounty.net/index1.php?taxdeed
		Payette – www.payettecounty.org/treasurer/Treasurer.htm
		Power – www.co.power.id.us/index.php?option=com_content&view=article&id=149&catid=114&Itemid=2
		Shoshone – www.shoshonecounty.org/index.php?option=com_content&view=article&id=30&Itemid=18
		Teton – www.tetoncountyidaho.gov/department.php?deptID=25&menuID=1
		Twin Falls – www.twinfallscounty.org
		Valley – www.co.valley.id.us/treasurer
		Washington – www.co.washington.id.us/treasurer
	Statute	Idaho Statute	Sections 31-808; 63-1003-1011
	Illinois		
13	Type of sale	Tax lien	Certificate of purchase or tax sale certificate

STATE		
Sale date	Varies by municipality	Tax liens that are not sold at the annual tax sale are offered for sale at what is termed a *scavenger sale*. Scavenger sales are held in odd years for properties with two years of delinquent taxes.
Bid method	Annual tax sale: bid down interest with penalties	Penalties are assessed as a percentage of the bid amount and are staggered across the redemption period.
	Scavenger sale: premium bid	Interest upon redemption is only applied to the opening bid amount. Redemption does not allow for a refund of the premium amount or that interest be applied to the premium amount.
Payment method	Annual tax sale	Preregistration procedures require that a deposit be made ten days before the tax sale in order to participate in the bidding. The balance of all purchases is due immediately upon winning a bid. Larger municipalities may require a letter of credit or bond for 1.5 times the amount of taxes and penalties for bids.
	Scavenger sale	Preregistration requires a $50 to $100 registration fee, paid five business days in advance of the sale. The minimum bid is $250, half of the tax amount or $500, and is due on the date of sale. If the bid is above the minimum, the balance of the bid is due the next day. Failure to pay the bid amount results in a forfeiture of the minimum bid amount and a possible lawsuit.
Interest	Annual tax sale: 18% penalty per 6 months	The penalty amount increases by the same amount that was bid, every six months.
	Scavenger sale: 24% per annum	Staggered penalty rates allow for differing payments, depending upon the date of redemption. The penalty to be applied to the redemption amount is calculated as a percentage of the certificate amount. If the interest upon redemption is bid down to 12%, the penalty is applied as follows: Within two months: 3% of the purchase amount per month - After two months, on or before six months: 12% of the purchase amount; 12% is the bid interest. - After six months, on or before one year: 24% of the purchase amount; 24% is equivalent to two times the bid interest. - After one year, on or before 18 months: 36% of the purchase amount; 36% is equivalent to three times the bid interest. - After 18 months, on or before two years: 48% of the purchase amount; 48% is equivalent to four times the bid interest. - After two years: 48% plus 6% per year thereafter

	STATE		
	Redemption period	2-3 years	The typical redemption period is two years. However, the tax lien certificate holder may extend the redemption period to three years beyond the annual tax sale by filing notice with the particular municipality. Improved residential properties with between one and six residential units have a redemption period of two years and six months. Improved residential properties with more than six residential units have a redemption period of six months, if the taxes are delinquent for more than two years. Vacant properties may be void of a redemption period and foreclosed by a petition filed with the courts.
	Subsequent taxes	Optional	If a tax lien certificate holder fails to pay back taxes, the property may be auctioned at a scavenger sale. Subsequent taxes are included in the calculation of the minimum bid for the scavenger sale.
	Foreclosure		A tax lien certificate becomes void if a petition for deed and record of the deed is not filed within five months of the end of the redemption period. Property owners may dispute a foreclosure up to five years after its issuance. Under certain circumstances, and in the absence of a quiet title judgment, the period may be extended to nine years. Foreclosed properties are free of liens and encumbrances, but not easements, such as those assessed by utility companies.
	Over the counter	No	
	Municipalities	102	Adams – www.co.adams.il.us/Treasurer Alexander – no website Bond – **http://bondcountyil.com** Boone – www.boonecountyil.org/department/treasurer Brown – no website Bureau – no website Calhoun – no website Carroll – www.carroll-county.net/index.asp?Type=B_BASIC&SEC={9DAE2E70-2888-4AC2-B826-7AED7E9724FC} Champaign – www.co.champaign.il.us/treas/taxsale.htm Christian – www.christiancountyil.com/treasurer.htm Clark – www.clarkcountyil.org/treasurer.htm Clay – www.claycountyillinois.org/index.aspx?page=24 Clinton – www.clintonco.illinois.gov/county_treasurer.htm Coles – www.co.coles.il.us/Treasurer Cook – www.cookcountytreasurer.com Crawford – www.crawfordcountycentral.com/treasurer Cumberland – www.cumberlandco.org/treasurer.aspx DeKalb – www.dekalbcounty.org De Witt – www.dewittcountyill.com/treasurer.htm

STATE	
	Douglas – **http://douglascountyil.com**
	Dupage – **www.dupageco.org/Treasurer/1834**
	Edgar – **www.edgarcountyillinois.com**
	Edwards – no website
	Effingham – **www.co.effingham.il.us/treasurer.html**
	Fayette – **www.fayettecountyillinois.org**
	Ford – **www.fordcountycourthouse.com/treasurer**
	Franklin – **www.franklincountyil.org**
	Fulton – **www.fultonco.org**
	Gallatin – no website
	Greene – no website
	Grundy – **www.grundyco.org/treasurer/treasurer.shtml**
	Hamilton – no website
	Hancock – **www.hancockcountycourthouse.org/county/treasurer**
	Hardin – no website
	Henderson – no website
	Henry – **www.henrycty.com/codepartments/treasurer**
	Iroquois – **www.co.iroquois.il.us**
	Jackson – **www.jacksoncounty-il.gov/index.php?option=com_content&task=view&id=63&Itemid=81**
	Jasper – no website
	Jefferson – **www.jeffil.us**
	Jersey – no website
	Jo Daviess – **www.jodaviess.org/index.asp?Type=B_BASIC&SEC={97CF9EC7-CA15-4A27-AB02-B3E-50DA8D8F2}**
	Johnson – no website
	Kane – **www.co.kane.il.us/treasurer**
	Kankakee – **www.co.kankakee.il.us/treasurer.html**
	Kendall – **www.co.kendall.il.us/treasurer**
	Knox – **www.knoxtreasurer.org**
	La Salle – **www.lasallecounty.org/treasurer**
	Lake – **www.lakecountyil.gov/Treasurer/Pages**
	Lawrence – **www.lawrencecountyillinois.com/treasurer.html**
	Lee – **www.countyoflee.org/treasurer/county_treasurer_main.html**
	Livingston – **http://livingstoncountyil.gov/?page_id=169**
	Logan – **www.co.logan.il.us/treasurer**
	Macon – **www.co.macon.il.us/treasurer.php#faq**
	Macoupin – **www.macoupincountyil.gov/treasurer.htm**
	Madison – **www.madcotreasurer.org**
	Marion – no website
	Marshall – **www.marshallcountyillinois.com/home/ElectedOfficials/CountyTreasurer.aspx**
	Mason – **www.masoncountyil.org/page8.html**

	STATE		
			Massac – no website
			McDonough – no website
			McHenry – **www.co.mchenry.il.us/Pages**
			McLean – **http://il-mcleancounty.civicplus.com/index.aspx?nid=97**
			Menard – **http://menardcountyil.com/County%20Treasurer.htm**
			Mercer – **www.mercercountyil.org**
			Monroe – **www.monroecountyil.org/index.aspx?NID=169**
			Montgomery – **www.montgomeryco.com/index.php/offices/treasurer-a-collector**
			Morgan – **www.morgancounty-il.com/County-Treasurer.html**
			Moultrie – no website
			Ogle – **www.oglecountytreasurer.org**
			Peoria – **www.peoriacounty.org/treasurer**
			Perry – no website
			Piatt – no website
			Pike – no website
			Pope – no website
			Pulaski – **www.pulaskicountyil.net/Pulaski_County**
			Putnam – **www.putnamcountyil.com/treasurer.htm**
			Randolph – **www.randolphco.org/gov**
			Richland – **no website**
			Rock Island – **www.rockislandcounty.org**
			Saline – no website
			Sangamon – **www.co.sangamon.il.us/Offices/treas/treasrer.asp**
			Schuyler – no website
			Scott – no website
			Shelby – **http://shelbycounty-il.com**
			St. Clair – **www.co.st-clair.il.us/Web+site+help.htm**
			Stark – **http://starkco.illinois.gov/countyOffice.php?officeID=63**
			Stephenson – **www.co.stephenson.il.us/treasurer**
			Tazewell – **www.tazewell.com/Treasurer/taz-treasurer.html**
			Union – no website
			Vermilion – **www.co.vermilion.il.us/Treas.htm**
			Wabash – no website
			Warren – **www.warrencountyil.com/countyOffice.php?officeID=11**
			Washington – no website
			Wayne – no website
			White – **www.whitecounty-il.gov**
			Whiteside – **www.whiteside.org/collector-treasurer**
			Will – **www.willcountyillinois.com**

Appendix 1: State Laws **205**

	STATE		
			Williamson – **http://williamsoncountycourthouse.com** Winnebago – **www.co.winnebago.il.us** Woodford – **www.woodford-county.org/index.php?section=27**
	Statute	35 Illinois Compiled Statutes	205/238, 200/21-350, 355, 385
	Indiana		
14	Type of sale	Tax lien	Certificate of sale or tax sale certificate
	Sale date	On or after 1 August, but before 1 November	Notice of the tax sale is displayed in a public location for 21 days and published once a week for 3 weeks.
	Bid method		The premium bid amount is referred to as a ***tax sale overbid***. The premium amount is held in the municipality's tax sale surplus fund.
	Payment method	Premium bid	Payment is required immediately upon winning the bid. Failure to pay results in a 25% penalty on the bid amount and also a lawsuit.
	Interest rate	10%–15% penalty; no interest	Staggered Interest rates allow for differing payments, dependent upon the date of redemption. The penalty to be applied to the redemption amount is calculated as follows: - Within six months: 10% of the opening bid amount - After six months, on or before one year: 15% of the opening bid amount - After one year: 25% of the opening bid amount The premium amount incurs no interest. Subsequent taxes and assessments incur interest at 12% per annum.
	Redemption period	1 year	The premium amount is refunded to the investor upon redemption. Three to five months before the end of the redemption period, the investor must give notice of the tax sale, the redemption period, the redemption amount, and the intent to petition for a deed. Notice must be delivered by certified mail to all individuals with interest in the property, as specified in public records. If an address is unknown, notice must be published for three consecutive weeks. If notice with specified details is not provided, the tax lien certificate expires 30 days after the end of the redemption period. A tax deed must be acquired within four years of filing a petition for it; otherwise, the tax lien certificate terminates.
	Subsequent taxes	Optional	Subsequent taxes earn interest at 12%.

STATE		
Foreclosure		Upon foreclosure, the property owner may file a claim to obtain the premium bid amount that was placed in the tax sale surplus fund. If the amount is not claimed within five years, the amount is forfeited and transferred from the municipality's surplus fund to its general fund.
Over the counter	No	
Municipalities	92	Adams – www.co.adams.in.us/county-offices/view/treasurers-office Allen – www.allencounty.us/tax-sale Bartholomew – www.bartholomewco.com/treasurer Benton – http://bentoncounty.in.gov/countygovernment.php Blackford – www.blackfordcountygov.us/pages.asp?PageIndex=371 Boone – http://boonecounty.in.gov/Default.aspx?tabid=171 Brown – no website Carroll – www.carrollcountyin.gov Cass – www.co.cass.in.us/dav/treasurer/treasurer.html Clark – www.co.clark.in.us/governmentdirectory.html Clay – www.claycountyin.gov/index.pl?id=4293;isa=Category;op=show Clinton – http://clintonco.com Crawford – no website Daviess – no website DeKalb – www.co.dekalb.in.us/dekalb/departments/Treasurer Dearborn – www.dearborncounty.org/Government/County-Offices/Treasurers-Office Decatur – www.decaturcounty.in.gov/treasurer/treasurer.htm Delaware – www.co.delaware.in.us/department/?fDD=13-0 Dubois – www.duboiscountyin.org/offices/treasurer.html Elkhart – www.elkhartcountyindiana.com/Departments/Treasurer Fayette – www.co.fayette.in.us/treasurer.htm Floyd – www.floydcounty.in.gov/county%20offices/treasurer.htm Fountain – http://fountainco.net Franklin – www.franklincounty.in.gov/countyoffices/treasurer-2 Fulton – www.co.fulton.in.us/treasurer Gibson – www.gibsoncounty-in.gov/departments/treasurer/default.aspx Grant – http://treasurer.grantcounty27.us

STATE	
	Greene – www.gcindiana.info/gov.shtml
Hamilton – www.hamiltoncounty.in.gov/departments.asp?id=2205
Hancock – http://hancockcoingov.org/hancock-county-government-departments/hancock-county-indiana-treasurers-office.html
Harrison – http://harrisoncounty.in.gov/treasurer.htm
Hendricks – www.co.hendricks.in.us/treasurer.html
Henry – www.henryco.net/index.php?option=com_content&view=article&id=24&Itemid=27
Howard – http://co.howard.in.us/Treasurer
Huntington – www.huntington.in.us/county/department/?fDD=45-0
Jackson – no website
Jasper – www.jaspercountyin.gov/Default.aspx?tabId=73
Jay – www.co.jay.in.us/treasurer.htm
Jefferson – no website
Jennings – www.jenningscounty-in.gov
Johnson – http://co.johnson.in.us/johnsoncounty/index.php?option=com_content&view=article&id=42&Itemid=52
Knox – www.knoxcountygov.com/modules.php?name=Content&pa=showpage&pid=3
Kosciusko – www.kcgov.com
Lagrange – www.lagrangecounty.org/index.php?option=com_frontpage&Itemid=132
Lake – www.lakecountyin.org/portal/media-type/html/group/treasurer/page/default;jsessionid=48F68817E9687A53D58C15F3EF102A42
La Porte – www.laportecounty.org/departments/treasurer/index.html
Lawrence – no website
Madison – www.madisoncty.com/TreasurersOffice.html
Marion – www.indy.gov/eGov/County/Treasurer/Pages/home.aspx
Marshall – www.co.marshall.in.us/departments/treasurer
Martin – no website
Miami – www.miamicountyin.gov/Departments/Treasurer
Monroe – www.co.monroe.in.us/tsd
Montgomery – www.montgomeryco.net/department/?fDD=14-0
Morgan – www.morgancounty.in.gov
Newton – www.newtoncountyin.com/gov_services.htm
Noble – http://nobleco.squarespace.com/treasurer
Ohio – no website

	STATE		
			Orange – www.co.orange.in.us
			Owen – www.owencounty.in.gov
			Parke – no website
			Perry – no website
			Pike – no website
			Porter – www.porterco.org/index.php?id=treasurer
			Posey – no website
			Pulaski – www.pulaskionline.org/content/view/39/50
			Putnam – http://co.putnam.in.us
			Randolph – http://randolphcounty.us
			Ripley – www.ripleycounty.com
			Rush – www.rushcounty.in.gov/Public/CountyOffices/Treasurer
			Scott – no website
			Shelby – www.co.shelby.in.us
			Spencer – http://spencercounty.in.gov/pages.cfm?Departmentid=413
			St. Joseph – www.stjosephcountyindiana.com/departments/treasurer
			Starke – no website
			Steuben – www.steubencounty.com/departments/treasurer/treasurer.aspx
			Sullivan – no website
			Switzerland – www.switzerland-county.com
			Tippecanoe – www.tippecanoe.in.gov/auditor/division.asp?fDD=7-50
			Tipton – www.tiptoncounty.in.gov/CountyOffices/Treasurer/tabid/252/Default.aspx
			Union – no website
			Vanderburgh – www.vanderburghgov.org
			Vermillion – www.vermilliongov.us
			Vigo – www.vigocounty.in.gov/office/?fDD=3-0
			Wabash – http://wabashcounty.in.gov/cgi.exe?PAGEID=0004
			Warren – no website
			Warrick – www.warrickcounty.gov/warrickassessor
			Washington – www.washingtoncounty.in.gov
			Wayne – www.co.wayne.in.us
			Wells – www.wellscounty.org/auditor.htm
			White – http://home.whitecountyindiana.us/index.php?option=com_content&view=category&id=65&Itemid=81
			Whitley – http://whitleygov.com
	Statute	Indiana Code	Sections 6-1,1-24 and 6-1.1-25
	Iowa		
15	Type of sale	Tax lien	Certificate of purchase or tax sale certificate

Appendix 1: State Laws

STATE		
Sale date	June, third Monday	The tax sale listing is published one to three weeks before the sale.
Bid method	Random or rotational	Random or rotational bidding is used in lieu of bidding down ownership.
Payment method		A nonrefundable fee may be required to register for the sale. Payment is required immediately upon winning the bid. If payment is not made, the tax lien certificate is offered for sale again.
Interest rate	24% per annum	
Redemption period	1 year and 9 months	If the tax lien on a property is more than one year old when it is acquired, the redemption period is nine months. Only the property owner or other individuals with recorded interest in a property may redeem a tax lien certificate.
Subsequent taxes		
Foreclosure	3 years	Ninety days before the expiration of the redemption period, the lien certificate holder must inform the property owner that the right of redemption is to expire in 90 days. The tax deed must be acquired within three years of the tax sale date. If the tax lien certificate holder does not notify the property owner within one year and nine months or obtain a tax deed within the specified three-year time frame, the tax lien certificate expires, and any amounts used to acquire the lien certificate are forfeited to the municipality. The treasurer cancels the sale.
Over the counter	No	Unsold tax lien certificates are adjourned and repeatedly offered for sale at two-month intervals until the next annual tax sale, when the process of repeatedly offering certificates for sale begins again.
Municipalities	99	Adair – www.adaircountyiowa.org Adams – www.adamscountyia.com Allamakee – www.co.allamakee.ia.us Appanoose – www.appanoosecounty.net Audubon – www.auduboncounty.com Benton – www.cobentoniaus.com Black Hawk – www.co.black-hawk.ia.us Boone – www.co.boone.ia.us Bremer – www.co.bremer.ia.us Buchanan – www.co.buchanan.ia.us Buena Vista – www.co.buena-vista.ia.us Butler – www.butlercoiowa.org Calhoun – www.calhouncountyiowa.com Carroll – www.co.carroll.ia.us Cass – www.casscountyiowa.us Cedar – www.cedarcounty.org Cerro Gordo – www.co.cerro-gordo.ia.us

STATE	
	Cherokee – www.cherokeecountyiowa.com
	Chickasaw – www.chickasawcoia.org
	Clarke – www.clarkecountyia.org/ClarkeCounty/mainhome.do
	Clay – www.co.clay.ia.us
	Clayton – www.claytoncountyia.gov
	Clinton – www.clintoncounty-ia.gov
	Crawford – www.crawfordcounty.org
	Dallas – www.co.dallas.ia.us
	Davis – www.daviscountyiowa.org
	Decatur – no website
	Delaware – http://co.delaware.ia.us
	Des Moines – www.co.des-moines.ia.us
	Dickinson – www.co.dickinson.ia.us
	Dubuque – www.dubuquecounty.org
	Emmet – www.emmetcountyia.com
	Fayette – www.fayettecountyiowa.org
	Floyd – www.floydcoia.org
	Franklin – http://co.franklin.ia.us
	Fremont – www.co.fremont.ia.us
	Greene – www.co.greene.ia.us
	Grundy – www.grundycounty.org
	Guthrie – www.guthriecounty.org
	Hamilton – www.hamiltoncounty.org
	Hancock – www.hancockcountyia.org
	Hardin – www.co.hardin.ia.us
	Harrison – www.harrisoncountyia.org
	Henry – www.henrycountyiowa.us
	Howard – www.co.howard.ia.us
	Humboldt – www.humboldtcountyia.org
	Ida – no website
	Iowa – www.co.iowa.ia.us
	Jackson – http://co.jackson.ia.us
	Jasper – www.co.jasper.ia.us
	Jefferson – www.jeffersoncountyiowa.com
	Johnson – www.johnson-county.com
	Jones – http://jonescountyiowa.org
	Keokuk – www.keokukcountyia.com
	Kossuth – www.co.kossuth.ia.us
	Lee – www.leecounty.org
	Linn – www.linncounty.org
	Louisa – www.louisacountyiowa.org
	Lucas – no website
	Lyon – www.lyoncountyiowa.com
	Madison – www.madisoncoia.us
	Mahaska – www.mahaskacounty.org
	Marion – www.co.marion.ia.us
	Marshall – www.co.marshall.ia.us

STATE			
			Mills – www.millscoia.us
			Mitchell – www.mitchellcoia.us
			Monona – no website
			Monroe – www.monroecoia.us
			Montgomery – www.montgomerycountyiowa.com
			Muscatine – www.co.muscatine.ia.us
			O'Brien – http://www.obriencounty.com/index.php?pageid=6d65726368616e745f69643a31302d31
			Osceola – www.osceolacountyia.org
			Page – http://co.page.ia.us
			Palo Alto – no website
			Plymouth – www.co.plymouth.ia.us
			Pocahontas – no website
			Polk – www.polkcountyiowa.gov
			Pottawattamie – www.pottcounty.com
			Poweshiek – www.poweshiekcounty.org
			Ringgold – no website
			Sac – www.saccounty.org
			Scott – www.scottcountyiowa.com
			Shelby – www.shco.org
			Sioux – www.siouxcounty.org
			Story – www.storycounty.com
			Tama – www.tamacounty.org
			Taylor – no website
			Union – www.unioncountyiowa.org
			Van Buren – http://vanburencoia.org
			Wapello – www.wapellocounty.org/index2.htm
			Warren – www.co.warren.ia.us
			Washington – http://co.washington.ia.us
			Wayne – no website
			Webster – http://webstercountyia.org
			Winnebago – www.winnebagocountyia.org
			Winneshiek – www.winnesheikcounty.org
			Woodbury – www.woodburyiowa.com
			Worth – www.worthcounty.org
			Wright – www.wrightcounty.org
	Statute	Code of Iowa	Chapters 446, 447.13
	Kansas		
16	Type of sale	Tax deed	
	Sale date	Varies by municipality	The tax sale is a public oral-bid foreclosure sale of real estate.
	Bid method	Premium bid	Some municipalities have no established minimum for bids. Bidding may start as low as $50, and properties may be purchased for less than the tax lien amount, that is, the delinquent tax, penalties, and costs.
	Payment method		

STATE		
Interest rate	N/A	
Redemption period	N/A	
Over the counter	No	
Municipalities	105	Allen – www.allencounty.org Anderson – http://andersoncountyks.org Atchison – www.atchisoncountyks.org Barber – no website Barton – www.bartoncounty.org Bourbon – www.bourboncountyks.org Brown – http://ks-brown.manatron.com Butler – www.bucoks.com Chase – www.chasecountyks.org/info/county_contacts.htm Chautauqua – www.chautauquacountyks.com Cherokee – http://cherokeecountyks.com Cheyenne – www.cheyennecounty.org Clark – www.clarkcountyks.com Clay – www.claycountykansas.org Cloud – www.cloudcountyks.org Coffey – www.coffeycountyks.org Comanche – www.comanchecounty.com Cowley – www.cowleycounty.org Crawford – www.crawfordcountykansas.org Decatur – http://oberlinks.com Dickinson – www.dkcoks.org Doniphan – www.dpcountyks.com Douglas – www.douglas-county.com Edwards – www.edwardscounty.org Elk – no website Ellis – www.ellisco.net Ellsworth – www.ellsworthcounty.org/home Finney – www.finneycounty.org Ford – www.fordcounty.net Franklin – www.franklincoks.org Geary – http://ks-geary.manatron.com Gove – no website Graham – www.grahamcountyks.com Grant – www.grantcoks.org Gray – www.grayco.org Greeley – no website Greenwood – www.greenwoodcounty.org Hamilton – www.hamiltoncountyks.com Harper – http://harpercountyks.gov Harvey – www.harveycounty.com Haskell – www.haskellcounty.org

STATE	
	Hodgeman – www.hodgemancountyks.com/courthouse.html
Jackson – http://ks-jackson.manatron.com
Jefferson – www.jfcountyks.com
Jewell – no website
Johnson – www.jocogov.org
Kearny – www.kearnycountykansas.com
Kingman – http://kingmancoks.com
Kiowa – www.kiowacountyks.org
Labette – www.labettecounty.com
Lane – no website
Leavenworth – www.leavenworthcounty.org/home.asp
Lincoln – www.lincolncoks.com
Linn – www.linncountyks.com
Logan – no website
Lyon – www.lyoncounty.org
Marion – www.marioncoks.net
Marshall – http://ks-marshall.manatron.com
McPherson – www.mcphersoncountyks.us
Meade – www.meadeco.org
Miami – www.miamicountyks.org
Mitchell – www.mcks.org
Montgomery – www.mgcountyks.org
Morris – www.morriscountyks.org
Morton – www.mtcoks.com
Nemaha – http://ks-nemaha.manatron.com
Neosho – www.neoshocountyks.org
Ness – www.nesscountyks.com
Norton – www.nortoncounty.net
Osage – www.osageco.org
Osborne – www.osbornecounty.org
Ottawa – www.ottawacounty.org
Pawnee – www.pawneecountykansas.com
Phillips – www.phillipscounty.org
Pottawatomie – www.pottcounty.org
Pratt – www.prattcounty.org
Rawlins – no website
Reno – www.renogov.org
Republic – www.republiccounty.org
Rice – www.ricecounty.us
Riley – www.rileycountyks.gov
Rooks – www.rookscounty.net
Rush – www.rushcountykansas.org
Russell – www.russell.kansasgov.com
Saline – www.saline.org
Scott – www.scott.kansasgov.com
Sedgwick – www.sedgwickcounty.org
Seward – www.sewardcountyks.org

	STATE		
			Shawnee – www.snco.us
Sheridan – no website
Sherman – http://ks-sherman.manatron.com
Smith – www.smithcoks.com
Stafford – www.staffordcounty.org
Stanton – www.stantoncountyks.com
Stevens – www.stevenscoks.org
Sumner – www.co.sumner.ks.us
Thomas – www.thomascountyks.com
Trego – no website
Wabaunsee – www.wabaunsee.kansasgov.com
Wallace – no website
Washington – www.washingtoncountyks.net
Wichita – no website
Wilson – www.wilson.kansasgov.com
Woodson – www.woodsoncounty.net
Wyandotte – www.wycokck.org/Internet2010Tab.aspx?id=16094&banner=27661
	Statute	K.S.A.	Section 79-2801
	Kentucky		
17	Type of sale	Tax lien	Certificate of delinquency or tax claims
	Sale date	April to May	The tax sale must be published 15 days before the tax sale date.
	Bid method	Premium bid	Bidding is not established by state statute.
	Payment method		Payment is due immediately upon winning a bid.
	Interest rate	12% per annum	Interest is calculated monthly with no consideration for portions of a month. The interest computed for the first day of the month is the same as that computed for any other day of the month.
	Redemption period	1 year	Within 50 days of purchase, the third-party purchaser must advise the delinquent taxpayer of the transaction, in a prescribed manner. After one year, the tax lien certificate holder may pursue formal collection from the property owner for amounts necessary to acquire the lien certificate or engage in enforcing the right to foreclose any right of redemption of the tax lien certificate. Tax deeds are obtained through a judicial foreclosure. The property owner must be notified of the intent to foreclose and the required redemption amount that will accrue 45 days before the date of the foreclosure.
	Over the counter	No	
	Municipalities	120	Adair – www.adaircounty.ky.gov
Allen – www.allencountykentucky.com
Anderson – www.andersoncounty.ky.gov
Ballard – www.ballardcounty.ky.gov

STATE	
	Barren – www.barrenco-ky.com
	Bath – no website
	Bell – http://bellcounty.ky.gov/default.htm
	Boone – www.boonecountyky.org
	Bourbon – no website
	Boyd – www.boydcountyky.net
	Boyle – www.boyleky.com
	Bracken – www.brackencounty.ky.gov
	Breathitt – http://breathittcounty.ky.gov
	Breckinridge – www.breckinridgecountyky.com
	Bullitt – www.bullittcounty.ky.gov
	Butler – www.butlercounty.ky.gov
	Caldwell – www.caldwellcounty.ky.gov
	Calloway – www.callowaycounty-ky.gov
	Campbell – www.campbellcountyky.org
	Carlisle – www.carlislecounty.ky.gov
	Carroll – www.carrollcountygov.us
	Carter – www.cartercounty.ky.gov
	Casey – www.caseycounty.ky.gov
	Christian – www.christiancountyky.gov/QCMS
	Clark – www.clarkcoky.com
	Clay – www.claycounty.ky.gov
	Clinton – www.clintoncounty.ky.gov
	Crittenden – no website
	Cumberland – www.cumberlandcounty.ky.gov
	Daviess – www.daviessky.org/homepage.asp
	Edmonson – www.edmonsoncounty.ky.gov
	Elliott – www.elliottcounty.ky.gov
	Estill – www.estillky.com
	Fayette – www.lexingtonky.gov
	Fleming – www.flemingcountyky.org/articles/home.asp
	Floyd – no website
	Franklin – http://franklincounty.ky.gov
	Fulton – www.fultoncounty.ky.gov
	Gallatin – http://gallatincounty.ky.gov
	Garrard – www.garrardcounty.ky.gov
	Grant – http://grantcounty.ky.gov
	Graves – http://gravescounty.ky.gov
	Grayson – www.graysoncounty.ky.gov
	Green – www.greencounty.ky.gov
	Greenup – www.greenupcounty.ky.gov
	Hancock – www.hancockky.us/Government/government.htm
	Hardin – www.hcky.org
	Harlan – no website
	Harrison – no website
	Hart – www.hartcounty.ky.gov
	Henderson – www.hendersonky.us

	STATE		
			Henry – www.henrycountygov.com
Hickman – www.hickmancounty.ky.gov
Hopkins – http://hopkinscounty.ky.gov
Jackson – www.jacksoncountyky.us
Jefferson – www.jeffersoncountyclerk.org
Jessamine – www.jessamineco.com
Johnson – no website
Kenton – www.kentoncounty.org
Knott – no website
Knox – no website
LaRue – www.laruecounty.org
Laurel – no website
Lawrence – www.lawrencecounty.ky.gov
Lee – www.leecounty.ky.gov
Leslie – www.lesliecounty.ky.gov
Letcher – www.letchercounty.ky.gov
Lewis – http://lewiscounty.ky.gov
Lincoln – www.lincolnky.com
Livingston – www.livingstonco.ky.gov
Logan – www.logancounty.ky.gov
Lyon – www.lyoncounty.ky.gov
Madison – www.madisoncountyky.us
Magoffin – http://magoffincounty.ky.gov
Marion – www.marioncounty.ky.gov
Marshall – http://marshallcounty.ky.gov
Martin – www.martincounty.ky.gov
Mason – www.masoncountykentucky.com/articles/home.asp
McCracken – www.mccrackenfiscalcourt.com
McCreary – www.mccrearycounty.com/Government.html
McLean – www.mcleancounty.ky.gov
Meade – www.visitmeadecounty.org/officials-meade.shtml
Menifee – www.menifeecounty.ky.gov
Mercer – www.mercercounty.ky.gov
Metcalfe – http://metcalfecounty.ky.gov
Monroe – www.monroecounty.ky.gov
Montgomery – www.montgomerycounty.ky.gov
Morgan – www.morgancounty.ky.gov
Muhlenberg – www.muhlenbergcounty.ky.gov
Nelson – www.nelsoncountyky.com
Nicholas – www.nicholascounty.ky.gov
Ohio – www.ohiocounty.ky.gov
Oldham – www.oldhamcounty.net
Owen – http://owencounty.ky.gov
Owsley – no website
Pendleton – www.pendletoncounty.ky.gov

Appendix 1: State Laws

	STATE		
			Perry – www.perrycounty.ky.gov
Pike – no website
Powell – www.powellcounty.ky.gov
Pulaski – www.pcgovt.com
Robertson – www.robertsoncounty.ky.gov
Rockcastle – www.rockcastlecountyky.com/government.html
Rowan – www.moreheadrowan.org/rowancounty
Russell – www.russellcounty.ky.gov
Scott – www.scottky.com/information/government/county/countygov.htm
Shelby – www.shelbycountykentucky.com
Simpson – www.simpsoncounty.us
Spencer – www.spencercountyky.gov/government.html
Taylor – www.taylorcounty.ky.gov
Todd – www.toddcounty.ky.gov
Trigg – www.triggcounty.ky.gov
Trimble – www.trimblecounty.ky.gov
Union – http://unioncounty.ky.gov
Warren – http://warrencountygov.com
Washington – www.washingtoncountyky.com
Wayne – www.waynecounty.ky.gov
Webster – http://webstercountyclerk.ky.gov
Whitley – www.whitleycountyfiscalcourt.com
Wolfe – no website
Woodford – http://woodfordcounty.ky.gov
	Statute	K.R.S.	Section 134.460
	Louisiana		
18	Type of sale	Hybrid tax deed	Tax deed or deed of sale
	Sale date	January to April	The tax sale date is not established by state statute.
	Bid method	Bid down interest	
	Payment method	Cash	Payment is required immediately upon winning the bid.
	Interest rate	12% per annum and 5% penalty	E.g. if the property is redeemed in one year, you will get 17%, two years – 29%, or the maximum three years – 41%
	Redemption period	3 years	Although this is one of the longest redemption periods set by states, the redemption period may be overridden, because Louisiana allows tax deed purchasers to petition the court for immediate possession of a property. Abandoned or blighted properties have the redemption period reduced to 18 months.
Louisiana is unique in allowing you to demand possession of the property during the redemption period.

STATE		
Subsequent taxes		Can be purchased at 12% interest.
Foreclosure		Statute does not dictate when a tax deed must be recorded, but a tax deed must be recorded after the sale, and the property owner is given three years from the date of the tax deed recording to redeem the property.
Over the counter	No	
Municipalities	64 Municipalities are called *parishes*.	Acadia – www.apso.org Allen – http://allenparishso.org/index.php?option=com_content&view=article&id=62&Itemid=107 Ascension – www.ascensionparish.net Assumption – http://assumptionla.com Avoyelles – no website Beauregard – www.beauparish.org Bienville – http://clerk.bienvilleparish.org Bossier – www.bossierparishla.gov Caddo – www.caddo.org Calcasieu – www.cppj.net Caldwell – no website Cameron – www.parishofcameron.net Catahoula – no website Claiborne – www.claiborneone.org Concordia – www.concordiasheriff.org DeSoto – www.desotoparishclerk.org East Baton Rouge – www.ebrso.org East Carroll – no website East Feliciana – www.eastfelicianaclerk.org Evangeline – no website Franklin – no website Grant – http://grantassessor.org Iberia – www.iberiaparishgovernment.com Iberville – www.ibervilleparish.com Jackson – http://jacksonparishclerk.org Jefferson – www.jeffparish.net Jefferson Davis – www.jeffdavis.net La Salle – no website Lafayette – www.lafayettela.gov Lafourche – www.lafourchegov.org Lincoln – www.lincolnparish.org Livingston – www.livingstonparishla.gov Madison – www.madisonso.com Morehouse – www.morehouseassessor.org Natchitoches – http://nppj.org Orleans – www.opcso.org Ouachita – www.oppj.org Plaquemines – www.plaqueminesparish.com

Appendix 1: State Laws

	STATE		
			Pointe Coupee – www.pcpolicejury.org
Rapides – www.rppj.com
Red River – www.redriversheriff.com
Richland – no website
Sabine – www.sabinesheriff.com
St. Bernard – www.sbpg.net
St. Charles – www.stcharlesgov.net
St. Helena – www.sthelenaso.org
St. James – www.stjamesla.com
St. John the Baptist – www.sjbparish.com
St. Landry – www.stlandryparishgovernment.org
St. Martin – http://stmartinparish-la.org
St. Mary www.parish.st-mary.la.us
St. Tammany – www.stpgov.org
Tangipahoa – www.tangipahoa.org
Tensas – no website
Terrebonne – www.tpcg.org
Union – http://unionparishassessor.com
Vermilion – http://vermilionparishpolicejury.com
Vernon – www.vernonclerk.com
Washington – www.wpgov.org
Webster – www.websterclerk.org
West Baton Rouge – www.wbrcouncil.org
West Carroll – no website
West Feliciana – www.westfelicianaparish-la.gov
Winn – no website
	Statute	L.R.S.	Section 47:2181,2183
	Maine		
19	Type of sale	Tax deed	Municipalities place liens against real property for delinquent property taxes. If the property owner does not redeem the property, the municipality may retain ownership of the property or sell the property. When the municipality decides to sell the property, title to the property is offered for sale through a tax lien foreclosure or sewer lien foreclosure.
	Sale date	Varies by municipality	
	Bid method	Sealed	The municipality offers property for sale that it has taken ownership of because the property owner failed to redeem the delinquent taxes assessed against him or her. The municipality uses its own discretion in accepting sealed bid offers or rejecting sealed bid offers as inadequate.
	Payment method		
	Interest rate	N/A	
	Redemption period	N/A	Property owners are given 18 months to redeem real property from the municipality.

	STATE		
	Over the counter	No	
	Municipalities	16	Androscoggin – no website Aroostook – www.aroostook.me.us Cumberland – www.cumberlandcounty.org Franklin – www.franklincountymaine.org/live_and_work/government.aspx Hancock – www.co.hancock.me.us Kennebec – www.kennebeccounty.org Knox – http://knoxcountymaine.gov Lincoln – www.lincolncountymaine.me Oxford – www.oxfordcounty.org Penobscot – www.penobscot-county.net Piscataquis – www.piscataquis.us Sagadahoc – www.sagcounty.com/government.html Somerset – www.somersetcounty-me.org Waldo – www.waldocountyme.gov Washington – www.washingtoncountymaine.com York – www.yorkcountyme.gov
	Statute	Maine Revised Statutes	Title 36
	Maryland		
20	Type of sale	Tax lien	Tax sale certificate or certificate of sale
	Sale date	Varies by municipality	The particular municipality establishes the tax sale date and the listing is published 30 to 60 days before the tax sale.
	Bid method	Premium bid	
	Payment method		Only the opening bid amount is required on the day of the tax sale. The tax lien certificate purchaser never pays the premium amount if the lien certificate is redeemed. If the lien certificate is redeemed, the premium amount must be paid in order to foreclose the right of redemption.
	Interest rate	6% to 24%	
	Redemption period	6 months	A redemption period is not established by statute. However, the lien certificate holder may foreclose judicially and end the redemption period six months after the tax sale, but before two years have expired. If the complaint is not filed within two years of the tax sale date, the tax lien certificate expires, and the purchaser forfeits all money used to acquire the certificate.
	Subsequent taxes		
	Foreclosure	Within 2 years	Foreclosure must be accomplished within two years, except in Baltimore City. Vacant or abandoned buildings or buildings in violation of building codes must be foreclosed within one year.

	STATE		
	Over the counter	Yes	
	Municipalities	23	Allegany – **www.gov.allconet.org** Anne Arundel – **www.aacounty.org** Baltimore City – **www.bidbaltimore.com/main?&unique_id=Szp1-goBBAEAAH4Zc9k&session=&auction_id=&use_this=view_faqs** Baltimore County – **www.baltimorecountymd.gov** Calvert – **www.co.cal.md.us** Caroline – **http://carolinemd.org/governmt** Carroll – **www.carr.org** Cecil – **www.ccgov.org** Charles – **www.charlescounty.org** Dorchester – **www.docogonet.com** Frederick – **www.frederickcountymd.gov** Garrett – **www.garrettcounty.org** Harford – **www.harfordcountymd.gov** Howard – **www.co.ho.md.us** Kent – **www.kentcounty.com/gov** Montgomery – **www.montgomerycountymd.gov/apps/taxliensale** Prince George's – **www.princegeorgescountymd.gov** Queen Anne's – **www.qac.org/index.aspx?pageid=33&template=2** Somerset – **www.co.somerset.md.us** St. Mary's – **www.co.saint-marys.md.us** Talbot – **www.talbotcountymd.gov** Washington – **www.washco-md.net** Wicomico – **www.wicomicocounty.org** Worcester – **http://co.worcester.md.us/trs/taxsale.aspx**
	Statute	Annotated Code of the Public Laws of Maryland	Section 14-817, 818, 820, 831, 833, 844
	Massachusetts		
21	Type of sale	Hybrid tax deed	Collector's deed, deed, or deed of the land
	Sale date	Varies by municipality	Notice of the tax sale must be published at least 14 days before the sale in a local newspaper and in two or more publicly accessible places.
	Bid method	Bid down ownership	
	Payment method		A good faith deposit is required immediately upon winning the bid, or else the sale is void. Full payment is required within 20 days of the sale, or the sale is void, and the deposit is forfeited.

STATE		
Interest rate	16% per annum	
Redemption period	6 months	A redemption period is not established by statute. The redemption amount may be paid to either the treasurer, the tax deed purchaser, a representative designated by the tax deed purchaser or an assignee of the tax deed purchaser. If a redemption payment is made to the treasurer for less than the full amount, the purchaser may sue for the balance within three months. Property owners are allowed to make payment in installments. Each installment must be at least 25% of the total redemption amount with the exception of the last installment payment, which should cover the balance of the amount due. When installment payments are made, the redemption period increases by one year. The tax deed holder must initiate a judicial foreclosure to end the redemption period. The tax deed holder may initiate the foreclosure six months after the tax sale date.
Subsequent taxes		
Foreclosure		The tax deed must be recorded within 60 days of the sale. The property owner is given six months to redeem the property, or the tax deed purchaser may foreclose on the property. Because of backlogs and the number of property owners requesting an extension of the redemption period, the actual foreclosure may be delayed up to three years. If a foreclosure is found to be invalid, the investor is refunded the amount of the purchase plus 6% interest for up to two years.
Over the counter	No	Unsold tax deeds are sold at another auction.
Municipalities (Massachusetts abolished many county governments in 2010; but the orderly transition brought them under the control of the commonwealth, and so business continues as usual)	14	Barnstable – www.barnstablecounty.org Berkshire – no county website Bristol – http://countyofbristol.net Dukes – http://dukescounty.org/Pages/index Essex – no website Franklin – www.frcog.org Hampden – www.registryofdeeds.co.hampden.ma.us Hampshire – www.hampshirecog.org Middlesex – no website Nantucket – www.nantucket-ma.gov/pages/index Norfolk – www.norfolkcounty.org Plymouth – http://plymouthdeeds.org Suffolk – www.suffolkdeeds.com Worcester – www.worcesterma.gov/finance/treasurer/public-auctions

Appendix 1: State Laws 223

	STATE		
	Statute	Annotated Law of Massachusetts	Sections 45, 62
	Michigan		
22	Type of sale	Tax deed	
	Sale date	May, first Tuesday	Tax lien certificates are offered for sale for properties in the third year of delinquency.
	Bid method	Bid down ownership	
	Payment method	Cash, certified check, or money order	Payment is required at the end of the tax sale day.
	Interest rate	First year, 15% Second year, 50% penalty	The Interest rate of 15% applies to redemption in the first year after the tax sale. Redemption at any point in the second year, but before the six-month redemption period that is initiated by the issuance of a tax deed, incurs a 50% penalty. The purchaser must provide the property owner with a quitclaim deed upon redemption.
	Redemption period	1 year	The property owner may redeem the tax lien certificate up until the time that a tax deed is obtained. The issuance of a tax deed initiates a new six-month redemption period.
	Subsequent taxes	Required	The time frame for converting a tax lien certificate into a tax deed is six months after the end of the redemption period. During this time frame, the purchaser is required to pay all subsequent taxes.
	Foreclosure		The tax deed expires in five years if a tax deed is not acquired and proper procedures are not followed to obtain title to the property.
	Over the counter	Yes	Unsold tax lien certificates are bought and offered for sale by the state. Tax lien certificates are offered for sale up to April 19 of the following year. The price includes interest at a rate of 15% per annum or 1.25% per month.
	Municipalities	83	Alcona – www.alconacountyml.com Alger – www.algercourthouse.com Allegan – www.allegancounty.org Alpena – www.alpenacounty.org Antrim – no website Arenac – www.arenaccountygov.com Baraga – www.baragacounty.org Barry – www.barrycounty.org Bay – www.baycounty-mi.gov Benzie – www.benzieco.net Berrien – www.berriencounty.org Branch – www.co.branch.mi.us Calhoun – www.calhouncountymi.gov Cass – www.casscountymi.org

STATE	
	Charlevoix – www.charlevoixcounty.org
	Cheboygan – www.cheboygancounty.net/home
	Chippewa – www.chippewacountymi.gov
	Clare – www.clareco.net
	Clinton – www.clinton-county.org
	Crawford – www.crawfordco.org
	Delta – www.deltacountymi.org
	Dickinson – www.dickinsoncountymi.gov
	Eaton – www.eatoncounty.org
	Emmet – www.emmetcounty.org
	Genesee – www.gc4me.com
	Gladwin – www.gladwinco.com
	Gogebic – www.gogebic.org
	Grand Traverse – www.co.grand-traverse.mi.us
	Gratiot – www.co.gratiot.mi.us
	Hillsdale – www.co.hillsdale.mi.us
	Houghton – www.houghtoncounty.net
	Huron – www.co.huron.mi.us/default.asp
	Ingham – www.ingham.org
	Ionia – www.ioniacounty.org
	Iosco – http://iosco.m33access.com
	Iron – www.iron.org
	Isabella – www.isabellacounty.org
	Jackson – www.mygovhelp.org/JACKSONCOUNTYMI/_cs/SupportHome.aspx?sSessionID=6566AA0C17074C56A00FE4A43C544C2FTIBPNRAI
	Kalamazoo – www.kalcounty.com
	Kalkaska – www.kalkaskacounty.net/treasurer.asp
	Kent – www.accesskent.com
	Keweenaw – http://keweenawcountyonline.org
	Lake – www.lakecounty-michigan.com
	Lapeer – http://lapeercountyweb.org
	Leelanau – www.leelanau.cc
	Lenawee – www.lenawee.mi.us
	Livingston – http://co.livingston.mi.us/default.asp
	Luce – www.lucecountymi.org
	Mackinac – www.mackinaccounty.net
	Macomb – http://macombcountymi.gov/index.htm
	Manistee – www.manisteecountymi.gov
	Marquette – www.co.marquette.mi.us
	Mason – www.masoncounty.net
	Mecosta – www.co.mecosta.mi.us
	Menominee – www.menomineecounty.com
	Midland – www.co.midland.mi.us
	Missaukee – www.missaukee.org
	Monroe – www.co.monroe.mi.us
	Montcalm – www.montcalm.org
	Montmorency – www.montmorencycountymichigan.us

STATE		
		Muskegon – www.co.muskegon.mi.us
Newaygo – www.countyofnewaygo.com/NC/Home.htm
Oakland – www.oakgov.com
Oceana – www.oceana.mi.us
Ogemaw – www.ogemawcountymi.gov
Ontonagon – no website
Osceola – www.osceola-county.org
Oscoda – www.oscodacountymi.com
Otsego – www.otsegocountymi.gov
Ottawa – www.co.ottawa.mi.us
Presque Isle – www.presqueislecounty.org
Roscommon – www.roscommoncounty.net
Saginaw – www.saginawcounty.com
Sanilac – www.sanilaccounty.net
Schoolcraft – www.schoolcraftcounty.net
Shiawassee – www.shiawassee.net
St. Clair – www.stclaircounty.org/Main
St. Joseph – www.stjosephcountymi.org
Tuscola – no website
Van Buren – www.vbco.org/government0002.asp
Washtenaw – www.ewashtenaw.org
Wayne – www.waynecounty.com
Wexford – www.wexfordcounty.org
Statute	Public Acts	Act 123 of 1999; Act 206 of Public Acts 1893 Sections 140-143
Minnesota		
23	Type of sale	Tax deed	Municipalities place liens against real property for delinquent property taxes. If the property owner does not redeem the property, the municipality may retain ownership of the property or sell the property. The municipality may:
- Offer the property for sale at public auction.
- Offer the property for sale to an adjacent property owner if the parcel of land is too small to build on.
- Transfer ownership to the city for authorized public use.
- Place the property on hold for an environmental review.
	Sale date	Varies by municipality	
	Bid method	Premium bid	Properties offered for sale at the public auction are sold to the highest bidder willing to pay the highest amount above the appraised market value of the property.
	Payment method		Some municipalities may finance the purchase of tax deeds at a rate of 10% per annum for up to ten years.
	Interest rate	N/A	

	STATE		
	Redemption period	N/A	The property owner loses title to the property as a result of foreclosure; however, the property owner may make application to repurchase the property. The municipality uses its own discretion in determining whether to accept or reject the application.
	Over the counter	Yes	
	Municipalities	87	Aitkin – www.co.aitkin.mn.us Anoka – www.co.anoka.mn.us Becker – www.co.becker.mn.us Beltrami – www.co.beltrami.mn.us Benton – www.co.benton.mn.us Big Stone – www.bigstonecounty.org Blue Earth – www.co.blue-earth.mn.us Brown – www.co.brown.mn.us Carlton – www.co.carlton.mn.us Carver – www.co.carver.mn.us Cass – www.co.cass.mn.us Chippewa – www.co.chippewa.mn.us Chisago – www.co.chisago.mn.us Clay – www.co.clay.mn.us Clearwater – www.co.clearwater.mn.us Cook – http://www.co.cook.mn.us/index.php/doing-business/public-sale-of-tax-forfeited-land Cottonwood – www.co.cottonwood.mn.us Crow Wing – www.co.crow-wing.mn.us Dakota – www.co.dakota.mn.us Dodge – www.co.dodge.mn.us Douglas – www.co.douglas.mn.us Faribault – www.co.faribault.mn.us Fillmore – www.co.fillmore.mn.us Freeborn – www.co.freeborn.mn.us Goodhue – www.co.goodhue.mn.us Grant – www.co.grant.mn.us Hennepin – www.co.hennepin.mn.us Houston – www.houstoncounty.govoffice2.com Hubbard – http://co.hubbard.mn.us Isanti – www.co.isanti.mn.us Itasca – www.co.itasca.mn.us/Home/Pages Jackson – www.co.jackson.mn.us Kanabec – www.kanabeccounty.org Kandiyohi – www.co.kandiyohi.mn.us Kittson – www.visitnwminnesota.com/Kittson.htm Koochiching – www.co.koochiching.mn.us Lac qui Parle – www.lqpco.com Lake – www.co.lake.mn.us Lake of the Woods – www.co.lake-of-the-woods.mn.us Le Sueur – www.co.le-sueur.mn.us Lincoln – www.lincolncounty-mn.us

	STATE		
			Lyon – **www.lyonco.org**
			Mahnomen – **www.co.mahnomen.mn.us**
			Marshall – **www.co.marshall.mn.us**
			Martin – **www.co.martin.mn.us**
			McLeod – **www.co.mcleod.mn.us**
			Meeker – **www.co.meeker.mn.us**
			Mille Lacs – **www.co.mille-lacs.mn.us**
			Morrison – **www.co.morrison.mn.us**
			Mower – **www.co.mower.mn.us**
			Murray – no website
			Nicollet – **www.co.nicollet.mn.us**
			Nobles – **www.co.nobles.mn.us**
			Norman – **www.co.norman.mn.us**
			Olmsted – **www.co.olmsted.mn.us/Pages/default.aspx**
			Otter Tail – **www.co.otter-tail.mn.us**
			Pennington – **http://co.pennington.mn.us**
			Pine – **www.co.pine.mn.us**
			Pipestone – **www.pipestone-county.com**
			Polk – **www.co.polk.mn.us**
			Pope – **www.co.pope.mn.us**
			Ramsey – **www.co.ramsey.mn.us/home**
			Red Lake – **www.visitnwminnesota.com/RedLake.htm**
			Redwood – **www.co.redwood.mn.us**
			Renville – **www.co.renville.mn.us**
			Rice – **www.co.rice.mn.us**
			Rock – **www.co.rock.mn.us**
			Roseau – **www.co.roseau.mn.us**
			Scott – **www.co.scott.mn.us/Pages/home.aspx**
			Sherburne – **www.co.sherburne.mn.us**
			Sibley – **www.co.sibley.mn.us**
			St. Louis – **www.stlouiscountymn.gov**
			Stearns – **www.co.stearns.mn.us**
			Steele – **www.co.steele.mn.us**
			Stevens – **www.co.stevens.mn.us**
			Swift – **www.swiftcounty.com**
			Todd – **www.co.todd.mn.us**
			Traverse – **www.co.traverse.mn.us**
			Wabasha – **www.co.wabasha.mn.us**
			Wadena – **www.co.wadena.mn.us**
			Waseca – **www.co.waseca.mn.us**
			Washington – **www.co.washington.mn.us**
			Watonwan – **www.co.watonwan.mn.us**
			Wilkin – **www.co.wilkin.mn.us**
			Winona – no website
			Wright – **www.co.wright.mn.us**
			Yellow Medicine – **http://co.ym.mn.gov**
	Statute	Minnesota Statutes	Sections 281, 282

	STATE		
	Mississipi		
24	Type of sale	Tax lien	Receipt showing the amount paid
	Sale date	Last Monday in August	The tax sale listing must be published in a local newspaper or posted for two weeks.
	Bid method	Premium bid	Interest upon redemption is only applied to the opening bid amount. Redemption does not allow a refund of the premium amount or interest on the premium amount.
	Payment method	Cash, certified check, money order or cashier's check	
	Interest rate	18% per annum plus 5% penalty	The 5% penalty is applied only once, in the first year of redemption. If the tax sale is found to have occurred in error, the investor receives a refund of the amount of the purchase with 18% interest and 5% penalty.
	Redemption period	2 years	The premium amount is refunded to the tax lien certificate holder.
	Subsequent taxes		
	Foreclosure		Tax deeds must be requested upon expiration of the redemption period. The investor is provided a deed with title and immediate possession of the property.
	Over the counter	No	
	Municipalities	82	Adams – www.adamscountyms.net/elected-officials/tax-collector Alcorn – http://alcorncounty.org/collector.aspx Amite – www.amitecounty.ms/elected-offices/tax Attala – www.attalacounty.net/elected-offices/tax-collector Benton – no website Bolivar – www.co.bolivar.ms.us/taxassessor.htm Calhoun – no website Carroll – www.carrollcountyms.com/electedofficials.htm#taxcollector Chickasaw – www.chickasawcoms.com Choctaw – no website Claiborne – http://claibornecountyms.org/info.htm Clarke – no website Clay – http://claycountyms.com/elected-offices/tax Coahoma – www.coahomacounty.net/taxassessor.html Copiah – www.copiahcounty.org/Tax%20Collector.htm Covington – no website Desoto – http://desotoms.com/officials/tax-assessor Forrest – http://forrestcountyms.us/main/index.php?option=com_content&task=view&id=59

	STATE	
		Franklin – www.franklincountyms.com/welcome.html
George – no website
Greene – no website
Grenada – www.tscmaps.com/mg/ms/grenada
Hancock – www.hancockcountyms.gov/assessor.htm
Harrison – www.co.harrison.ms.us/elected/taxassessor/mapping.asp
Hinds – www.co.hinds.ms.us/pgs/elected/taxcollector.asp
Holmes – no website
Humphreys – no website
Issaquena – no website
Itawamba – no website
Jackson – www.co.jackson.ms.us/officials/tax-collector
Jasper – www.co.jasper.ms.us/tax_assessor.html
Jefferson – no website
Jefferson Davis – no website
Jones – www.co.jones.ms.us/taxcollect.php
Kemper – no website
Lafayette – www.lafayettecoms.com
Lamar – www.lamarcounty.com/11
Lauderdale – www.lauderdalecounty.org/officerservices/tax_collector.htm
Lawrence – www.tscmaps.com/mg/ms/lawrence
Leake – www.leakeida.com/1RP109.html
Lee – www.tscmaps.com/mg/ms/lee
Leflore – www.lefloretax.com
Lincoln – no website
Lowndes – www.lowndesassessor.com
Madison – http://madison-co.com/elected_offices/tax_collector
Marion – www.marioncounty-ms.us/contact.html
Marshall – no website
Monroe – http://monroecountyms.org/tax_collector.htm
Montgomery – http://montgomerycountyms.com
Neshoba – www.neshobacounty.net/elected-offices/tax-collector
Newton – no website
Noxubee – no website
Oktibbeha – http://tscmaps.com/mg/ms/oktibbeha
Panola – www.panolacoms.com
Pearl River – www.pearlrivercounty.net/tax
Perry – no website
Pike – www.co.pike.ms.us/tax.html
Pontotoc – no website
Prentiss – no website
Quitman – no website
Rankin – www.rankincounty.org/tc

STATE		
		Scott – no website
Sharkey – no website
Simpson – www.simpsontax.com
Smith – www.smithcounty.ms.gov/tax_collector.html
Stone – www.stonecounty.com
Sunflower – no website
Tallahatchie – no website
Tate – no website
Tippah – no website
Tishomingo – no website
Tunica – www.tunicamaps.com
Union – no website
Walthall – no website
Warren – www.co.warren.ms.us/Tax/tax_Collector.htm
Washington – http://washingtoncountyms.us/tax_collector.html
Wayne – no website
Webster – www.webstercountymo.gov/pages/collectors_office
Wilkinson – no website
Winston – www.winstonassessor.com
Yalobusha – no website
Yazoo – no website
Statute	Mississippi Code of 1972	Amended Sections 27-41-55, 59 27-45-3
Missouri		
25	Type of sale	Tax lien	Certificate of purchase
	Sale date	August, fourth Monday	The tax sale listing is published two to three weeks before the tax sale.
	Bid method	Bid up ownership	Bidding is limited to residents of the particular municipality only. Nonresidents must designate a resident of the particular municipality to act as a resident agent on their behalf and bid at the tax sale.
	Payment method	Cash, certified check, or cashier's check	Payment is required immediately upon winning the bid, or a penalty may be imposed on the purchaser.
	Interest rate	10% per annum	An 8% Interest rate is applied to subsequent taxes paid by the lien certificate holder.
	Redemption period	2 years	The lien certificate holder must apply for a tax deed within six months of the expiration of the redemption period.
	Over the counter	No	
	Municipalities	114	Adair – no website
Andrew – www.andrewcounty.org
Atchison – www.atchisoncounty.org/index.php/county-goverment-andcourthouse

	STATE		
			Audrain – **http://audraincounty.org**
Barry – **http://barrycountycollector.com**
Barton – no website
Bates – **www.batescounty.net**
Benton – **www.bentoncountycollector.com/delinquent.php**
Bollinger – no website
Boone – **www.showmeboone.com/COLLECTOR**
Buchanan – **www.co.buchanan.mo.us/offices/collector/index.html**
Butler – no website
Caldwell – no website
Callaway – **www.callawaycollector.com/Events.aspx**
Camden – **www.camdenmo.org/collector/delinquent-taxsales.htm**
Cape Girardeau – **www.capecounty.us**
Carroll – no website
Carter – no website
Cass – **www.casscounty.com/collector/delinqtax.html**
Cedar – no website
Charlton – no website
Christian – **www.christiancountycollector.com**
Clark – no website
Clay – **www.claycountymo.gov/taxsale**
Clinton – no website
Cole – **www.colecountycollector.org/collector.htm?id=108&cat=2**
Cooper – **www.coopercountymo.org/coopercounty%20goverment.htm**
Crawford – **http://crawfordcountymo.net**
Dade – no website
Dallas – no website
Daviess – no website
DeKalb – **www.dekalbcountymo.org/ElectedOfficials.aspx**
Dent – no website
Douglas – no website
Dunklin – no website
Franklin – **www.franklinmo.org**
Gasconade – **www.gscnd.com/government.html**
Gentry – no website
Greene – **www.greenecountymo.org/spane/taxsale2.htm**
Grundy – **www.grundycountymo.com/collector.php**
Harrison – no website
Henry – **http://henrycomo.com/treasurer_collector.htm**
Hickory – no website
Holt – no website

STATE	
	Howard – no website
	Howell – www.howellcounty.net/directory.php
	Iron – no website
	Jackson – www.jacksongov.org/content/3310/3324
	Jasper – www.jaspercountycollector.com
	Jefferson – www.jeffcomo.org/Collector.aspx?nodeID=collector
	Johnson – www.jcmtax.com/DelinquentTaxSale.php
	Knox – www.knoxcountymo.org/index.cgi
	Laclede – www.lacledecountymissouri.org
	Lafayette – www.lafayettecountycollector.com
	Lawrence – no website
	Lewis – no website
	Lincoln – www.co.lincoln.or.us/treasurer
	Linn – no website
	Livingston – www.livingstoncountymo.com/treasurer.htm
	Macon – http://maconcountymo.com/Government/Collector/tabid/81/language/en-US/Default.aspx
	Madison – http://madisoncountymo.us
	Marion – no website
	Maries – no website
	McDonald – http://mcdonaldcountygov.com/depts/collector.html
	Mercer – no website
	Miller – http://millercountymissouri.org/collector.html
	Mississippi – www.misscomo.net/countyofficeindex/collector.html
	Moniteau – no website
	Monroe – no website
	Montgomery – no website
	Morgan – www.morgan-county.org
	New Madrid – www.new-madrid.mo.us/index.aspx?NID=38
	Newton – www.newtoncountycollector.com
	Nodaway – www.nodawaycountymo.com/content/view/35/47
	Oregon – no website
	Osage – http://osagecountygov.com/Osage-County-Missouri/collector-of-revenue
	Ozark – no website
	Pemiscot – no website
	Perry – http://perrycountymo.us/index.aspx?nid=254
	Pettis – www.pettiscomo.com/coll.html
	Phelps – www.phelpscounty.org/collector/delinquent-taxcertificatesale.htm

	STATE		
			Pike – **www.pikecountymo.org/courthouse.htm#Collector**
Platte – **www.co.platte.mo.us**
Polk – no website
Pulaski – **www.pulaskicollector.com/page5.html**
Putnam – no website
Ralls – no website
Randolph – **www.randolphcounty-mo.com**
Ray – no website
Reynolds – no website
Ripley – no website
Saline – no website
Schuyler – no website
Scotland – no website
Scott – **www.scottcountymo.com/collector.html**
Shannon – no website
Shelby – no website
St. Charles – **http://collector.sccmo.org/collector**
St. Clair – **http://stclaircountymissouri.com/stclaircountymissouricomcollectorofrevenuecom.aspx**
St. Francois – **www.sfcgov.org/Collector.html**
Ste. Genevieve – **www.stegencounty.org**
St. Louis City – **http://stlcin.missouri.org/collector**
St. Louis County – **www.co.st-louis.mo.us**
Stoddard – no website
Stone – **www.stoneco-mo.us**
Sullivan – no website
Taney – **www.co.taney.mo.us/cgi-bin/County/index.cgi?department=10**
Texas – **www.texascountymissouri.org/collector_treasurer.html**
Vernon – **www.vernoncountymo.org/?page_id=23**
Warren – **www.warrencountymo.org**
Washington – **www.washingtoncountymo.org**
Wayne – no website
Webster – **http://www.webstercountymo.gov/**
Worth – **www.worthcounty.us**
Wright – no website
	Statute	Missouri Revised Statutes	140
	Montana		
26	Type of sale	Tax lien	
	Sale date	July	The tax sale listing must be published in a local newspaper or public place for three weeks, beginning no later than the last Monday in June
	Bid method	Random or rotational	

	STATE		
	Payment method	Cash	Payment is required on the day of the sale.
	Interest rate	10% per annum plus 2% penalty	
	Redemption period	3 years	A tax deed is granted to the lien certificate holder upon expiration of the redemption period. The tax deed must then be recorded.
	Over the counter	Yes	
	Municipalities	57	Beaverhead – www.beaverheadcounty.org Big Horn – http://bighorn.mt.gov Blaine – http://co.blaine.mt.gov Broadwater – no website Carbon – www.co.carbon.mt.us Carter – www.cartercountymt.info Cascade – www.co.cascade.mt.us Chouteau – www.co.chouteau.mt.us Custer – no website Daniels – no website Dawson – www.dawsoncountymontana.org Deer Lodge – www.anacondadeerlodge.mt.gov Fallon – http://falloncounty.net Fergus – www.co.fergus.mt.us Flathead – http://flathead.mt.gov Gallatin – www.gallatin.mt.gov/Public_Documents/index Garfield – no website Glacier – www.glaciercountygov.com Golden Valley – www.co.golden-valley.mt.us Granite – www.co.granite.mt.us Hill – http://co.hill.mt.us Jefferson – www.jeffco.mt.gov Judith Basin – http://co.judith-basin.mt.us Lake – www.lakecounty-mt.org Lewis and Clark – www.co.lewis-clark.mt.us Liberty – http://co.liberty.mt.us Lincoln – www.lincolncountymt.us Madison – http://madison.mt.gov McCone – www.mccone.mt.gov Meagher – no website Mineral – http://co.mineral.mt.us Missoula – www.co.missoula.mt.us Musselshell – no website Park – www.parkcounty.org Petroleum – www.petroleumcountymt.com Phillips – no website

	STATE		
			Pondera – www.ponderacountymontana.org
Powder River – http://prco.mt.gov
Powell – www.powellcountymt.gov
Prairie – http://prairie.mt.gov
Ravalli – http://rc.mt.gov/default.mcpx
Richland – www.richland.org
Roosevelt – no website
Rosebud – www.rosebudmontana.com
Sanders – www.sanderscounty.mt.gov
Sheridan – www.co.sheridan.mt.us
Silver Bow – http://co.silverbow.mt.us
Stillwater – www.stillwater.mt.gov
Sweet Grass – www.co.sweetgrass.mt.us
Teton – www.tetoncomt.org/inside.aspx
Toole – www.toolecountymt.gov
Treasure – no website
Valley – http://valleycountymt.net
Wheatland – no website
Wibaux – no website
Yellowstone – www.co.yellowstone.mt.gov
	Statute	Montana Code	Annotated Sections 15-16-102; 15-18-211 through 216
	Nebraska		
27	Type of sale	Tax lien	Certificate of purchase, certificate of sale or tax certificate
	Sale date	March, first Monday	The tax sale listing must be compiled between four and six weeks before the tax sale date. The listing must be published weekly for three consecutive weeks.
	Bid method	Bid down ownership or rotational	The tax lien holder is required to pay subsequent taxes on the securing property. The amounts are added to the tax lien amount.
	Payment method	Payment methods are determined by the particular municipality	Payment is required on the day of the sale.
	Interest rate	14% per annum	
	Redemption period	3 years	A tax lien certificate holder must serve notice to the property owner of the intent to foreclose the right to redemption three months before making application for a tax deed.
	Over the counter	Yes	
	Municipalities	93	Adams – www.adamscounty.org
Antelope – www.co.antelope.ne.us
Arthur – no website
Banner – www.bannercounty-gov.us

STATE	
	Blaine – www.blainecounty.ne.gov
	Boone – www.co.boone.ne.us
	Box Butte – www.co.box-butte.ne.us
	Boyd – no website
	Brown – www.co.brown.ne.us
	Buffalo – www.buffalocounty.ne.gov
	Burt – www.burtcounty.ne.gov
	Butler – www.co.butler.ne.us
	Cass – www.cassne.org
	Cedar – www.co.cedar.ne.us
	Chase – www.co.chase.ne.us
	Cherry – www.co.cherry.ne.us
	Cheyenne – www.co.cheyenne.ne.us
	Clay – www.claycounty.ne.gov
	Colfax – www.colfaxcounty.ne.gov
	Cuming – http://cumingcounty.ne.gov
	Custer – www.co.custer.ne.us
	Dakota – www.dakotacountyne.org
	Dawes – www.co.dawes.ne.us
	Dawson – www.dawsoncone.com
	Deuel – www.co.deuel.ne.us
	Dixon – www.co.dixon.ne.us
	Dodge – www.dodgecounty.ne.gov
	Douglas – www.douglascounty-ne.gov
	Dundy – www.co.dundy.ne.us
	Fillmore – www.fillmorecounty.org
	Franklin – www.co.franklin.ne.us
	Frontier – www.co.frontier.ne.us
	Furnas – www.furnascounty.ne.gov
	Gage – www.gagecountynebraska.us
	Garden – www.co.garden.ne.us
	Garfield – www.garfieldcounty.ne.gov
	Gosper – www.co.gosper.ne.us
	Grant – no website
	Greeley – www.greeleycounty.ne.gov
	Hall – www.hcgi.org
	Hamilton – www.co.hamilton.ne.us
	Harlan – no website
	Hayes – www.hayescounty.ne.gov
	Hitchcock – www.co.hitchcock.ne.us
	Holt – www.co.holt.ne.us
	Hooker – www.co.hooker.ne.us
	Howard – www.howardcounty.ne.gov
	Jefferson – www.co.jefferson.ne.us
	Johnson – www.co.johnson.ne.us
	Kearney – www.kearneycounty.ne.gov
	Keith – www.co.keith.ne.us
	Keya Paha – www.co.keya-paha.ne.us

	STATE		
			Kimball – www.co.kimball.ne.us
			Knox – www.co.knox.ne.us
			Lancaster – www.lincoln.ne.gov
			Lincoln – www.co.lincoln.ne.us
			Logan – no website
			Loup – www.co.loup.ne.us
			Madison – www.co.madison.ne.us
			McPherson – no website
			Merrick – www.merrickcounty.ne.gov
			Morrill – www.co.morrill.ne.us
			Nance – www.co.nance.ne.us
			Nemaha – www.nemahacounty.ne.gov
			Nuckolls – www.nuckollscounty.ne.gov
			Otoe – www.co.otoe.ne.us
			Pawnee – www.co.pawnee.ne.us
			Perkins – www.co.perkins.ne.us
			Phelps – www.justtheplacenebraska.com
			Pierce – www.co.pierce.ne.us
			Platte – www.plattecounty.net
			Polk – www.polkcounty.ne.gov
			Red Willow – www.co.red-willow.ne.us
			Richardson – www.co.richardson.ne.us
			Rock – www.rockcounty.ne.gov
			Saline – www.co.saline.ne.us
			Sarpy – www.sarpy.com
			Saunders – www.saunderscounty.ne.gov
			Scotts Bluff – www.scottsbluffcounty.org
			Seward – http://connectseward.org/cgov
			Sheridan – www.sheridancountynebraska.com
			Sherman – www.co.sherman.ne.us
			Sioux – www.co.sioux.ne.us
			Stanton – www.co.stanton.ne.us
			Thayer – www.thayercounty.ne.gov
			Thomas – www.thomascountynebraska.us
			Thurston – www.thurstoncountynebraska.us
			Valley – www.co.valley.ne.us
			Washington – www.co.washington.ne.us
			Wayne – www.waynecountyne.org
			Webster – www.co.webster.ne.us
			Wheeler – www.wheelercounty.ne.gov
			York – www.yorkcounty.ne.gov
	Statute	Revised Statutes of Nebraska	Sections 77-1807, 1824
	Nevada		
28	Type of sale	Tax deed	The tax sale is a public oral-bid foreclosure sale of real estate.

	STATE		
	Sale date	Varies by municipality	
	Bid method	Premium bid	
	Payment method		
	Interest rate	12%	
	Redemption period	120 days 2 years	The Redemption period is 120 days for vacant properties and two years for developed properties
	Over the counter	No	
	Municipalities	17	Carson City – www.carson.org/Index.aspx?page=1 Churchill – www.churchillcounty.org Clark – www.clarkcountynv.gov Douglas – www.douglascountynv.gov/sites/main Elko – www.elkocountynv.net Esmeralda – www.accessesmeralda.com Eureka – www.co.eureka.nv.us Humboldt – www.hcnv.us Lander – http://landercountynv.org Lincoln – www.lincolncountynv.org Lyon – www.lyon-county.org Mineral – no website Nye – www.co.nye.nv.us Pershing – http://pershingcounty.net Storey – www.storeycounty.org Washoe – www.co.washoe.nv.us White Pine – www.whitepinecounty.net
	Statute	Nevada Revised Statutes	Sections 361.590-595
	New Hampshire		
29	Type of sale	Tax lien	Tax lien
	Sale date	Varies by municipality	The tax sale listing must be published in at least two places, at least 25 days before the tax sale.
	Bid method	Bid down ownership	The tax lien certificate purchaser is required to notify any mortgage holders of record of the purchase of the certificate before the tax sale is considered valid.
	Payment method		Payment is required immediately upon winning the bid.
	Interest rate	18%	
	Redemption period	2 years	Partial payments are allowed for redemption in multiples of $5. Part owners may redeem only their share of the redemption amount.

	STATE		
	Subsequent taxes	Optional	The tax lien holder must notify mortgage holders of record of the payment within 30 days of the making the payment. Subsequent taxes incur interest at a rate of 18%.
	Foreclosure		The lien certificate holder must apply for a tax deed at the expiration of the redemption period. The tax lien holder must serve notice of the lien purchase to the property owner, mortgage company, or other entity with a security interest in the property by certified mail. If the tax lien certificate is still not redeemed within 30 days, a deed is issued to the purchaser. The statute of limitations to contest the tax sale and tax deed is ten years.
	Over the counter	No	
	Municipalities	10	Belknap – www.belknapcounty.org/Pages/index Carroll – www.carrollcountynh.net Cheshire – www.co.cheshire.nh.us Coos – www.cooscountynh.us Grafton – www.co.grafton.nh.us Hillsborough – www.hillsboroughcountynh.org Merrimack – www.merrimackcounty.net Rockingham – www.co.rockingham.nh.us Strafford – www.co.strafford.nh.us Sullivan – www.sullivancountynh.gov
	Statute	New Hampshire Revised Statutes	Annotated Section 80:24
	New Jersey		
30	Type of sale	Tax lien	Certificate of purchase or certificate of tax sale
	Sale date	Varies by municipality	The tax sale must be published in a local newspaper for four weeks before the sale and posted in five of the most public places of the municipality.
	Bid method	Bid down interest or premium bid	If the Interest rate is bid down to less than 1%, the bidders then may engage in the bidding up of premiums on the lien amount.
	Payment method		Payment is required immediately upon winning the bid.
	Interest rate	18% per annum plus 2% to 6% penalty	

STATE		

Redemption period	2 years	The purchase of a tax lien certificate must be recorded within three months of the tax sale in order for the lien certificate to be considered valid. If the tax lien certificate is redeemed, the property owner is required to pay the following:
		- Within ten days: cost of lien certificate and 18% interest.
		- After ten days: cost of lien certificate, 18% interest, and subsequent municipal liens plus penalty on the redemption amount as:
		  2%, if the redemption amount is in excess of $200
		  4%, if the redemption amount is over $5,000
		  6%, if the redemption amount is over $10,000
		The redemption period is two years, provided the property owner is provided written notice of the right to redemption within 18 months of the sale date. If the notice is served after the expiration of 18 months, the redemption period is six months from the date of the notice.

Subsequent taxes	Optional	The lien holder is not required to make subsequent tax payments. Newly assessed and delinquent taxes will cause a new tax lien certificate to be offered for sale.
Foreclosure	Within 20 years	After 20 years, no further action can be taken upon the foreclosure, except when the tax lien certificate holder pays the subsequent taxes. The foreclosure period extends for as long as taxes continue to be paid. Upon expiration of the redemption period, the holder of a valid lien certificate may obtain a deed of conveyance, which indicates that all procedures have been followed with regard to redemption. The investor must issue a 30-day notice of the intent to foreclose. The investor must initiate a judicial foreclosure of the property owner's right of redemption.
Over the counter	Yes	Unsold tax lien certificates are sold at auction at a private sale or public auction for not less than the cost of the lien. If the tax lien is valued at an amount that is more than the assessed value of the property, the tax lien certificate is sold at the assessed value of the property, unless by resolution, the municipality allows the lien certificate to be sold for less than the assessed value.
Municipalities	21	Atlantic – www.aclink.org Bergen – www.co.bergen.nj.us Burlington – www.co.burlington.nj.us Camden – www.camdencounty.com Cape May – www.capemaycountygov.net Cumberland – www.co.cumberland.nj.us/content/161 Essex – www.essex-countynj.org Gloucester – www.co.gloucester.nj.us Hudson – www.hudsoncountynj.org Hunterdon – www.co.hunterdon.nj.us Mercer – www.state.nj.us/counties/mercer/about

	STATE		
			Middlesex – **www.co.middlesex.nj.us**
			Monmouth – **http://www.co.monmouth.nj.us**
			Morris – **www.co.morris.nj.us/generalHTML/generalinfo.asp**
			Ocean – **www.oceancountygov.com/governmt.htm**
			Passaic – **www.passaiccountynj.org**
			Salem – **www.salemcountynj.gov/cmssite**
			Somerset – **www.co.somerset.nj.us/government.html**
			Sussex – **www.sussex.nj.us/index.cfm**
			Union – **http://ucnj.org**
			Warren – **www.co.warren.nj.us/About.html**
	Statute	New Jersey Code	Annotated Sections 54:5-32, 54
	New Mexico		
31	Type of sale	Tax deed	Real property is offered for sale subject to any encumbrances on the property, such as outstanding mortgages.
	Sale date	Varies by municipality	
	Bid method	Premium bid	
	Payment method		
	Interest rate	N/A	
	Redemption period	N/A	The tax lien certificate does not represent a priority lien.
	Over the counter	No	
	Municipalities	33	State website – **www.tax.newmexico.gov/About-Us/Property-Tax-Division/Delinquent-Property-Tax-Bureau/Pages/Upcoming-Auctions.aspx**
Bernalillo – no website
Catron – **https://mylocalgov.com/catroncountynm**
Chaves – **www.co.chaves.nm.us**
Cibola – **www.co.cibola.nm.us**
Colfax – **www.co.colfax.nm.us**
Curry – **https://mylocalgov.com/currycountynm**
Debaca – no website
Doña Ana – **www.co.dona-ana.nm.us**
Eddy – **www.co.eddy.nm.us**
Grant – **www.grantcountynm.com**
Guadalupe – no website
Harding – no website
Hidalgo – **www.hidalgocounty.org**
Lea – **www.leacounty.net**
Lincoln – **www.lincolncountynm.net**
Los Alamos – **www.losalamosnm.us/Pages**
Luna – **www.lunacountynm.us**

	STATE		
			McKinley – www.co.mckinley.nm.us
Mora – www.countyofmora.com
Otero – no website
Quay – www.quaycounty-nm.gov
Rio Arriba – www.rio-arriba.org
Roosevelt – www.rooseveltcounty.com
San Juan – www.sjcounty.net
San Miguel – www.smcounty.net
Sandoval – www.sandovalcounty.com
Santa Fe – www.santafecounty.org
Sierra – www.sierracountynm.gov
Socorro – http://sites.google.com/site/socorrocounty intranet
Taos – www.taoscounty.org
Torrance – www.torrancecountynm.org
Union – no website
Valencia – www.co.valencia.nm.us
	Statute	New Mexico Statutes	Annotated Chapter 7, articles 38-38
	New York		
32	Type of sale	Deed	Tax lien certificate or tax lien
	Sale date	Varies by municipality, often April or August	The city of New York is allowed to offer the sale of tax lien certificates, but does not sell to the public. Nassau county also conducts lien sales.
	Bid method	Premium bid	
	Payment method		
	Interest rate	14%	
	Redemption period	1 year	
	Over the counter	No	
	Municipalities	62	Albany – www.albanycounty.com
Allegany – www.alleganyco.com
Bronx – no website
Broome – www.gobroomecounty.com
Cattaraugus – www.co.cattaraugus.ny.us
Cayuga – www.co.cayuga.ny.us
Chautauqua – www.chautauqua-ny.com/pages
Chemung – www.chemungcounty.com
Chenango – www.co.chenango.ny.us
Clinton – www.clintoncountygov.com
Columbia – www.columbiacountyny.com
Cortland – www.cortland-co.org
Delaware – www.co.delaware.ny.us

STATE	
	Dutchess – **www.dutchessny.gov**
	Erie – **www2.erie.gov**
	Essex – **www.co.essex.ny.us**
	Franklin – **http://franklincony.org/content**
	Fulton – **www.fultoncountyny.gov**
	Genesee – **www.co.genesee.ny.us**
	Greene – **www.greenegovernment.com**
	Hamilton – **www.hamiltoncounty.com**
	Herkimer – **http://herkimercounty.org/content**
	Jefferson – **www.co.jefferson.ny.us**
	Kings – **www.countyofkings.com**
	Lewis – **http://lewiscountyny.org/content**
	Livingston – **www.co.livingston.state.ny.us**
	Madison – **www.madisoncounty.org**
	Monroe – **www.monroecounty.gov**
	Montgomery – **www.co.montgomery.ny.us**
	Nassau – **www.nassaucountyny.gov**
	New York – no website
	New York City – **www.nyc.gov/html/dof/html/property/property_bill_taxlien.shtml**
	Niagara – **www.niagaracounty.com**
	Oneida – **http://ocgov.net**
	Onondaga – **http://ongov.net**
	Ontario – **www.co.ontario.ny.us**
	Orange – **www.co.orange.ny.us**
	Orleans – **www.orleansny.com**
	Oswego – **www.co.oswego.ny.us**
	Otsego – **www.otsegocounty.com**
	Putnam – **www.putnamcountyny.com**
	Queens – no website
	Rensselaer – **www.rensco.com**
	Richmond – no website
	Rockland – **www.co.rockland.ny.us**
	Saratoga – **www.saratogacountyny.gov**
	Schenectady – **www.schenectadycounty.com**
	Schoharie – no website
	Schuyler – **www.schuylercounty.us**
	Seneca – **www.co.seneca.ny.us**
	St. Lawrence – **www.co.st-lawrence.ny.us**
	Steuben – **www.steubencony.org**
	Suffolk – **www.suffolkcountyny.gov**
	Sullivan – **http://co.sullivan.ny.us**
	Tioga – **www.tiogacountyny.com**
	Tompkins – **www.tompkins-co.org**
	Ulster – **www.co.ulster.ny.us**
	Warren – **www.co.warren.ny.us**
	Washington – **http://co.washington.ny.us**
	Wayne – **www.co.wayne.ny.us**

	STATE		
			Westchester – www3.westchestergov.com Wyoming – www.wyomingco.net/Welcome.html Yates – www.yatescounty.org
	Statute	Uniform Delinquent Tax Enforcement Act	
	North Carolina		
33	Type of sale	Deed	The tax sale is a public oral-bid foreclosure sale of real estate.
	Sale date	Varies by municipality	Any person taking exception or claiming an irregularity of the tax sale may challenge the sale within ten days of the commissioner reporting foreclosure sales to the court. Also, anyone who wishes to increase the amount that was accepted at bid may file court action to increase the bid. This process is termed an upset bid. The upset bid must increase the bid amount by the maximum of $25 or 10% of the first $1,000 PLUS 5% of the excess above $1,000. The court will negate the first tax sale purchase and order a "resale" of the property.
	Bid method	Premium bid	
	Payment method		
	Interest rate	N/A	
	Redemption period	N/A	But North Carolina allows "upset bids" within ten days of the sale, which could overturn the sale.
	Over the counter	No	
	Municipalities	100	Alamance – www.alamance-nc.com Alexander – www.alexandercountync.gov Alleghany – www.alleghanycounty-nc.gov Anson – www.co.anson.nc.us Ashe – www.ashecountygov.com Avery – www.averycountync.gov Beaufort – www.co.beaufort.nc.us Bertie – www.co.bertie.nc.us Bladen – www.bladeninfo.org Brunswick – www.brunsco.net Buncombe – www.buncombecounty.org Burke – www.co.burke.nc.us Cabarrus – www.cabarruscounty.us/Pages Caldwell – www.caldwellcountync.org Camden – http://camdencountync.besavvy2.egovlink.com Carteret – www.carteretcountygov.org

	STATE		
			Caswell – www.caswellcountync.gov
Catawba – www.catawbacountync.gov
Chatham – www.chathamnc.org
Cherokee – www.cherokeecounty-nc.gov
Chowan – www.chowancounty-nc.gov
Clay – www.clayconc.com
Cleveland – www.clevelandcounty.com/ccmain
Columbus – www.columbusco.org
Craven – www.cravencountync.gov
Cumberland – www.co.cumberland.nc.us
Currituck – www.co.currituck.nc.us
Dare – www.co.dare.nc.us
Davidson – www.co.davidson.nc.us
Davie – www.co.davie.nc.us
Duplin – www.duplincountync.com
Durham – www.co.durham.nc.us
Edgecombe – www.edgecombecountync.gov
Forsyth – www.co.forsyth.nc.us
Franklin – www.franklincountync.us
Gaston – www.gastontax.com
Gates – www.gatescounty.govoffice2.com
Graham – www.grahamcounty.org
Granville – http://granvillenc.govoffice2.com
Greene – www.co.greene.nc.us
Guilford – http://countyweb.co.guilford.nc.us
Halifax – www.halifaxnc.com
Harnett – www.harnett.org
Haywood – www.haywoodnc.net
Henderson – www.hendersoncountync.org
Hertford – www.hertfordcountync.gov
Hoke – www.hokecounty.org
Hyde – www.hydecountync.gov
Iredell – www.co.iredell.nc.us
Jackson – www.jacksonnc.org
Johnston – www.johnstonnc.com
Jones – www.co.jones.nc.us
Lee – http://leecountync.gov
Lenoir – www.co.lenoir.nc.us
Lincoln – www.lincolncounty.org
Macon – http://maconnc.org
Madison – www.madisoncountync.org
Martin – www.martincountycgov.com
McDowell – www.mcdowellgov.com
Mecklenburg – http://charmeck.org/Pages/default.aspx
Mitchell – www.mitchellcounty.org
Montgomery – www.montgomerycountync.com
Moore – www.moorecountync.gov
Nash – www.co.nash.nc.us

	STATE		
			New Hanover – www.nhcgov.com/Pages Northampton – www.northamptonnc.com Onslow – www.onslowcountync.gov Orange – www.co.orange.nc.us Pamlico – www.pamlicocounty.org Pasquotank – www.co.pasquotank.nc.us Pender – www.pendercountync.gov Perquimans – www.perquimanscountync.gov Person – www.personcounty.net Pitt – www.pittcountync.gov Polk – www.polknc.org Randolph – www.co.randolph.nc.us Richmond – www.richmondnc.com Robeson – www.co.robeson.nc.us Rockingham – www.co.rockingham.nc.us Rowan – www.rowancountync.gov Rutherford – www.rutherfordcountync.gov Sampson – www.sampsonnc.com Scotland – www.scotlandcounty.org Stanly – www.co.stanly.nc.us Stokes – www.co.stokes.nc.us Surry – www.co.surry.nc.us Swain – www.swaincountync.gov Transylvania – www.transylvaniacounty.org Tyrrell – www.visittyrrellcounty.com/Government Union – www.co.union.nc.us Vance – www.vancecounty.com Wake – www.wakegov.com Warren – www.warrencountync.com Washington – www.washconc.org Watauga – www.wataugacounty.org Wayne – www.waynegov.com Wilkes – www.wilkescounty.net Wilson – www.wilson-co.com Yadkin – www.yadkincountync.gov Yancey – www.yanceycountync.gov
	Statute	North Carolina General Statutes	Chapter 44A
	North Dakota		
34	Type of sale	Tax lien	Tax sale certificate or certificate of sale

STATE		
Sale date	November, third Tuesday	Municipalities place liens against real property for delinquent property taxes. If the property owner does not redeem the property, the municipality may retain ownership of the property or sell the property. Notice of the tax sale must be published in the local newspaper, once each week, for two consecutive weeks and posted in at least four public places.
Bid method	Bid down interest	The board of commissioners of the particular municipality must appraise properties owned and offered for sale before the tax sale. If the appraised fair market value is more than the amount due on the property, the opening bid is set to the amount due on the property. If the appraised fair market value is less than the amount due on the property, the opening bid is fixed as determined by the board of commissioners. The property must be sold for at least the opening bid.
Payment method	Cash	The winning bidder may pay the total bid price or 25% of the bid price with the balance to paid, as set by a contractual agreement, over a period of ten years.
Interest rate	9%–12% per annum	The Interest rate upon redemption is 12% for the tax lien certificate and 9% for subsequent tax lien certificates purchased.
Redemption period	3 years	Upon expiration of the redemption period, notice of the redemption is served on the property owner, occupants of the property, mortgage holders, and others with a recorded interest in the property. If any of the parties resides out-of-state, the notice must be served by registered or certified mail, and it must be published once a week for three consecutive weeks in the local newspaper. If no redemption occurs within 90 days of serving notice, a tax deed is issued to the tax lien certificate purchaser. As an exception, individuals with mental challenges, minor children, and prisoners of war are allowed a redemption period that extends three years after the end of their disability.
Subsequent taxes	Optional	Only the purchaser of the original tax lien certificate is entitled to purchase subsequent tax lien certificates.
Foreclosure		Processes to acquire a tax deed and foreclose the right of redemption must be initiated within ten years of the tax sale.
Over the counter	Yes	Unsold tax lien certificates are offered for sale at 6% per annum interest.
Municipalities	53	Adams – no website Barnes – **www.co.barnes.nd.us** Benson – **www.bensoncountynd.com** Billings – **www.billingscountynd.gov** Bottineau – **http://botco.homestead.com** Bowman – **www.bowmannd.com/county** Burke – **www.burkecountynd.com** Burleigh – **http://burleighco.com** Cass – **www.casscountynd.gov**

STATE		
		Cavalier – www.cavaliercounty.us
Dickey – www.dickeynd.com
Divide – no website
Dunn – www.dunncountynd.org
Eddy – no website
Emmons – http://emmonscounty.tripod.com
Foster – https://mylocalgov.com/FosterCountyND
Golden Valley – www.beachnd.com
Grand Forks – http://gfcounty.nd.gov
Grant – www.grantcountynd.com
Griggs – www.griggscountynd.gov
Hettinger – no website
Kidder – no website
Lamoure – www.lamourecountynd.com
Logan – no website
McHenry – no website
Mcintosh – no website
McKenzie – www.4eyes.net
McLean – www.visitmcleancounty.com
Mercer – www.mercercountynd.com
Morton – www.co.morton.nd.us
Mountrail – no website
Nelson – www.nelsonco.org
Oliver – no website
Pembina – http://pembinacountynd.gov
Pierce – no website
Ramsey – www.co.ramsey.nd.us
Ransom – www.ransomcountynd.com
Renville – www.renvillecountynd.org
Richland – https://mylocalgov.com/richlandcountynd
Rolette – www.rolettecounty.com
Sargent – https://mylocalgov.com/SargentCountyND
Sheridan – https://mylocalgov.com/SheridanCountyND
Sioux – no website
Slope – no website
Stark – https://mylocalgov.com/starkcountynd
Steele – www.co.steele.nd.us
Stutsman – www.co.stutsman.nd.us
Towner – http://townercounty.org
Traill – www.co.traill.nd.us
Walsh – www.walshcountynd.com
Ward – www.co.ward.nd.us
Wells – https://mylocalgov.com/wellscountynd
Williams – www.williamsnd.com
	Statute	North Dakota Century Code	Chapters 57-24, 38
	Ohio		

Appendix 1: State Laws

35	STATE		
	Type of sale	Tax deed	Tax certificate or certificate
	Sale date	Varies by municipality	Counties with populations in excess of 200,000 may offer the sale of tax lien certificates. Otherwise, the tax sale is a public oral-bid foreclosure sale of real estate. The courts must confirm all sales.
	Bid method	Premium bid	The opening bid for deed sales is two-thirds of the appraised value of the property.
	Payment method		
	Interest rate	18% per annum (tax liens)	
	Redemption period	1 year 15 days (tax deeds)	Property owners may redeem property up until such time as the sale is confirmed. This usually takes about 15 days.
	Over the counter	No	
	Municipalities	88	Adams – www.adamscountyoh.com/recorder.asp Allen – www.co.allen.oh.us/treasurer Ashland – no website Ashtabula – www.co.ashtabula.oh.us/web/framesets/ElecOfils.html Athens – www.athenssheriff.com/real-estate.htm Auglaize – www2.auglaizecounty.org/elected-officials/sheriff/sales Belmont – no website Brown – no website Butler – www.butlersheriff.org/geninfo/gen_info_sheriff_sales.htm Carroll – no website Champaign – http://champaignoh.ddti.net Clark – www.clarkcountyohio.gov/sheriff/CivilSales.html Clermont – www.clermontsheriff.org/RealEstateSales.aspx Clinton – http://clintonsheriff.com/public-services/property-sales Columbiana – www.colcountysheriff.com/sales/main.htm Coshocton – www.coshcoauditor.org/Main/Home.aspx Crawford – www.crawfordcountysheriffohio.com Cuyahoga – http://sheriff.cuyahogacounty.us Darke – www.darkecountyrealestate.org Defiance – www.defiance-county.com/dcso Delaware – www.delawarecountysheriff.com/sales/sheriff_sales.htm Erie – www.erie-county-ohio.net/sheriff/salesfaq.shtml

STATE	
	Fairfield – www.sheriff.fairfield.oh.us
	Fayette – www.fayette-co-oh.com
	Franklin – http://treasurer.franklincountyohio.gov
	Fulton – www.fultoncountyoh.com/fcso/Sheriff%20Sales.htm
	Gallia – http://galliasheriff.org
	Geauga – www.sheriff.co.geauga.oh.us/Divisions/Civil/Sale.aspx
	Greene – www.co.greene.oh.us/Sheriff/SO_Foreclosures.asp
	Guernsey – www.guernseysheriff.com/geninfo/sheriffssalesfaq.html
	Hamilton – www.hamiltoncountyohio.gov/treasurer
	Hancock – www.hancocksheriff.org/sheriff2_005_sales.htm
	Hardin – www.co.hardin.oh.us
	Harrison – no website
	Henry – www.henrycountysheriff.com/Sheriff_Sales.htm
	Highland – www.highlandcoso.com/sales.htm
	Hocking – no website
	Holmes – www.holmescountysheriff.org/sheriff%20sales.htm
	Huron – no website
	Jackson – no website
	Jefferson – www.jeffersoncountyoh.com/OnLine Services/TaxSales.aspx
	Knox – www.knoxcountysheriff.com/civildivision.htm
	Lake – www.lakecountyohio.gov/LakeCountyOhio SheriffsSales/tabid/1252/Default.aspx
	Lawrence – no website
	Licking – www.lcounty.com/Treasurer/frmDelinquent Tax.aspx
	Logan – www.co.logan.oh.us/sheriff/sales.htm
	Lorain – www.loraincountysheriff.com/Page.aspx?id=148
	Lucas – www.co.lucas.oh.us/index.aspx?NID=572
	Madison – www.madisonsheriff.org/sheriffs_sales.htm
	Mahoning – www.mahoningcountyoh.gov/DepartmentsAgencies/Departments/Sheriff/TaxDollarsatWork/TaxDollarsatWorkBreakdown/tabid/1051/Default.aspx
	Marion – no website
	Medina – www.medinasheriff.com/Sheriff%20Sales.htm
	Meigs – no website
	Mercer – www.mercercountysheriff.org
	Miami – www.co.miami.oh.us
	Monroe – no website
	Montgomery – www.mcohio.org/government/treasurer/tax_lien_sale.html

Appendix 1: State Laws   **251**

	STATE		
			Morgan – no website
			Morrow – no website
			Muskingum – **www.ohiomuskingumsheriff.org/sales.htm**
			Noble – no website
			Ottawa – no website
			Paulding – **www.pauldingohsheriff.com**
			Perry – no website
			Pickaway – no website
			Pike – no website
			Portage – **www.co.portage.oh.us/sheriffsales.htm**
			Preble – **www.preblecountysheriff.org/sheriffsales.html**
			Putnam – **www.sheriffoff.com**
			Richland – **www.richlandcountyauditor.org/Main/Home.aspx**
			Ross – no website
			Sandusky – no website
			Scioto – **www.sciotocountyohio.com**
			Seneca – no website
			Shelby – **www.co.shelby.oh.us**
			Stark – **http://webapp.co.stark.oh.us/sheriff_sales/DelinquentTaxSales.aspx**
			Summit – **www.co.summit.oh.us/sheriff/sales.htm**
			Trumbull – no website
			Tuscarawas – **www.co.tuscarawas.oh.us/Auditors/DelinquentTaxList.htm**
			Union – no website
			Van Wert – no website
			Vinton – **www.vintoncounty.com**
			Warren – **www.co.warren.oh.us**
			Washington – no website
			Wayne – no website
			Williams – **www.co.williams.oh.us**
			Wood – **www.woodcountysheriff.com/pages/sheriff-sales.php**
			Wyandot – no website
	Statute	Ohio Revised Code	Sections 2329.17, 20; 5721.23; 315.251
	Oklahoma		
36	Type of sale	Tax lien	Certificate of purchase or tax sale certificate
	Sale date	October, first Monday	
	Bid method	Random or rotational	
	Payment method		
	Interest rate	8% per annum	

STATE		
Redemption period	2 years	
Over the counter	Yes	
Municipalities	77	Adair – no website Alfalfa – no website Atoka – no website Beaver – http://beaver.okcounties.org Beckham – http://beckham.okcounties.org Blaine – http://blainecountyok.com Bryan – http://bryan.okcountytreasurers.com Caddo – http://caddo.okcountytreasurers.com Canadian – www.canadiancounty.org Carter – www.brightok.net/cartercounty Cherokee – no website Choctaw – no website Cimarron – no website Cleveland – www.ccok.us Coal – no website Comanche – www.comanchecounty.us Cotton – no website Craig – http://craig.okcountytreasurers.com Creek – http://creekcountyonline.com Custer – http://custer.okcounties.org Delaware – www.delawareclerk.org Dewey – no website Ellis – no website Garfield – no website Garvin – http://garvin.okcountytreasurers.com Grady – www.gradycountyok.com Grant – www.grantcountyok.com Greer – http://greer.okcounties.org Harmon – no website Harper – no website Haskell – no website Hughes – no website Jackson – www.jacksoncountyok.com Jefferson – www.jeffcoinfo.org Johnston – http://johnston.okcountytreasurers.com Kay – www.courthouse.kay.ok.us/home.html Kingfisher – no website Kiowa – no website Latimer – http://latimer.okcountytreasurers.com LeFlore – http://leflore.okcountytreasurers.com Lincoln – no website Logan – www.logancountyok.com Love – http://love.okcounties.org Major – no website

Appendix 1: State Laws **253**

	STATE		
			Marshall – **http://marshall.okcounties.org**
			Mayes – **http://mayes.okcounties.org**
			McClain – **http://mcclain-co-ok.us**
			McCurtain – no website
			McIntosh – no website
			Murray – **www.murrayok.com**
			Muskogee – no website
			Noble – no website
			Nowata – no website
			Okfuskee – no website
			Oklahoma – **www.oklahomacounty.org**
			Okmulgee – no website
			Osage – no website
			Ottawa – no website
			Pawnee – **http://pawnee.okcountytreasurers.com**
			Payne – **www.paynecounty.org**
			Pittsburg – no website
			Pontotoc – **http://pontotoc.okcountytreasurers.com**
			Pottawatomie – no website
			Pushmataha – no website
			Roger Mills – no website
			Rogers – **www.rogerscounty.org**
			Seminole – no website
			Sequoyah – **www.sequoyahcountygovernment.com**
			Stephens – **http://stephens.okcountytreasurers.com**
			Texas – **www.txcountyok.com**
			Tillman – **www.tillmancounty.org**
			Tulsa – **www.tulsacounty.org/Tulsacounty**
			Wagoner – **www.ok.gov/wagonercounty/Elected_ Officials/County_Clerk**
			Washington – **www.countycourthouse.org**
			Washita – no website
			Woods – **http://woods.okcountytreasurers.com**
			Woodward – **http://woodwardcounty.org**
	Statute	68 Oklahoma State Statutes	Sections 3107; 3135
	Oregon		
37	Type of sale	Tax deed	Municipalities place liens against real property for delinquent property taxes. If the property owner does not redeem the property, the municipality may retain ownership of the property or sell the property.
	Sale date	Varies by municipality	The tax sale is a public oral-bid foreclosure sale of real estate.
	Bid method	Premium bid	Some municipalities may set the opening bid as a percentage of the appraised value of the property.
	Payment method		Some municipalities may finance the purchase of tax deeds.

	STATE		
	Interest rate	N/A	
	Redemption period	N/A	
	Over the counter	Yes	Some municipalities offer over-the-counter sales.
	Municipalities	36	Baker – www.bakercounty.org Benton – www.co.benton.or.us Clackamas – www.co.clackamas.or.us Clatsop – www.co.clatsop.or.us Columbia – www.co.columbia.or.us Coos – www.co.coos.or.us Crook – www.co.crook.or.us Curry – www.co.curry.or.us Deschutes – www.deschutes.org Douglas – www.co.douglas.or.us Gilliam – www.co.gilliam.or.us Grant – no website Harney – www.co.harney.or.us Hood River – www.co.hood-river.or.us Jackson – www.co.jackson.or.us Jefferson – www.co.jefferson.or.us Josephine – www.co.josephine.or.us Klamath – www.klamathcounty.org Lake – www.lakecountyor.org Lane – www.lanecounty.org/Pages Lincoln – www.co.lincoln.or.us Linn – www.co.linn.or.us Malheur – www.malheurco.org Marion – www.co.marion.or.us Morrow – www.morrowcountyoregon.com Multnomah – http://web.multco.us Polk – www.co.polk.or.us Sherman – www.sherman-county.com Tillamook – www.co.tillamook.or.us Umatilla – www.co.umatilla.or.us Union – www.union-county.org Wallowa – www.co.wallowa.or.us Wasco – www.co.wasco.or.us Washington – www.co.washington.or.us Wheeler – www.wheelercounty-oregon.com Yamhill – www.co.yamhill.or.us
	Pennsylvania		
38	Type of sale	Hybrid tax deed	The tax sale is a public oral-bid foreclosure sale of real estate.
	Sale date	Monthly	

STATE		
Bid method	Premium bid	Properties are offered for sale at the opening bid amount during an upset sale. Properties not sold at the upset sale are offered for sale at a private sale. If a property is not sold at the private sale, the property is offered for sale at a Judicial sale, which is governed by court order. If the property is not sold at the judicial sale, the property is offered for sale to county commissioners who bid up the cost of the tax lien at a repository sale.
Payment method		
Interest rate	10% per annum	
Redemption period	1 year	
Over the counter	Yes	Some municipalities offer over-the-counter sales.
Municipalities	67	Adams – www.adamscounty.us Allegheny – www.county.allegheny.pa.us Armstrong – www.armstrongcounty.com Beaver – www.beavercountypa.gov Bedford – http://bedford.pacounties.org/Pages Berks – www.co.berks.pa.us/Pages Blair – www.blairco.org/Pages Bradford – www.bradfordcountypa.org Bucks – www.buckscounty.org Butler – www.co.butler.pa.us Cambria – www.co.cambria.pa.us/Pages Cameron – www.cameroncountypa.com Carbon – www.carboncounty.com Centre – www.co.centre.pa.us Chester – www.chesco.org/chesco/site Clarion – www.co.clarion.pa.us Clearfield – www.clearfieldco.org Clinton – www.clintoncountypa.com Columbia – www.columbiapa.org Crawford – www.crawfordcountypa.net/portal/page?_pageid=393%2C1%2C393_812452&_dad=portal&_schema=PORTAL Cumberland – www.ccpa.net Dauphin – www.dauphincounty.org Delaware – www.co.delaware.pa.us Elk – www.co.elk.pa.us Erie – www.eriecountygov.org Fayette – www.co.fayette.pa.us/Pages Forest – www.co.forest.pa.us Franklin – www.co.franklin.pa.us/Pages Fulton – www.co.fulton.pa.us

STATE		
		Greene – www.co.greene.pa.us
Huntingdon – www.huntingdoncounty.net/Pages/HuntingdonCountyHome.aspx
Indiana – no website
Jefferson – no website
Juniata – www.co.juniata.pa.us
Lackawanna – www.lackawannacounty.org
Lancaster – www.co.lancaster.pa.us/lanco/site
Lawrence – www.co.lawrence.pa.us
Lebanon – www.lebcounty.org/Pages/default.aspx
Lehigh – www.lehighcounty.org
Luzerne – www.luzernecounty.org
Lycoming – www.lyco.org
McKean – www.mckeancountypa.org
Mercer – www.mcc.co.mercer.pa.us
Mifflin – www.co.mifflin.pa.us/Pages
Monroe – www.co.monroe.pa.us/monroe/site/default.asp
Montgomery – www2.montcopa.org/montco/site
Montour – www.montourco.org/Pages/default.aspx
Northampton – www.northamptoncounty.org/northampton/site
Northumberland – www.northumberlandco.org/default.asp?iId=HILHG
Perry – www.perryco.org/Pages
Philadelphia – no website
Pike – www.pikepa.org
Potter – www.pottercountypa.net
Schuylkill – www.co.schuylkill.pa.us
Snyder – www.snydercounty.org/Pages/default.aspx
Somerset – www.co.somerset.pa.us
Sullivan – www.sullivancounty-pa.org
Susquehanna – www.susqco.com
Tioga – www.tiogacountypa.us/Pages
Union – www.unioncountypa.org
Venango – www.co.venango.pa.us
Warren – www.warrencountypa.net
Washington – www.co.washington.pa.us
Wayne – www.co.wayne.pa.us
Westmoreland – www.co.westmoreland.pa.us/westmoreland/site
Wyoming – no website
York – www.york-county.org
	Statute	Act of Assembly	May 16, 1923, P.L. 207; March 15, 1956, No. 388
	Rhode Island		

Appendix 1: State Laws 257

	STATE		
39	Type of sale	Hybrid tax deed	Collector's deed or deed
	Sale date	April to October	The tax sale must be published in the newspaper and at least two public places for three weeks before the sale. The purchaser is required to make subsequent tax payments.
	Bid method	Bid down interest or premium bid	
	Payment method		Payment is required immediately upon winning the bid.
	Interest rate	10% penalty	The Interest rate upon redemption is 10% of the purchase plus 1% percent month for each month over six months.
	Redemption period	1 year	A tax deed is issued immediately and must be recorded within 60 days of the tax sale. The tax deed holder must petition the court to foreclose the owner's right of redemption at the expiration of the redemption period.
	Over the counter	No	
	Municipalities	5	Bristol – www.bristolri.us Kent – no website Newport – no website Providence – no website Washington – no website
	Statute	Rhode Island General Laws	Sections 44-9-12,19,21
	South Carolina		
40	Type of sale	Tax lien	Receipt for the purchase money or tax sale receipt
	Sale date	December, third Monday	The tax sale listing must be published within four weeks before the tax sale.
	Bid method	Premium bid	Payment is required immediately upon winning the bid.
	Payment method		
	Interest rate	8%–12% per annum	The Interest rate upon redemption is dependent upon when the redemption takes place. - First three months: 3% - Months four though six: 6% - Months seven through nine: 9% - Months nine through 12: 12%
	Redemption period	12 to 18 months	If the property owner fails to redeem the tax lien certificate, the lien certificate holder is provided a quitclaim deed within 30 days of the expiration of the redemption period. Neither the taxing municipality nor the state makes warranty as to the quality of title acquired.

STATE		
Over the counter	Yes	
Municipalities	46	Abbeville – www.abbevillecountysc.com
Aiken – www.aikencountysc.gov
Allendale – www.allendalecounty.com
Anderson – www.andersoncountysc.org
Bamberg – www.bambergcountysc.gov
Barnwell – www.barnwellcounty.sc.gov
Beaufort – www.bcgov.net
Berkeley – www.berkeleycountysc.gov
Calhoun – www.calhouncounty.sc.gov/Pages/default.aspx
Charleston – www.charlestoncounty.org
Cherokee – http://delisac.site.aplus.net/cherokeecountysouthcarolina
Chester – www.chestercounty.org
Chesterfield – www.chesterfieldcountysc.com
Clarendon – www.clarendoncounty.sc.gov
Colleton – www.colletoncounty.org/default.aspx?pageID=1
Darlington – www.darcosc.com
Dillon – http://dilloncounty.sc.gov/Pages/default.aspx
Dorchester – www.dorchestercounty.net
Edgefield – www.edgefieldcounty.sc.gov
Fairfield – www.fairfieldsc.com
Florence – http://florenceco.org
Georgetown – www.georgetowncountysc.org
Greenville – www.greenvillecounty.org
Greenwood – www.greenwoodsc.gov
Hampton – www.hamptoncountysc.org
Horry – www.horrycounty.org/hcgPortal.asp
Jasper – www.jaspercountysc.org
Kershaw – www.kershaw.sc.gov
Lancaster – www.mylancastersc.org
Laurens – www.laurenscountysc.org
Lee – no website
Lexington – www.lex-co.com
Marion – www.marionsc.org
Marlboro – www.marlborocounty.sc.gov/Pages/default.aspx
McCormick – www.mccormickcountysc.com
Newberry – www.newberrycounty.net
Oconee – www.oconeesc.com
Orangeburg – www.orangeburgcounty.org
Pickens – www.co.pickens.sc.us
Richland – www.rcgov.us
Saluda – www.saludacountysc.com
Spartanburg – www.spartanburgcounty.org

Appendix 1: State Laws 259

	STATE		
			Sumter – **www.sumtercountysc.org** Union – **www.countyofunion.org** Williamsburg – **www.williamsburgcounty.sc.gov** York – **www.yorkcountygov.com**
	Statute	South Carolina Statutes	Section 12-51-90
	South Dakota		
	Important Note		In 2006, South Dakota adopted a resolution that there would be no more tax certificates sold, unless the particular board of county commissioners adopted a contrary resolution. Some counties have done this, and all are included here in case more do in the future.
41	Type of sale	Tax lien	Tax certificate, tax sale certificate, or certificate of sale
	Sale date	December, third Monday	The tax sale listing must be published in the newspaper and one other public place, once in the week before the tax sale.
	Bid method	Premium bid	The tax lien certificate holder has the option of paying subsequent taxes. Subsequent taxes earn 12% interest calculated from the date they would have become delinquent, if not paid.
	Payment method		Payment is required immediately upon winning the bid.
	Interest rate	12% per annum	
	Redemption period	3 or 4 years	The redemption time is three years for properties within the limits of the municipality and four years for properties located outside of the municipality.
	Over the counter	Yes	The winning bidder must initiate the process to obtain a tax deed by providing the property owner with a notice of the intent to obtain deed to the property within 60 days and also inform the property owner of the redemption expiration date. The county will issue a tax deed 60 days after making such notice.
	Municipalities	66	Aurora – no website Beadle – no website Bennett – no website Bon Homme – no website Brookings **http://www.brookingscountysd.gov/county offices/finance-office** Brown – **www.brown.sd.us** Brule – **http://brulecounty.org** Buffalo – no website Butte – **http://butte.sdcounties.org** Campbell – no website Charles Mix – **http://charlesmix.sdcounties.org** Clark – no website Clay – **www.claycountysd.org**

	STATE		
			Codington – www.codington.org
			Corson – http://corson.sdcounties.org
			Custer – www.custercountysd.com
			Davison – www.davisoncounty.org
			Day – http://day.sdcounties.org
			Deuel – www.deuelcountysd.com
			Dewey – no website
			Douglas – no website
			Edmunds – http://edmunds.sdcounties.org
			Fall River – http://fallriver.sdcounties.org
			Faulk – no website
			Grant – no website
			Gregory – no website
			Haakon – no website
			Hamlin – no website
			Hand – http://hand.sdcounties.org
			Hanson – no website
			Harding – no website
			Hughes – www.hughescounty.org
			Hutchinson – no website
			Hyde – no website
			Jackson – no website
			Jerauld – no website
			Jones – no website
			Kingsbury – http://kingsbury.sdcounties.org
			Lake – www.lakecountysd.com
			Lawrence – www.lawrence.sd.us
			Lincoln – www.lincolncountysd.org
			Lyman – www.lymancounty.org/page.php?2
			Marshall – no website
			McCook – no website
			McPherson – www.rootsweb.ancestry.com/~sdmcpher
			Meade – www.meadecounty.org
			Mellette – no website
			Miner – www.minercountysd.org
			Minnehaha – www.minnehahacounty.org
			Moody – http://www.moodycounty.net/
			Pennington – www.co.pennington.sd.us
			Perkins – no website
			Potter – no website
			Roberts – http://roberts.sdcounties.org
			Sanborn – http://sanborn.sdcounties.org
			Shannon – http://shannon.sdcounties.org/
			Spink – www.spinkcounty-sd.org
			Stanley – www.stanleycounty.org
			Sully – www.sullycounty.net
			Todd – no website
			Tripp – no website

Appendix 1: State Laws   **261**

	STATE		
			Turner – **http://turner.sdcounties.org** Union – **http://unioncountysd.org** Walworth – **http://walworthco.org** Yankton – **www.co.yankton.sd.us** Ziebach – no website
	Statute	South Dakota Codified Laws	Titles 10, 44
	Tennessee		
42	Type of sale	Hybrid tax deed	Tax deed
	Sale date	Varies by municipality	
	Bid method	Premium bid	
	Payment method		Payment is required within 24 hours of the tax sale. Failure to pay the bid amount may result in legal action.
	Interest rate	10% per annum	
	Redemption period	1 year	The court must confirm the tax deed sale, and the tax deed may be requested following such confirmation, which usually takes about 30 days.
	Over the counter	No	
	Municipalities	95	Anderson – **www.andersontn.org** Bedford – **www.bedfordcountytn.org** Benton – **www.bentoncounty.us** Bledsoe – no website Blount – **www.blounttn.org** Bradley – **www.bradleyco.net** Campbell – no website Cannon – no website Carroll – no website Carter – **www.cartercountytn.gov** Cheatham – **http://cheathamcountytn.gov/government** Chester – **http://chestercountytn.org/county_offices** Claiborne – **www.claibornecounty.com/community/local-government** Clay – no website Cocke – **www.cockecounty.net** Coffee – **www.coffeecountytn.org** Crockett – no website Cumberland – **http://cumberlandcountytn.gov** Davidson – **www.nashville.gov** DeKalb – **www.dekalbtennessee.com** Decatur – **www.decaturcountytn.org** Dickson – **http://dicksoncounty.net** Dyer – no website

STATE	
	Fayette – www.fayettetn.us
	Fentress – no website
	Franklin – www.franklincotn.us
	Gibson – no website
	Giles – www.gilescounty-tn.us
	Grainger – http://graingertn.com
	Greene – www.greenecountytngovt.com
	Grundy – www.grundycountytn.net
	Hamblen – www.hamblencountygovernment.us
	Hamilton – www.hamiltontn.gov
	Hancock – www.hancockcountytn.com
	Hardeman – http://hardemancountytn.com
	Hardin – no website
	Hawkins – www.hawkinscountytn.gov
	Haywood – www.haywoodcountybrownsville.com/HaywoodCounty
	Henderson – no website
	Henry – www.henryco.com
	Hickman – www.hickmanco.com
	Houston – no website
	Humphreys – www.humphreystn.com
	Jackson – www.jacksonco.com
	Jefferson – www.jeffersoncountytn.gov
	Johnson – no website
	Knox – www.knoxcounty.org
	Lake – www.lakecountytn.com
	Lauderdale – no website
	Lawrence – www.lawcotn.org
	Lewis – www.lewiscountytn.com
	Lincoln – www.lincolncountytngov.com
	Loudon – www.loudoncounty-tn.gov
	Macon – www.maconcountytn.com
	Madison – www.co.madison.tn.us
	Marion – no website
	Marshall – www.marshallcountytn.com
	Maury – www.maurycounty-tn.gov
	McMinn – http://mcminncountytn.gov
	McNairy – www.mcnairycountytn.com
	Meigs – no website
	Monroe – www.monroegovernment.org
	Montgomery – www.mcgtn.org
	Moore – no website
	Morgan – www.morgancountytn.org/service.htm
	Obion – no website
	Overton – www.overtoncountytn.com
	Perry – www.perrycountytennessee.com/government/perry-county-government

Appendix 1: State Laws **263**

	STATE		
			Pickett – www.dalehollow.com/info-resources/government Polk – www.polkgovernment.com Putnam – www.putnamcountytn.gov Rhea – no website Roane – www.roanegov.org Robertson – www.robertsoncountytn.org Rutherford – www.rutherfordcountytn.gov Scott – www.scottcounty.com Sequatchie – www.sequatchiecounty-tn.gov Sevier – www.seviercountytn.org Shelby – www.shelbycountytn.gov Smith – no website Stewart – www.stewartcountygovernment.com Sullivan – www.sullivancountytn.gov Sumner – www.sumnertn.org Tipton – http://tiptonco.com Trousdale – www.hartsvilletrousdale.com Unicoi – www.unicoicountytn.gov Union – www.unioncountytn.com Van Buren – no website Warren – www.warrencountytn.gov Washington – www.washingtoncountytn.org Wayne – www.waynecountytn.org Weakley – no website White – no website Williamson – www.williamsoncounty-tn.gov Wilson – www.wilsoncountytn.com
	Statute	Tennessee Code	Title 67
	Texas		
43	Type of sale	Hybrid tax deed	Deed
	Sale date	Each month, first Tuesday	
	Bid method	Premium bid	
	Payment method		
	Interest rate	25% penalty	The penalty is applied to the lien amount, the premium amount, and any costs associated with the administration of the deed.
	Redemption period	6 months or 2 years	The redemption period is six months for non-homestead and non-agricultural properties and two years for homestead and agricultural properties.
	Over the counter	Yes	

STATE		
Municipalities	254	Anderson – www.co.anderson.tx.us
		Andrews – www.co.andrews.tx.us
		Angelina – www.angelinacounty.net
		Aransas – www.aransascountytx.gov/main
		Archer – www.co.archer.tx.us/ips/cms
		Armstrong – www.co.armstrong.tx.us/ips/cms
		Atascosa – no website
		Austin – www.austincounty.com/ips/cms
		Bailey – www.co.bailey.tx.us/ips/cms
		Bandera – www.banderacounty.org
		Bastrop – www.co.bastrop.tx.us
		Baylor – no website
		Bee – www.co.bee.tx.us/ips/cms
		Bell – www.bellcountytx.com
		Bexar – www.co.bexar.tx.us
		Blanco – www.co.blanco.tx.us/ips/cms
		Borden – www.co.borden.tx.us/ips/cms
		Bosque – www.bosquecounty.us
		Bowie – www.co.bowie.tx.us/ips/cms
		Brazoria – www.brazoria-county.com
		Brazos – www.co.brazos.tx.us
		Brewster – http://brewstercountytx.com
		Briscoe – www.co.briscoe.tx.us/ips/cms
		Brooks – www.co.brooks.tx.us/ips/cms
		Brown – www.browncountytx.org/ips/cms
		Burleson – www.co.burleson.tx.us
		Burnet – www.burnetcountytexas.org
		Caldwell – www.co.caldwell.tx.us/ips/cms
		Calhoun – www.calhouncotx.org
		Callahan – www.co.callahan.tx.us/ips/cms
		Cameron – www.co.cameron.tx.us
		Camp – www.co.camp.tx.us/ips/cms
		Carson – www.co.carson.tx.us/ips/cms
		Cass – www.co.cass.tx.us/ips/cms
		Castro – www.co.castro.tx.us/ips/cms
		Chambers – www.co.chambers.tx.us
		Cherokee – www.co.cherokee.tx.us/ips/cms
		Childress – no website
		Clay – www.co.clay.tx.us/ips/cms
		Cochran – www.co.cochran.tx.us/ips/cms
		Coke – www.co.coke.tx.us/ips/cms
		Coleman – www.co.coleman.tx.us/ips/cms
		Collin – www.co.collin.tx.us
		Collingsworth – www.co.collingsworth.tx.us/ips/cms
		Colorado – www.co.colorado.tx.us/ips/cms
		Comal – www.co.comal.tx.us
		Comanche – no website
		Concho – www.co.concho.tx.us/ips/cms

STATE	
	Cooke – www.co.cooke.tx.us/ips/cms
Coryell – www.coryellcounty.org
Cottle – no website
Crane – www.co.crane.tx.us/ips/cms
Crockett – www.co.crockett.tx.us/ips/cms
Crosby – www.co.crosby.tx.us/ips/cms
Culberson – www.co.culberson.tx.us/ips/cms
Dallam – www.dallam.org/county
Dallas – www.dallascounty.org
Dawson – www.co.dawson.tx.us/ips/cms
Deaf Smith – www.co.deaf-smith.tx.us/ips/cms
Delta – www.co.delta.tx.us/ips/cms
Denton – www.co.denton.tx.us
DeWitt – www.co.dewitt.tx.us/ips/cms
Dickens – www.co.dickens.tx.us/ips/cms
Dimmit – no website
Donley – www.co.donley.tx.us/ips/cms
Duval – no website
Eastland – www.eastlandcountytexas.com
Ector – www.co.ector.tx.us/ips/cms
Edwards – no website
El Paso – www.epcounty.com
Ellis – www.co.ellis.tx.us
Erath – http://co.erath.tx.us
Falls – no website
Fannin – www.co.fannin.tx.us/ips/cms
Fayette – www.co.fayette.tx.us/ips/cms
Fisher – www.co.fisher.tx.us/ips/cms
loyd – no website
Foard – no website
Fort Bend – www.co.fort-bend.tx.us
Franklin – http://co.franklin.tx.us/ips/cms
Freestone – www.co.freestone.tx.us/Ips/cms
Frio – www.co.frio.tx.us/ips/cms
Gaines – www.co.gaines.tx.us/ips/cms
Galveston   www.co.galveston.tx.us
Garza – www.garzacounty.net
Gillespie – www.gillespiecounty.org
Glasscock – www.co.glasscock.tx.us/ips/cms
Goliad   www.co.goliad.tx.us/ips/cms
Gonzales – www.co.gonzales.tx.us/ips/cms
Gray – www.co.gray.tx.us/ips/cms
Grayson – www.co.grayson.tx.us
Gregg – www.co.gregg.tx.us
Grimes – www.co.grimes.tx.us/ips/cms
Guadalupe – www.co.guadalupe.tx.us/guadalupe2010
Hale – no website
Hall – no website

STATE	
	Hamilton – **http://hamiltoncountytx.org**
Hansford – **www.co.hansford.tx.us/ips/cms**
Hardeman – no website
Hardin – **www.co.hardin.tx.us/ips/cms**
Harris – **www.co.harris.tx.us**
Harrison – **www.co.harrison.tx.us**
Hartley – **www.co.hartley.tx.us/ips/cms**
Haskell – **www.co.haskell.tx.us/ips/cms**
Hays – **www.co.hays.tx.us**
Hemphill – no website
Henderson – **www.co.henderson.tx.us/ips/cms**
Hidalgo – **www.co.hidalgo.tx.us**
Hill – **www.co.hill.tx.us/ips/cms**
Hockley – **www.co.hockley.tx.us/ips/cms**
Hood – **www.co.hood.tx.us**
Hopkins – **www.hopkinscountytx.org**
Houston – **www.co.houston.tx.us/ips/cms**
Howard – **www.co.howard.tx.us/ips/cms**
Hudspeth – no website
Hunt – **www.huntcounty.net**
Hutchinson – **www.co.hutchinson.tx.us/ips/cms**
Irion – **www.co.irion.tx.us/ips/cms**
Jack – **www.jackcounty.org**
Jackson – **www.co.jackson.tx.us/ips/cms**
Jasper – **www.co.jasper.tx.us/ips/cms**
Jeff Davis – **www.co.jeff-davis.tx.us/ips/cms**
Jefferson – **www.co.jefferson.tx.us**
Jim Hogg – no website
Jim Wells – **www.co.jim-wells.tx.us/ips/cms**
Johnson – **www.johnsoncountytx.org**
Jones – **www.co.jones.tx.us/ips/cms**
Karnes – **www.co.karnes.tx.us/ips/cms**
Kaufman – **www.kaufmancounty.net**
Kendall – **www.co.kendall.tx.us/ips/cms**
Kenedy – **www.co.kenedy.tx.us/ips/cms**
Kent – **www.co.kent.tx.us/ips/cms**
Kerr – **www.co.kerr.tx.us**
Kimble – **www.co.kimble.tx.us/ips/cms**
King – no website
Kinney – **www.co.kinney.tx.us/ips/cms**
Kleberg – **www.co.kleberg.tx.us/ips/cms**
Knox – **www.knoxcountytexas.org**
La Salle – no website
Lamar – **www.co.lamar.tx.us/ips/cms**
Lamb – **www.co.lamb.tx.us/ips/cms**
Lampasas – **www.co.lampasas.tx.us/ips/cms**
Lavaca – **www.co.lavaca.tx.us/ips/cms**
Lee – **www.co.lee.tx.us/ips/cms**

STATE	
	Leon – www.co.leon.tx.us/ips/cms
	Liberty – www.co.liberty.tx.us/ips/cms
	Limestone – www.co.limestone.tx.us/ips/cms
	Lipscomb – www.co.lipscomb.tx.us/ips/cms
	Live Oak – www.co.live-oak.tx.us/ips/cms
	Llano – www.co.llano.tx.us/ips/cms
	Loving – no website
	Lubbock – www.co.lubbock.tx.us
	Lynn – www.co.lynn.tx.us/ips/cms
	Madison – www.co.madison.tx.us/ips/cms
	Marion – www.co.marion.tx.us/ips/cms
	Martin – no website
	Mason – www.co.mason.tx.us/ips/cms
	Matagorda – www.co.matagorda.tx.us/ips/cms
	Maverick – www.co.maverick.tx.us/ips/cms
	McCulloch – www.co.mcculloch.tx.us/ips/cms
	McLennan – www.co.mclennan.tx.us
	McMullen – no website
	Medina – www.medinacountytexas.org/ips/cms
	Menard – www.menardtexas.com/county.htm
	Midland – www.co.midland.tx.us
	Milam – http://ccserving.com/www/mcinfo
	Mills – www.co.mills.tx.us/ips/cms
	Mitchell – no website
	Montague – www.co.montague.tx.us/ips/cms
	Montgomery – www.co.montgomery.tx.us
	Moore – www.co.moore.tx.us/ips/cms
	Morris – www.co.morris.tx.us/ips/cms
	Motley – www.co.motley.tx.us/ips/cms
	Nacogdoches – www.co.nacogdoches.tx.us
	Navarro – www.co.navarro.tx.us/ips/cms
	Newton – www.co.newton.tx.us/ips/cms
	Nolan – www.co.nolan.tx.us/ips/cms
	Nueces – www.co.nueces.tx.us
	Ochiltree – www.co.ochiltree.tx.us/ips/cms
	Oldham – www.co.oldham.tx.us/ips/cms
	Orange – www.co.orange.tx.us
	Palo Pinto – www.co.palo-pinto.tx.us/ips/cms
	Panola – www.co.panola.tx.us/ips/cms
	Parker – www.co.parker.tx.us/ips/cms
	Parmer – www.co.parmer.tx.us/ips/cms
	Pecos – www.co.pecos.tx.us
	Polk – www.co.polk.tx.us/ips/cms
	Potter – www.co.potter.tx.us
	Presidio – no website
	Rains – www.co.rains.tx.us/ips/cms
	Randall – www.randallcounty.org
	Reagan – no website

	STATE		
			Real – www.co.real.tx.us/ips/cms
			Red River – www.co.red-river.tx.us/ips/cms
			Reeves – no website
			Refugio – www.co.refugio.tx.us/ips/cms
			Roberts – www.co.roberts.tx.us/ips/cms
			Robertson – no website
			Rockwall – www.rockwallcountytexas.com
			Runnels – www.co.runnels.tx.us/ips/cms
			Rusk – www.co.rusk.tx.us/ips/cms
			Sabine – no website
			San Augustine – www.co.san-augustine.tx.us
			San Jacinto – www.co.san-jacinto.tx.us/ips/cms
			San Patricio – www.co.san-patricio.tx.us/ips/cms
			San Saba – www.co.san-saba.tx.us/ips/cms
			Schleicher – www.co.schleicher.tx.us/ips/cms
			Scurry – www.co.scurry.tx.us/ips/cms
			Shackelford – www.co.shackelford.tx.us/ips/cms
			Shelby – www.co.shelby.tx.us/ips/cms
			Sherman – www.co.sherman.tx.us/ips/cms
			Smith – www.smith-county.com
			Somervell – http://co.somervell.tx.us/ips/cms
			Starr – www.co.starr.tx.us/ips/cms
			Stephens – www.co.stephens.tx.us/ips/cms
			Sterling – www.co.sterling.tx.us/ips/cms
			Stonewall – no website
			Sutton – no website
			Swisher – www.co.swisher.tx.us/ips/cms
			Tarrant – www.tarrantcounty.com/egov/site
			Taylor – www.taylorcountytexas.org
			Terrell – www.sandersontx.info
			Terry – www.co.terry.tx.us/ips/cms
			Throckmorton – no website
			Titus – www.co.titus.tx.us
			Tom Green – www.co.tom-green.tx.us/ips/cms
			Travis – www.co.travis.tx.us
			Trinity – www.co.trinity.tx.us/ips/cms
			Tyler – www.co.tyler.tx.us/ips/cms
			Upshur – www.countyofupshur.com
			Upton – www.co.upton.tx.us/ips/cms
			Uvalde – http://uvaldecounty.com
			Val Verde – no website
			Van Zandt – www.vanzandtcounty.org/ips/cms
			Victoria – www.victoriacountytx.org
			Walker – www.co.walker.tx.us
			Waller – www.co.waller.tx.us/ips/cms
			Ward – www.co.ward.tx.us/ips/cms
			Washington – www.co.waller.tx.us/ips/cms
			Webb – www.webbcounty.com

	STATE		
			Wharton – www.co.wharton.tx.us/ips/cms
Wheeler – www.co.wheeler.tx.us/ips/cms
Wichita – www.co.wichita.tx.us
Wilbarger – www.co.wilbarger.tx.us
Willacy – http://co.willacy.tx.us/ips/cms
Williamson – www.wilco.org
Wilson – www.co.wilson.tx.us/ips/cms
Winkler – www.co.winkler.tx.us
Wise – www.co.wise.tx.us
Wood – www.mywoodcounty.com
Yoakum – www.co.yoakum.tx.us/ips/cms
Young – www.co.young.tx.us/ips/cms
Zapata – www.co.zapata.tx.us/ips/cms
Zavala – www.co.zavala.tx.us/ips/cms
	Statute	Texas Tax Code	Section 34.21
	Utah		
44	Type of sale	Tax deed	
	Sale date	May, last Wednesday	The tax sale is a public oral-bid foreclosure sale of real estate.
	Bid method	Premium bid	
	Payment method		
	Interest rate	N/A	
	Redemption period	N/A	
	Over the counter	No	
	Municipalities	29	Beaver – http://beaver.utah.gov
Box Elder – www.boxeldercounty.org
Cache – www.cachecounty.org
Carbon – http://carbon.utah.gov
Daggett – www.daggettcounty.org
Davis – www.daviscountyutah.gov
Duchesne – http://duchesne.utah.gov
Emery – www.co.emery.ut.us
Garfield – http://garfield.utah.gov
Grand – www.grandcountyutah.net
Iron – www.ironcounty.net
Juab – www.co.juab.ut.us
Kane – http://kane.utah.gov
Millard – www.millardcounty.org
Morgan – www.morgan-county.net
Piute – www.piute.org
Rich – www.richcountyut.org
Salt Lake – www.slco.org

Appendix 1: State Laws **269**

	STATE		
			San Juan – www.sanjuancounty.org Sanpete – http://sanpete.com Sevier – www.sevierutah.net Summit – www.co.summit.ut.us Tooele – www.co.tooele.ut.us Uintah – www.co.uintah.ut.us Utah – www.co.utah.ut.us Wasatch – www.co.wasatch.ut.us Washington – www.washco.utah.gov Wayne – www.waynecountyutah.org Weber – www.co.weber.ut.us
	Statute	Utah Code	Title 59
	Vermont		
45	Type of sale	Tax lien	
	Sale date	Varies by municipality	The tax sale is a public oral-bid foreclosure sale of real estate.
	Bid method	Premium bid	
	Payment method		
	Interest rate	12% per annum	
	Redemption period	1 year	
	Over the counter	No	
	Municipalities	14	Addison, Bennington, Caledonia, Chittenden, Essex, Franklin, Grand Isle, Lamoille, Orange, Orleans, Rutland, Washington, Windham, Windsor The counties of Vermont do not have government websites. Towns are the municipalities responsible for tax lien sales. See for example the Town of Wilmington: **www.wilmingtonvermont.us/index.asp?Type=B_BASIC&SEC=%7B24AA671F-E780-4B85-8383-C0D1418312DE%7D.**
	Statute	Vermont Statutes	Title 32, Section 5260
	Virginia		
46	Type of sale	Tax deed	The tax sale is a public oral-bid foreclosure sale of real estate.
	Sale date	Varies by municipality	The county of Arlington does not hold a sale every year.
	Bid method	Premium bid	
	Payment method		
	Interest rate	N/A	

Appendix 1: State Laws

STATE		
Redemption period	N/A	
Over the counter	No	
Municipalities	95	Accomack – www.co.accomack.va.us Albemarle – www.albemarle.org Alleghany – www.co.alleghany.va.us Amelia – no website Amherst – www.countyofamherst.com Appomattox – no website Arlington – www.arlingtonva.us Augusta – www.co.augusta.va.us Bath – www.bathcountyva.org Bedford – www.co.bedford.va.us Bland – no website Botetourt – www.co.botetourt.va.us Brunswick – no website Buchanan – no website Buckingham – www.buckinghamcountyva.org Campbell – www.co.campbell.va.us/Pages Caroline – www.co.caroline.va.us Carroll – no website Charles City – www.co.charles-city.va.us Charlotte – www.co.charlotte.va.us Chesterfield – www.chesterfield.gov Clarke – www.clarkecounty.gov Craig – no website Culpeper – http://web.culpepercounty.gov Cumberland – www.cumberlandcounty.virginia.gov Dickenson – www.dickensoncountyvirginia.org Dinwiddie – www.dinwiddieva.us Essex – www.essex-virginia.org Fairfax – www.fairfaxcounty.gov Fauquier – www.fauquiercounty.gov Floyd – www.floydcova.org Fluvanna – www.co.fluvanna.va.us Franklin – www.franklincountyva.org Frederick – www.co.frederick.va.us Giles – www.gilescounty.org Gloucester – www.co.gloucester.va.us Goochland – www.co.goochland.va.us Grayson – www.graysongovernment.com Greene – www.gcva.us Greensville – www.greensvillecountyva.gov Halifax – no website Hanover – www.co.hanover.va.us Henrico – www.co.henrico.va.us Henry – no website Highland – www.highlandcova.org

STATE	
	Isle of Wight – www.co.isle-of-wight.va.us
	James City – www.jccegov.com
	King and Queen – no website
	King George – www.king-george.va.us
	King William – www.kingwilliamcounty.us
	Lancaster – www.lancova.com
	Lee – no website
	Loudoun – no website
	Louisa – www.louisacounty.com
	Lunenburg – no website
	Madison – no website
	Mathews – www.co.mathews.va.us
	Mecklenburg – no website
	Middlesex – www.co.middlesex.va.us
	Montgomery – www.montva.com
	Nelson – http://nelsoncounty.com
	New Kent – www.co.new-kent.va.us
	Northampton – www.co.northampton.va.us
	Northumberland – www.co.northumberland.va.us
	Nottoway – www.nottoway.org
	Orange – www.orangecova.com
	Page – no website
	Patrick – www.co.patrick.va.us
	Pittsylvania – www.pittgov.org
	Powhatan – no website
	Prince Edward – www.co.prince-edward.va.us
	Prince George – www.princegeorgeva.org
	Prince William – www.pwcgov.org
	Pulaski – www.pulaskicounty.org
	Rappahannock – no website
	Richmond – www.co.richmond.va.us
	Roanoke – www.roanokecountyva.gov
	Rockbridge – www.co.rockbridge.va.us
	Rockingham – no website
	Russell – www.russellcountyva.us
	Scott – www.scottcountyva.com
	Shenandoah – www.shenandoahcountyva.us
	Smyth – www.smythcounty.org
	Southampton – www.southamptoncounty.org/T0.aspx?PID=2
	Spotsylvania – www.spotsylvania.va.us
	Stafford – www.co.stafford.va.us
	Surry – no website
	Sussex – no website
	Tazewell – no website
	Warren – www.warrencountyva.net
	Washington – www.washcova.com
	Westmorland – www.westmoreland-county.org

Appendix 1: State Laws

	STATE		
			Wise – www.wisecounty.org Wythe – no website York – www.yorkcounty.gov
	Statute	Code of Virginia	Title 58, Chapter 32
	Washington		
47	Type of sale	Tax deed	
	Sale date	Varies by municipality	The tax sale is a public oral-bid foreclosure sale of real estate.
	Bid method	Premium bid	
	Payment method		
	Interest rate	N/A	
	Redemption period	N/A	
	Over the counter	No	
	Municipalities	39	Adams – www.co.adams.wa.us Asotin – www.co.asotin.wa.us Benton – www.co.benton.wa.us Chelan – www.co.chelan.wa.us Clallam – www.clallam.net Clark – www.clark.wa.gov Columbia – www.columbiaco.com Cowlitz – www.co.cowlitz.wa.us Douglas – www.douglascountywa.net Ferry – www.ferry-county.com Franklin – www.co.franklin.wa.us Garfield – www.co.garfield.wa.us Grant – www.co.grant.wa.us Grays Harbor – www.co.grays-harbor.wa.us Island www.islandcounty.net Jefferson – www.co.jefferson.wa.us King – www.kingcounty.gov Kitsap – www.kitsapgov.com Kittitas – www.co.kittitas.wa.us Klickitat – www.klickitatcounty.org Lewis – http://lewiscountywa.gov Lincoln – www.co.lincoln.wa.us Mason – www.co.mason.wa.us Okanogan – www.okanogancounty.org Pacific – www.co.pacific.wa.us Pend Oreille – www.pendoreilleco.org Pierce – www.co.pierce.wa.us/pc/ San Juan – www.sanjuanco.com Skamania – www.skamaniacounty.org

	STATE		
			Snohomish – www1.co.snohomish.wa.us Spokane – www.spokanecounty.org Stevens – www.co.stevens.wa.us Thurston – www.co.thurston.wa.us/home Wahkiakum – www.co.wahkiakum.wa.us Walla Walla – www.co.walla-walla.wa.us Whatcom – www.co.whatcom.wa.us Whitman – www.whitmancounty.org Yakima – www.yakimacounty.us
	Statute	Revised Code of Washington	Chapters 36, 60
	West Virginia		
48	Type of sale	Tax lien	Certificate of sale, certificate of purchase, tax certificate of sale, or tax certificate
	Sale date	Varies by municipality	Usually October or November
	Bid method	Premium bid	Upon redemption, the premium amount is not returned; nor is interest applied to the amount.
	Payment method		
	Interest rate	12% per annum	
	Redemption period	18 months	
	Over the counter	Yes – liens No – deeds	
	Municipalities	55	Barbour – www.barbourcounty.wv.gov/Pages/default.aspx Berkeley – www.berkeleycountycomm.org Boone – www.boonecountywv.org Braxton – www.braxtoncounty.wv.gov Brooke – www.brookewv.org Cabell – www.cabellcounty.org Calhoun – www.calhouncounty.wv.gov Clay – www.claycounty.wv.gov Doddridge – www.doddridgecounty.wv.gov Fayette – www.fayettecounty.wv.gov Gilmer – www.gilmercounty.wv.gov Grant – www.grantcounty.wv.gov Greenbrier – www.greenbriercounty.net Hampshire – www.hampshirecounty.wv.gov Hancock – http://hancockcountywv.org Hardy – www.hardycounty.com Harrison – www.harrisoncountywv.com Jackson – www.jacksoncounty.wv.gov Jefferson – www.jeffersoncountywv.org Kanawha – www.kanawha.us

	STATE		
			Lewis – www.lewiscounty.wv.gov
			Lincoln – www.lincolncountywv.org
			Logan – no website
			Marion – www.marioncountywv.com
			Marshall – www.marshallcountywv.org
			Mason – www.masoncounty.wv.gov
			McDowell – www.mcdowellcounty.wv.gov
			Mercer – www.mercercounty.wv.gov
			Mineral – www.mineralcountywv.com
			Mingo – www.mingocountywv.com
			Monongalia – www.co.monongalia.wv.us
			Monroe – www.monroecountywv.net
			Morgan – http://morgancountywv.gov
			Nicholas – www.nicholascountywv.org
			Ohio – www.ohiocounty.wv.gov
			Pendleton – www.pendletoncounty.wv.gov
			Pleasants – no website
			Pocahontas – www.pocahontascounty.wv.gov
			Preston – www.prestoncountywv.org
			Putnam – www.putnamcounty.org
			Raleigh – www.raleighcounty.com
			Randolph – no website
			Ritchie – www.ritchiecounty.wv.gov
			Roane – www.roanecounty.wv.gov
			Summers – http://summerscountywv.org
			Taylor – www.taylorcounty.wv.gov
			Tucker – www.tuckercounty.wv.gov
			Tyler – www.tylercountywv.com
			Upshur – www.upshurcounty.org
			Wayne – www.waynecountywv.org
			Webster – www.webstercounty.wv.gov
			Wetzel www.wetzelcounty.wv.gov
			Wirt – www.wirtcounty.wv.gov
			Wood www.woodcountywv.com
			Wyoming – www.wyomingcounty.com
	Statute	West Virginia Code	Section 11A-3-23
	Wisconsin		
49	Type of sale	Tax deed	Tax liens are owned by the counties, which sell tax deeds after two years.
	Sale date	Varies by municipality	
	Bid method	Premium bid	The opening bid for deed sales is set equal to the **appraised value** of the property and not just for the outstanding **taxes**. However, the appraised value may be significantly less than the fair market value of the property.

STATE		
Payment method		
Interest rate		
Redemption period	2 years	In county possession
Over the counter	No	
Municipalities	72	Adams – www.co.adams.wi.gov Ashland – www.co.ashland.wi.us Barren – www.barroncountywi.gov Bayfield – www.bayfieldcounty.org Brown – www.co.brown.wi.us Buffalo – www.buffalocounty.com Burnett – www.burnettcounty.com Calumet – www.co.calumet.wi.us Chippewa – www.co.chippewa.wi.us Clark – www.co.clark.wi.us/ClarkCounty Crawford – http://crawfordcountywi.org Columbia – www.co.columbia.wi.us Dane – www.countyofdane.com Dodge – www.co.dodge.wi.us Door – www.co.door.wi.gov Douglas – www.douglascountywi.org Dunn – http://dunncountywi.govoffice2.com Eau Claire – www.co.eau-claire.wi.us Florence – www.florencewisconsin.com Fond du Lac – www.fdlco.wi.gov Forest – www.co.forest.wi.gov Grant – www.co.grant.wi.gov Green – www.co.green.wi.gov Green Lake – www.co.green-lake.wi.us Iowa – www.iowacounty.org Iron – www.co.iron.wi.gov Jackson – www.co.jackson.wi.us Jefferson – www.jeffersoncountywi.gov/jc/public/jchome.php Juneau – www.juneaucounty.com Kenosha – www.co.kenosha.wi.us Kewaunee – www.kewauneeco.org La Crosse – www.co.la-crosse.wi.us Lafayette – www.co.lafayette.wi.gov Langlade – www.co.langlade.wi.us Lincoln – www.co.lincoln.wi.us Manitowoc – www.co.manitowoc.wi.us Marathon – www.co.marathon.wi.us Marinette – www.marinettecounty.com Marquette – www.co.marquette.wi.us Menominee – www.menomineecounty.com

STATE			
			Milwaukee – **http://county.milwaukee.gov/CountyTreasurer7712.htm** Monroe – **www.co.monroe.wi.us** Oconto – **www.co.oconto.wi.us** Oneida – **www.co.oneida.wi.gov** Outagamie – **www.co.outagamie.wi.us** Ozaukee – **www.co.ozaukee.wi.us** Pepin – **www.co.pepin.wi.us** Pierce – **www.co.pierce.wi.us** Polk – **www.co.polk.wi.us** Portage – **www.co.portage.wi.us** Price – **www.co.price.wi.us** Racine – **www.racineco.com** Richland – **www.co.richland.wi.us** Rock – **www.co.rock.wi.us** Rusk – **www.ruskcounty.org** Sauk – **www.co.sauk.wi.us** Sawyer – **www.sawyercountygov.org** Shawano – **www.co.shawano.wi.us** Sheboygan – **www.co.sheboygan.wi.us** St. Croix – **www.co.saint-croix.wi.us** Taylor – **www.co.taylor.wi.us** Trempealeau – **www.tremplocounty.com** Vernon – **www.co.vernon.wi.gov** Vilas – **http://co.vilas.wi.us** Walworth – **www.co.walworth.wi.us** Washburn – **www.co.washburn.wi.us** Washington – **www.co.washington.wi.us** Waukesha – **www.waukeshacounty.gov** Waupaca – **www.co.waupaca.wi.us** Waushara – **www.1waushara.com** Winnebago – **www.co.winnebago.wi.us** Wood – **www.co.wood.wi.us**
	Statute	Wisconsin Statutes	Chapter 75
	Wyoming		
50	Type of sale	Tax lien	Certificate of purchase
	Sale date	July –September	Notice of the tax sale is published once each week for three weeks in a local newspaper. The first notice must be published four weeks before the sale and end before the first week of September.
	Bid method	Random selection or bid down ownership	
	Payment method		Payment is required immediately upon purchase.

STATE		
Interest rate	15% per annum plus 3% penalty	
Redemption period	4 years	The property owner, mortgage holders, and other individuals with a recorded interest in the property must be served notice of the redemption. Notice must be served by certified or registered mail. Service by publication is once a week for three weeks. The first notice must be published no more than five months before the application of tax deed is made. The investor must apply for a tax deed before four years have expired, but not more than six years after the tax sale. Once notification is served and three months have passed, the investor may apply for a tax deed that entitles the holder to right of possession of the property. If a tax lien certificate or tax deed is issued in error and the municipality causes the error, the municipality pays the investor an amount equal to the redemption amount. If the error was due to some other factor, the investor receives a first lien with an 8% Interest rate. The lien is superior to all liens, except tax liens sold for subsequent taxes and the payment of taxes by another individual.
Subsequent taxes	Optional	If subsequent taxes are not paid by the original tax lien holder, the subsequent delinquent taxes become cause for the sale of subsequent tax lien certificates.
Foreclosure	Within 10 years	The tax lien certificate holder must foreclose the right of redemption between four and ten years of the tax sale.
Over the counter	Yes	Unsold tax lien certificates may be offered for sale at either public or private auctions at any time determined by the municipality.
Municipalities	23	Albany – www.co.albany.wy.us/tax-lien-sale.aspx Big Horn – www.bighorncountywy.gov Campbell – www.ccgov.net Carbon – www.carbonwy.com Converse – http://conversecounty.org Crook – www.crookcounty.wy.gov Fremont – http://fremontcountywy.org Goshen – http://goshencounty.org Hot Springs – www.hscounty.com Johnson – www.johnsoncountywyoming.org Laramie – http://webgate.co.laramie.wy.us Lincoln – www.lcwy.org Natrona – www.natrona.net Niobrara – www.niobraracounty.org Park – www.parkcounty.us Platte – www.plattecountywyoming.com Sheridan – www.sheridancounty.com Sublette – www.sublettewyo.com Sweetwater – www.sweet.wy.us

Appendix 1: State Laws 279

STATE			
			Teton – **http://tetonwyo.org** Uinta – **www.uintacounty.com** Washakie – **www.washakiecounty.net** Weston – **www.westongov.com**
	Statute	Wyoming Statutes	Section 39-3-108, 39-4-102
District of Columbia			
	Type of sale	Lien	Certificate of sale or tax lien
	Sale date	July	
	Bid method	Premium bid	Any action to foreclose must be preceded by a title search from a qualified title company. The title search may be ordered after expiration of four months of the redemption period. However, actions to foreclose may not be initiated until the six-month redemption period has expired.
	Payment method		
	Interest rate	12% per annum	
	Redemption period	6 months	
	Over the counter	No	
	Municipalities		
	Statute	D.C. Code	Section 47-1304
Guam			
	Type of sale	Hybrid deed	Tax sold property or deed
	Sale date		
	Bid method	Premium bid	
	Payment method		
	Interest rate	12% per annum	
	Redemption period	1 year	
	Over the counter	No	
	Municipalities		www.guamtax.com
	Statute	11 Guam Law	Section 24812
Puerto Rico			
	Type of sale	Tax lien	Certificate of purchase
	Sale date		

STATE		
Bid method		
Payment method		
Interest rate	20% penalty	
Redemption period	1 year	
Over the counter		
Municipalities		
Statute		
Puerto Rico		
Type of sale	Tax lien	Certificate of purchase
Sale date		
Bid method		
Payment method		
Interest rate	20% penalty	
Redemption period	1 year	
Over the counter		
Municipalities		
Statute		
U.S. Virgin Islands		
Type of sale	Tax lien	Certificate of purchase
Sale date		
Bid method		
Payment method		
Interest rate	12%	On total payment, including any premium
Redemption period	1 year	
Over the counter		
Municipalities		St. Croix
		St. John
		St. Thomas
Statute		

Bibliography

Allen, C.W., C. Hill, D. Kennedy, and G. Sutton. *Inc. & Grow Rich*, 2nd Ed.. Sage International, 1999.

Ashby, D. *Make Money Trading Mortgages*. The Wellington Company, Inc., PDF file, 2004.

Bbyrd2100@centurytel.net. *Real Estate Investing*. PDF file, 2005.

Carey, C.H., and B. Carey B. *Make Money in Real Estate Tax Liens*. John Wiley & Sons, Inc., 2005.

Loftis, L.B., Esq. *Profit by Investing in Real Estate Tax Liens*. Dearborn Trade Publishing, 2005.

Moskowitz, J., J.D. *The 16% Solution*. Andrews and McMeel, 1994.

Pellegrino, M, Esq. *Tax Lien$ — The Complete Guide to Investing in New Jersey Tax Liens*. Lake Neepaulin Publishing, 2005.

USA Properties, *Tax Lien Certificates*, PDF file.

USA Properties, *Tax Lien Sales*, PDF file.

Villanova, L. *The "You Can Do It" Guide to Success in Tax Lien and Tax Deed Investing*, Vol. 1. 1st Books Library, 2002.

Yocom, J. *Tax Lien Certificates — A Little Known Government Program That Can Make You Financially Independent.* 1st Books Library, 2002.

Author Biography

Alan Northcott is a successful financial author, freelance writer, trading educator, professional engineer, radio broadcaster, farmer, karaoke jockey, and wedding officiant, along with other pursuits. He and his wife live in Florida where they share their house with many dogs and cats. They have three children living on three different continents and two grandchildren.

Originating from England, Northcott was educated at Eltham College in London and obtained his degree from the University of Surrey, also in England. He immigrated with his wife to America in 1992. His engineering career spanned more than 30 years, on both sides of the Atlantic, and recent years have found him seeking and living a more diverse, fulfilling lifestyle. This is his tenth book with Atlantic Publishing Group, Inc.

He offers a free newsletter on various related and unrelated topics. You can email him directly at **alannorthcott@msn.com** for more details.

THIS NOTE IS LEGAL TENDER
FOR ALL DEBTS, PUBLIC AND PRIVATE
Treasurer of the United States

Index

A

abandoned properties 33, 144

administrative filing of foreclosure 76, 156, 159

ad valorem taxes 27

adverse possession 169, 191

arrearages 30

assignment 23, 24, 41, 66, 95, 107, 111, 116, 117, 147, 148, 149, 154

   deed 149

automatic stay 162, 163

B

bidding down 60, 61, 63

ownership 24, 52, 61, 132, 209

C

collector's scavenger sale 115

cram-down 163

D

delinquent

   property owner 19, 24, 25, 110, 149

   property taxes 15, 19, 21, 25, 30, 43, 59, 106, 107, 116, 149, 152, 184, 219, 225, 247, 253

E

equity 73, 74, 92, 98, 106, 108, 148, 156, 162, 163, 164
 -sharing 74, 98
escrow account 11, 30

F

flipping 106, 107, 147
force of sale foreclosure 156, 160
foreclosure 29, 40, 41, 56, 61, 62, 63, 70, 76, 84, 85, 98, 125, 136, 149, 150, 151, 152, 153, 155, 156, 157, 158, 159, 160, 161, 162, 163, 164, 168, 169, 181, 182, 184, 187, 190, 191, 194, 198, 202, 206, 211, 214, 219, 222, 226, 237, 240, 244, 249, 253, 254, 269, 270, 273

G

general partner 89, 90
grant deed 56, 57

H

homestead property 29, 191
hybrid tax deed states 16, 17

I

independent investors 78
institutional investors 24, 78, 79

L

landlocked 32, 146
late-entry bidding 60, 64, 65
lien priority 152, 153, 161
limited partner 89
liquidity risk 40

M

market risk 39
metes and bounds 174
multiple-family housing units 28

N

notice of intent 157, 194

O

opening bid 23, 49, 59, 60, 61, 70, 99, 100, 111, 112, 115, 124, 126, 127, 128, 129, 130, 131, 182, 116, 199, 201, 205, 220, 228, 247, 249, 253, 255

Index **287**

overencumbered 151

overhead risk 41

ownership interest 136

owner's right of redemption 20, 24, 56, 87, 125, 150, 155, 240, 257

P

partition action 62

premium
  bid amount 60, 128, 205, 206
  bidding 60, 61, 69, 78, 99, 123, 128

public oral bid 25, 26, 51, 112

pure tax
  deed states 17
  lien states 19

Q

quiet title action 158, 160, 168, 169

quitclaim deed 73, 98, 107, 108, 194, 223

R

rate of return 29, 70, 71, 76, 92, 101, 117, 118, 124, 149, 172

real property 15, 16, 21, 23, 27, 28, 29, 30, 118, 131, 135, 136, 137, 139, 140, 143, 144, 151, 153, 154, 219, 225, 247, 253

  tax sale 15, 28

redemption period 16, 17, 20, 24, 25, 26, 36, 61, 62, 63, 69, 70, 72, 76, 77, 78, 90, 98, 100, 101, 102, 103, 105, 110, 113, 118, 121, 123, 131, 132, 136, 145, 148, 149, 150, 152, 153, 154, 155, 156, 159, 179, 189, 190, 194, 198, 201, 202, 205, 209, 217, 220, 222, 223, 228, 230, 234, 238, 239, 240, 247, 257, 263, 279

relief of stay 162, 163

Rule of 72 100

S

safety risk 39

scavenger sale 67, 78, 115, 201, 202

security interest 15, 136, 142, 167, 239

short sale provision 163

single-family unit 28

squatter's rights 169

T

tax

  deed states 15, 16, 17, 18, 20, 43, 57, 67, 69, 159

  -defaulted land sale 184

  -delinquent sale 182

  lien certificates 28, 29, 31, 32, 35, 36, 37, 38, 39, 41, 43, 45, 48, 49, 50, 51, 52, 53, 54, 55, 60, 61, 63, 65, 66, 68, 69, 71, 72, 76, 77, 78, 79, 81, 83, 84, 85, 86, 87, 88, 90, 91, 92, 97, 100, 101, 106, 109, 110, 111, 112, 113, 114, 115, 116, 117, 121, 123, 124, 126, 128, 129, 130, 131, 132, 133, 134, 135, 136, 137, 139, 142, 146, 147, 148, 149, 150, 151, 153, 154, 155, 164, 181, 184, 190, 209, 223, 240, 242, 247, 249, 278

  lien states 15, 19, 20, 43, 57, 67, 110, 115, 156, 19

  sale overbid 205

tenants-in-common 21, 62

tract indexing method 139

treasurer's deed 62, 132

trust deed 31, 163

U

undivided portion 132

unlawful detainer 168

upset sale 255

upside down 29

V

vacant lots 27, 31, 32, 143

W

warranty deed 56, 57

Y

yield 79, 98, 101, 102, 103, 104, 105, 106, 125, 161

Z

zoning 32, 34, 44, 173